Social Work Practice With Asian Americans

SAGE SOURCEBOOKS FOR THE HUMAN SERVICES SERIES

Series Editors: ARMAND LAUFFER and CHARLES GARVIN

Recent Volumes in this Series

Social Work Practice With Asian Americans

edited by

Sharlene Maeda Furuto
Renuka Biswas
Douglas K. Chung
Kenji Murase
Fariyal Ross-Sheriff

Sage Sourcebooks for
SSHS
the Human Services Series

20

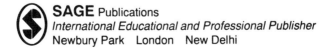

SAGE Publications
International Educational and Professional Publisher
Newbury Park   London   New Delhi

10-16-95

This book includes papers presented at the Asian American Social Work Educators Symposia.

For information address:

SAGE Publications, Inc.
2455 Teller Road
Newbury Park, California 91320

SAGE Publications Ltd.
6 Bonhill Street
London EC2A 4PU
United Kingdom

SAGE Publications India Pvt. Ltd.
M-32 Market
Greater Kailash I
New Delhi 110 048 India

Printed in the United States of America

Library of Congress Cataloging-in-Publication Data

Main entry under title:

Social work practice with Asian Americans / edited by Sharlene Maeda
    Furuto . . . [et al.].
        p.   cm.—(Sage sourcebooks for the human services series;
    v. 20)
    Includes bibliographical references and index.
    ISBN 0-8039-3809-8.—ISBN 0-8039-3810-1 (pbk.)
    1. Asian Americans—Services for.   2. Social work with minorities—
United States.   I. Furuto, Sharlene Maeda.   II. Series.
HV3186.A2S63   1992   92-7770
362.84'095073—dc20   CIP

92   93   94   95   10   9   8   7   6   5   4   3   2   1

Sage Production Editor: Judith L. Hunter

CONTENTS

FOREWORD

Ever since William Petersen coined the term "model minority" in 1966, Asian Americans have come to be regarded by many with a complex mix of envy, awe, jealousy, suspicion, and hostility. What this label masks is the plight and poverty of Laotian, Cambodian, and Vietnamese refugees, the loneliness and isolation of older Asian Americans, the battering and violence suffered by many Asian American women, the turbulence of intergenerational conflicts experienced by Asian families, and the marginalization at the workplace and in the larger society of vast numbers of Asian American men and women. This ostensibly complimentary epithet also conveniently ignores the discrimination that Asian Americans, like other minorities of color, continue to encounter in contemporary America. Such discrimination ranges all the way from the phenomenon of the "glass ceiling" to downright harassment, vandalism, intimidation, assault, and violence.

Often described as a nation of immigrants, the United States has benefited immensely from the toil and talents of emigrants from abroad. Asians have been the largest recent emigration to this country. Although a richly diverse people within themselves, the many common elements in their worldview set them apart in discernible ways from the mainstream Euro American community. Yet little systematic information is available to social work students and faculty that deals with practice issues in working with this rapidly growing segment of the American population.

Social Work Practice With Asian Americans, capably edited by Sharlene Maeda Furuto and the four unit editors—Renuka Biswas,

Kenji Murase, Douglas K. Chung, and Fariyal Ross-Sheriff—fills a void in the literature on social work practice. One does not have to agree with every premise, every argument, and every conclusion advanced in the 14 chapters of this pioneering volume in order to appreciate the contribution it makes to the understanding of the culture, historical roots, adaptation and integration patterns, and mental health and social service needs of Asian Americans.

This book is a product of the collaborative effort of a number of social work educators and practitioners, most of whom are themselves Asian Americans. Its contents include synthesizing essays, reports of exploratory and ethnographic studies, case vignettes, census data analyses, and descriptive and interpretive articles about Asian Americans. It covers important issues of cultural identity, integration, adaptation, maladaptation, alienation, marginality, empowerment, diversity, pluralism, cultural conflict, and cultural confluence, albeit with varying degrees of depth and detail. The authors write about the problems of discrimination, neglect, and poor services facing Asian Americans. Fortunately, however, they go beyond lamenting such problems. They make a cogent case for developing a network of social services that is delivered in a culturally sensitive and culturally competent fashion. Unlike some other writings on this subject, *Social Work Practice With Asian Americans* is generally free from the shrill rhetoric of recrimination and bitterness.

While its various chapters make a persuasive plea for Asian Americans retaining their healthy cultural identity, the book does not succumb to the tendency toward reverse ethnocentrism: It never asserts that ancient cultures are necessarily superior since, in one form or another, they have survived so long. Neither does the book fall prey to the psychology of victimization. It recognizes the ambivalence of the host culture toward newcomers, including Asians, but it also alludes to the noteworthy gains made by Asian Americans in education, in the professions, in business, and in commerce.

In discussing diversity and multiculturalism, this collection of original articles addresses one of the most critical issues facing America today. It warns against the recent rise of ethno-violence. It explodes many extant myths and stereotypes about Asian Americans and pointedly draws the reader's attention to the conditions of unskilled new immigrants, refugees, the elderly, and single-parent families. It suggests policies and programs that counter racism and xenophobia, while it emphasizes the need for unified efforts by Asians and non-Asians alike in support of programs that enhance the adaptation, integration, and empowerment of Asian Americans.

Unfortunately, diversity in our day and age is often viewed as a problem. The coexistence of diverse cultures and peoples is one of the greatest strengths of the United States. Model minority or not, Asian Americans enhance this strength. The challenge facing them is to transcend the conflict of cultures and to fully partake of the rich cultural confluence that is America. When they are successfully able to blend the Asian and the American perspectives, when they fully embrace the liberating pluralism and multiculturalism of the modern age, and when they actively and responsibly participate in the political process not only for advancing their own interests but also for enhancing the common good, then they will become worthy of emulation by other groups—minority as well as majority.

Shanti K. Khinduka

To Asian Americans
and
to all of our families

Part I

ASIAN AMERICANS: *History, Culture, and Adaptation*

RENUKA BISWAS

According to the 1990 Census, there are 7 million Asians living in the United States (U.S. Bureau of the Census, 1991). During the 1980s, Asians were the fastest growing ethnic group in the United States, and they may well retain that position in the 1990s. Asians were labled the "model minority" in the 1960s because of their educational and economic accomplishments; however, that description is premature and these chapters will show that only some Asians have achieved a comfortable level economically and educationally, whereas collectively Asians continue to remain in poverty, underserved and poorly served in social services, and undercompensated in the work force. There is little in the literature regarding the resolution of these and other issues facing the Chinese, Japanese, Koreans, Filipinos, Asian Indians, and Southeast Asians. Asians, by nature quiet and reticent, frequently mingle only with other Asians and thus remain misunderstood by non-Asians.

Part I of this book is an effort to help the reader better understand Asians by providing the background of Asians as newcomers, their values, and how they adapt and integrate into the American society.

The first chapter, "A History of Asian Americans," by Rowena Fong, presents an overview of Asians in the United States. It traces the diversity of immigrants and refugees from the mid-nineteenth century to the present, their economic motives for coming, racist discrimination, and aggressive responses to that discrimination. The serious discrimination Asian Americans encounter in the United States in the form of unfair laws, denial of due process, and even outright murder is described in terms of discrimination fostered and integration prohibited. Asian Americans have made an effort to combat discrimination, and more effort by all Americans needs to develop.

In the second chapter, "Asian Cultural Commonalities: A Comparison With Mainstream American Culture," Douglas K. Chung contrasts the values Asian groups share that distinguish them collectively from Euro Americans. Asian values are high-context and, for example, emphasize relationships with people, while Euro American values are medium low-context and, in contrast, focus less on individuals and more on objective facts. The philosophies and religions of Confucianism in particular and also Buddhism, Hinduism, Christianity, and Islam have widely influenced Asian lives, relationships, worldviews, and values as well as adaptation and integration into the American society.

Dr. Fariyal Ross-Sheriff discusses Asian adaptation and integration in the next chapter, "Adaptation and Integration Into American Society: Major Issues Affecting Asian Americans." Adaptation of Asians involves acculturation to Euro American values, norms, attitudes, and expectations at both the individual and group levels. The adaptation process, which moves from welcome-acceptance to opposition-hostility to marginalization and finally to assimilation-integration, is analyzed in structural, economic, social, and political dimensions. Asians face many critical issues as they attempt to adapt into American society, and undeniably the most far-reaching one is discrimination. Perhaps the media and individuals should place greater emphasis on Asians as models of self-discipline, hard work, family cohesion, and orientation toward education and achievement to help control the pronounced anti-Asian hostility that is growing today.

The three above-mentioned chapters provide information helpful to better understand Asians and social work intervention in the United States today.

REFERENCE

U.S. Bureau of the Census. (1991).

Chapter 1

A HISTORY OF ASIAN AMERICANS

ROWENA FONG

Asian Americans are now a visible group. They are the fastest-growing minority group in the United States today. Historian Ronald Takaki reports that in 1960 there were 877,934 Asians in the United States, representing one-half of 1% of the country's population (Takaki, 1989). The 1990 census counted 6,908,638 Asian Americans, an increase of nearly 800% in 30 years; Asians today comprise nearly 3% of the total American population (U.S. Bureau of the Census, 1991). Asians today are regarded by some as a "model minority," but many of them would not only deny but also strongly refute that characterization. In any case, they have not always been thought of or treated that way.

Historically Asians, because initially their numbers were small, were an invisible group, just droplets in the sea of immigrants who came to the United States in the latter decades of the nineteenth century and the first decades of the twentieth. They came to the United States for a variety of reasons: political freedom, economic advancement, personal aspirations, or family pressure. Individual reasons may have varied, but the treatment they received on arrival and thereafter was much the same. Asian Americans were ridiculed, harassed, beaten; and Euro Americans even stripped some of their rights as citizens of the United States.

This chapter will outline the history of Asian Americans. The term *Asian Americans* refers to people living in the United States whose ancestors were native inhabitants of Asia: Chinese, Japanese, Koreans, Filipinos, Asian Indians, and Southeast Asians, and who are categorized by the U.S. Census Bureau as being Asian American. These different

Asian American ethnic groups will be looked at over the course of time, from the middle of the nineteenth century to the present. Many of these groups came to Hawaii as well as to the U. S. Mainland. Although periodic reference will be made to Asian experiences in Hawaii, the main focus of the present chapter will be on the Mainland.

EARLY IMMIGRATION—THE FIRST WAVES

Chinese Immigration

The first Asian group to come to the United States as immigrants were the Chinese. They came as individual fortune-seekers and as contract laborers to work on the sugar plantations of Hawaii, in the gold mines of California, and on the railroads that spanned the Western part of the United States. Although those were the main occupations, some Chinese immigrants moved quickly to other jobs, such as cooks, launderers, shopkeepers, and agricultural laborers in California.

The Chinese began to come in the late 1840s. Most were single men from two provinces of southeast China—Kwangtung and Fukien—which had for centuries sent laborers overseas to other places such as Southeast Asia (Chen, 1940; Mei, 1984). Some of these men were married and left wives behind in China. Their home provinces were plagued with banditry, rebellions, incursions by foreign troops, and natural disasters. When gold was discovered in California in 1848, thousands of young Chinese men, like men from many parts of the world, were enticed to leave their homes and families and try their luck in the United States. They were not immigrants in the strictest sense; few intended to live out their days in the United States. Like many who came from southern and eastern Europe, they were sojourners (Saloutos, 1956). They left China and came to the United States, hoping to make enough money to return to China, buy land or a business, and live a prosperous life. They called America *gum san*, their "mountain of gold" (Sung, 1967).

However, the chief reactions the Chinese received were not friendly. European Americans (referred to hereafter as Euro Americans), many of them laborers themselves who refused to do the menial jobs the Chinese were doing, and who in any case refused to work for the low wages most Chinese were receiving, protested against the Chinese. The main complaint was that Chinese immigrants worked too hard for wages that were too low, and thereby undercut the wages of Euro American workers. Chinese miners were regularly driven off their claims in the gold country. Some were killed in either planned or random acts of violence. In 1871, for example, a Euro American riot in Los Angeles Chinatown left 19 dead and hundreds homeless; dozens of similar incidents followed (Sandmeyer, 1973).

The protests were heard in the halls of government and sometimes led to discrimination or harassment. For example, in 1853 California, the state that had the most Chinese, levied a Foreign Miner's Tax. This forced the Chinese, Mexicans, and other pigmented, noncitizen miners to pay a tax that United States citizens (and noncitizens of European descent) did not have to pay. Other states followed California's lead. In 1870 San Francisco passed a Cubic Air Ordinance, designed to harass the young Chinese who slept several men to a room in order to save money to send home. Six years later, San Francisco decreed that all Chinese men must cut off their queues, the long pigtails that Chinese law required them to wear. To appear in China without a queue was punishable by death, but California's Euro American citizens insisted the queues must go (Coolidge, 1909).

Chinese immigrants could not become United States citizens. In 1868 China and the United States signed the Burlingame Treaty, which was an agreement for reciprocal immigration, travel, and trade. But there were no provisions for citizenship for foreign-born Chinese. At the founding of this country, only "free white" people could apply for naturalization as United States citizens. After the Civil War, that law was amended so that Africans—people born in Africa and people of African descent—could be eligible for naturalization. But Asians still were barred. The only way a Chinese could be an American citizen was by virtue of birth in the United States (Daniels, 1988).

In 1882 Congress finally knuckled under to the anti-Chinese lobby and passed the Chinese Exclusion Law, which halted Chinese immigration by barring the entry of Chinese laborers. Exemptions were made for merchants, students, teachers, diplomats, and travelers who showed certificates signed by the Chinese government and the U. S. consul in China (Chan, 1991). Although these merchants, students, and others could enter the United States, they still had to go through a grueling ordeal at Angel Island in California. Angel Island was not like Ellis Island, the New York immigration station that processed the millions of Europeans who came to the United States in those decades. Angel Island was a prison where Chinese would-be entrants were questioned for days and weeks before they could get clearance from immigration officials to enter the United States (Lai, Lim, & Yung, 1981; Yung, 1977).

The 1882 law was renewed several times and affected the Chinese for the next 61 years. Finally, in 1943, in a lukewarm gesture to a wartime ally, the Exclusion Act was repealed and an annual quota of 105 immigrants was set for the Chinese (Knoll, 1982).

Legal exclusion did not satisfy the fomenters of the anti-Chinese movement. Protests and violence continued against those Chinese who remained. In 1885 white mineworkers in Rock Springs, Wyoming, murdered 28 Chinese fellow workers for voting against a strike, and drove hundreds more out of their homes. That same year, hundreds of Chinese farm workers and city folk were killed or driven out of Tacoma and several other Washington communities (Karlin, 1948). In such confrontations, the usual pattern was that European American workers and labor organizations demanded the death or ouster of the Chinese as unfair competitors, while employers and clergy defended the right of Chinese people to remain. The clergy were motivated by humanitarian concern, but the employers saw this as an opportunity to divide the working class along racial lines, setting up competition between Euro American and Chinese American workers, thereby keeping wages low and avoiding strikes (Cheng & Bonacich, 1984).

Many Chinese buckled under all this pressure and went back to China. But most had not yet saved enough money to go back in the style they had set as their goal. Others decided to try to make a life for themselves and future generations in the United States. They found the harassment from Euro Americans to be constant. But they also found ways to cope with the discrimination they encountered. With the mining work opportunities dwindling, and railroad and agricultural labor opportunities increasingly denied them, the Chinese men moved to the growing cities of the American West—San Francisco, Seattle, Los Angeles, and a host of smaller towns. There they were segregated from the white population and, for self-protection as well, came to live close together in Chinatown communities. They would eat familiar Chinese foods, tell favorite stories about their lives and families in China, and dream dreams of becoming rich someday (Chin & Chin, 1973; Lee, 1978).

By the first decades of the twentieth century, these informal Chinatown communities had begun to organize formal social institutions. In every American Chinatown there appeared an organization called *Chung*

Wah, the Chinese Consolidated Benevolent Association (in San Francisco, the largest Chinatown, this was called the Chinese Six Companies, for the six major organizations it comprised). The Chinese Consolidated Benevolent Association (CCBA) acted as an authority structure within Chinatown, settling disputes and controlling debts, labor, and commerce (Lyman, 1974). The CCBA also acted as the Chinese voice, speaking to American officials. However, the voice of the CCBA was not able to prevent the passage of discriminatory laws. For the most part, during the first two-thirds of this century, the European American power structure left the people of Chinatowns alone and under the control of the CCBA (Armentrout-Ma, 1983; Hoy, 1942).

Besides the CCBA, which was run mainly by merchants, the Chinese developed two other major social institutions, *tongs* and family associations. The *tongs* styled themselves as social clubs, but in fact were branches of Old World secret societies that organized such social life as gambling, prostitution, and other small-time criminal activities (Chu, 1973). The family associations brought together all the members of a locality who bore the same surname, and organized social and benevolent activities. For example, the Wong Family Association would give clothing or small loans to a newcomer whose last name was Wong, and held an annual picnic that all local Wongs would attend (Lyman, 1974).

The family associations, the *tongs*, and the CCBA were indicators of how the Chinese were organizing themselves to cope with their new environment in the United States. That was no small task, since the pressures on these Chinese men were intense. Not the least of their problems was that they were destined to remain members of a bachelor society. They had come as sojourners, many leaving wives at home in China. With the passage of the Exclusion Act, any hope of being reunited with their families depended on their making enough money to return to China as they had hoped, for alien Chinese laborers were not allowed to bring wives to the United States. The Chinese bachelors coped with their isolation by playing mah jong, by recreating Chinese plays and operas, and by visiting prostitutes. Some of the prostitutes were Euro Americans; others were Chinese women sold or kidnapped into slavery and then brought to the United States, ostensibly as the wives of men of the merchant class (Li, 1980; Nee & Nee, 1973).

A small window of opportunity opened in 1906, when the San Francisco earthquake and fire destroyed that city's records. Immediately, savvy Chinese claimed they had been born in San Francisco and were U. S. citizens by virtue of their birth; they could not be contradicted by the recordless authorities. Then those who could afford to sent for wives and began to form a small number of families in Chinatown. Others made visits back to China, each time recording the birth of a son on their return. Such "sons"—real or fictional—would be United States citizens because their fathers were citizens. In time, after acquiring enough wealth to go back to China, a man would sell his own citizenship papers and those of his "sons" to others from his village who wanted to come to the United States. These people were reckoned as "paper sons." By this subterfuge, a small but significant number of people circumvented the Exclusion Act, and Chinese immigration continued throughout the period of formal exclusion (Daniels, 1988).

For most of the bachelors, however, there would be no U. S. citizenship, no wives in the United States, no real or paper sons. There would be only unrelenting work, and sending money back to relatives whose memory grew ever more distant, and finally a lonely death.

Japanese Immigration

Japanese immigrants were similar to the Chinese in certain respects: Both groups were overwhelmingly young and male in the early years, both sought economic improvement, both came primarily to the West Coast and Hawaii, and both intended to return to their homeland once their fortunes were made. But the Japanese were determined to learn from the mistakes of the Chinese. The Japanese government carefully screened those men who would go to the United States and actively intervened on behalf of its citizens in the United States. Seeking to avoid the pitfalls of a bachelor society where prostitution, gambling, and drunkenness prevailed, the Japanese government in time came to promote the emigration of Japanese women and the establishment of family life in the United States (Wakatsuki, 1979).

The first Japanese settlers arrived in California in 1869, more than a decade before the enactment of Chinese exclusion. But large numbers of immigrants did not begin to arrive until the 1880s. The first large group was contract laborers, nearly all male, recruited by agents of Hawaiian sugar plantations. Some served out the years of their contracts and then went back to Japan with cash in hand, but others left the plantations and became independent farmers or city tradespeople (Moriyama, 1985; Ogawa, 1978). By the 1890s Japanese laborers were also making their way to the U. S. Mainland to fill spots on farms and railroads and in canneries that had fallen vacant at the expulsion of the Chinese.

The Japanese government sought, by selecting a higher class of emigrant, to avoid the wrath of Euro Americans that had plagued the Chinese. They screened out criminal elements and chose men with some education. But those efforts did not prevent Euro Americans from applying to the Japanese all the racism that had characterized the anti-Chinese movement. Japanese agricultural laborers and other workers experienced as much hostility from Euro American workers as had the Chinese (Ichioka, 1988). While employers welcomed laborers who would work for low wages, Euro American workers did not. Takaki (1989) reports: "While agricultural and railroad employers of Japanese laborers were willing to include Japanese in subordinate economic and social roles, whites generally scorned their presence and white workers waged hostile and sometimes even violent campaigns to keep the Japanese out of the labor market."

An anti-Japanese movement mirroring the anti-Chinese movement began early in the 1900s. The Asiatic Exclusion League called for the ouster of all Japanese, Koreans, and Chinese. In 1906 the San Francisco School Board ordered the city's Japanese, Chinese, and Korean students to attend a segregated Asian school in Chinatown. But, unlike the Chinese, the Japanese immigrants were citizens of a nation that possessed growing military power and diplomatic influence. The Japanese government protested and U. S. President Theodore Roosevelt ordered an investigation. Secretary of Commerce Metcalf reported to President Roosevelt that Japanese students were being attacked by gangs and that there was exaggeration about the "Mongol hordes" overrunning the school system (Knoll, 1982). President Roosevelt, on Metcalf's advice, strong-armed the San Francisco School Board into rescinding its decision against the Japanese students, although the Chinese and Korean students remained segregated (Daniels, 1968).

President Roosevelt's actions may seem to indicate some understanding or sympathy toward the situation of Japanese immigrants, but his real motive was to avoid a confrontation with a growing Asian power. In 1907 President Roosevelt and the Japanese government concluded a Gentlemen's Agreement that restricted the emigration of Japanese laborers. The impact of this agreement was evident in the numbers recorded for Japanese immigrants. From 1902 through 1908, immigrants to the Pacific Coast States and to Hawaii averaged 16,000 a year. In the 2 years following the Gentlemen's Agreement, the average dropped to less than 3,000 per year (Knoll, 1982).

Although the Gentlemen's Agreement restricted male laborer immigrants, it did not restrict female immigrants. At this point, the Japanese

American community changed from a bachelor society to a family society. Some Japanese men went back to Japan, married, and returned with their wives. Others arranged by letter to acquire spouses in the famous "picture bride" system. Many of the picture brides were shocked to find on arrival that the successful businessmen they had been led to believe they were marrying were actually laborers and keepers of tiny shops. But they had cast their lot and there was no going back. Men who had wandered throughout the American West, following the crops and working in mines, canneries, and fishing operations, now settled down and started families (Uchida, 1987).

The Japanese immigrants built not just families but other institutions as well. Primary among these was the Japanese Association in each town that had a substantial Japanese population. This organization brought together businessmen, religious leaders, and consular officials, served as a conduit for communicating with the Japanese government, and acted as a speaker for the community. Also important were *kenjinkai*, social organizations made up of all the people who hailed from a particular prefecture in Japan. The Japanese immigrants also began to build Buddhist and Christian churches, Japanese language schools to train the young in Japanese culture, and various other organs of community cohesion (Ichioka, 1988). Some began to think of the United States as a permanent home. They moved out of wage labor and began to buy farms and build small businesses of their own (Miyamoto, 1984; Modell, 1977).

Euro Americans had thought they were getting rid of the Japanese with the Gentlemen's Agreement and were angered to learn that Japanese people were still immigrating. There was no subterfuge on the part of the Japanese. Their government had simply thought that Americans would be more accepting of Japanese people if they were family people, not just footloose young men, and so they encouraged the brides to emigrate. Euro American antagonists regarded the picture bride phenomenon as a dastardly deception and resolved to drive the Japanese out. In 1913 the California legislature passed an Alien Land Law, quickly copied by other states, that made it illegal for "aliens ineligible to citizenship"—Asians—to own real estate. Seven years later the legislature tightened the law. But those Japanese immigrants who had American-born children circumvented this requirement by registering their property in the names of their sons and daughters and went on with their business. Finally, in 1924, as part of an act that sharply limited immigration from southern and eastern Europe, Congress and the President cut off Asian immigration entirely (Ichioka, 1988).

Early Korean and Punjabi Immigration

Smaller numbers of immigrants came from other parts of Asia in the first decades of this century. At the high point, there were 110,000 Chinese on the U. S. Mainland in 1890, and another 17,000 in Hawaii. In 1920 there were 110,000 Japanese Americans on the Mainland, and an equal number in Hawaii (Knoll, 1982). By comparison, in 1903 there were only 7,000 Koreans working sugar cane and pineapple fields in Hawaii (Knoll, 1982), and fewer than 2,000 on the Mainland as late as 1920 (Takaki, 1989).

Those Koreans who came to Hawaii were laborers from Japanese territory who were emigrating along with Japanese workers. Korea was dominated by Japan beginning in the 1870s and was formally annexed in 1910. The Koreans who came to the U. S. Mainland, on the other hand, were mainly students and political exiles. From bases in San Francisco and other U. S. cities, they mounted a decades-long campaign to liberate their homeland from Japanese colonialism (Lyu, 1976). Unlike other Asian groups, the Koreans were predominately Christians— Methodists and Presbyterians—and their churches were the primary organizations of political resistance to the Japanese as well as the main social institutions in the immigrant communities. Korean Americans were victims of the same anti-Asian movement that harassed and finally excluded the Japanese. In fact, since Koreans were officially represented by the Japanese consul, most people never knew of their separate identity. Like the Chinese, Filipinos, and others, Korean Americans soon became a bachelor society of lonely men who, in the Korean case, could not go back to their country for political reasons (Choy, 1979).

Asian Indians were the other Asian group that came in the early phase of immigration, first arriving shortly after the turn of the century. Although they were Euro Americans, that did not save Asian Indians from the racism of the anti-Asian movements of the first three decades of this century. Anthropologists classified people from India, like people from Europe, as descendants of the ancient Aryans, but most Americans saw dark skin and disclaimed any kinship. Nearly all these immigrants came from Punjab, in what is now northwest India and Pakistan. Americans referred to them all as "Hindoos," but in fact most were Sikhs, perhaps one-third were Muslims, and only a tiny number were Hindus (Takaki, 1989). Immigration from the Punjab began in the middle of the first decade of this century, as the Gentlemen's Agreement cut off entry of Japanese farm laborers, and West Coast farm owners sought replacements. The numbers were never very big, however— 5,000 in California, the most populous state, in 1914 (Takaki, 1989).

At first some Asian Indian immigrants applied for and were awarded citizenship. But a series of court decisions in the 1910s and 1920s ruled that, despite the anthropologists' opinions, these were Asians and hence ineligible for citizenship. Some even had their citizenship revoked and were made stateless. As with the other Asian groups, part of the Euro American complaint was that Asian Indians were culturally incompatible and unwilling to assimilate. But in the Asian Indian case there was the added American fear of the caste system and its anti-democratic implications (Jensen, 1988).

Legal discrimination, political opposition, and physical violence befell the Asian Indians. For example, in 1907 hundreds of Euro American workers attacked the Asian Indian community in Bellingham, Washington, and drove 700 Asian Indians across the border into Canada. After the citizenship issue was decided against them, Asian Indians were subjected to the Alien Land Law, the Immigration Restriction Act, and other forms of legal discrimination (Leonard, 1985; Takaki, 1989).

A 1917 immigration law forbade Asian men already in the United States to send for their wives; but unlike the other Asian groups, the Asian Indians did not let this prevent them from having families. Several hundred went to great lengths to circumvent anti-miscegenation laws and marry Euro American or Mexican women. The children of many of the latter couples blended into the Chicano population in succeeding decades (Leonard, 1982).

Filipino Immigration

The presence of Filipinos in the United States in the first third of this century is attributable to the expansion of U. S. power overseas at the turn of the century and the web of colonial connectedness that was set up in succeeding decades. The United States' colonial role in the Philippines began in 1898, when it acquired the Philippines in the Spanish-American War. Filipinos had an unusual legal status: They were not citizens, but "U. S. nationals." They were the one group exempted by Congress from the exclusion provisions of the Immigration Act of 1924 (Lasker, 1969).

As Japanese and Korean labor immigration ended about 1905, Hawaiian plantation owners began to look elsewhere for cheap workers. Like the Chinese and Japanese laborers, the Filipinos were persuaded by sugar plantation owners to go to Hawaii and work under contract. In 1907, 150 Filipinos were sent to Hawaii (Chan, 1991). Others soon arrived on the Mainland and the Filipinos became successors to Chinese and Japanese in Western farms and canneries. They numbered about 100,000 from the 1930s through the 1950s, with about equal numbers on the Mainland and in Hawaii. Besides working on farms and in canneries, Filipinos also worked as cooks and did domestic labor. They also worked in sawmills and in other industrial plants (Bulosan, 1973; Lasker, 1969).

The Filipinos were not excluded from the discrimination and harassment that the three previous Asian groups endured. In 1928 there began violent incidents against the Filipinos on the Mainland. In 1930 in Monterey, California, a mob of 400 attacked a Filipino club, beating up many Filipinos and killing one. That same year a Filipino lettuce picker was shot to death in California, and although seven suspects were arrested, none was indicted (Chan, 1991).

These acts of violence toward the Filipinos may or may not have been related to the fact that Filipinos, unlike the earlier Chinese, Japanese, and Korean immigrants, sought to marry Euro and Mexican American women. Although U. S. nationals, Filipinos were still discriminated against because of race. Since Filipinos were not "Mongolians" like Chinese, Japanese, and Koreans, they were not under the jurisdiction of the miscegenation laws. However, in 1930 a Superior Court judge in California prohibited a county court clerk from issuing a marriage license to a Filipino man and a Euro American woman (Chan, 1991). In 1931 that decision was overturned because, in the opinion of the appellate court, Filipinos were "Malays" and not "Mongolians"; thus they could intermarry, and some began to form families. Still, the majority of the Filipinos, like other Asians except for the Japanese, remained unattached to families in the United States (Posadas, 1981).

Not only could the Filipinos intermarry but, unlike other Asians, they could also become citizens through service in the military. Many Filipino men became citizens after stints in the Navy. However, even with provisions for citizenship, immigrant Filipinos were restricted to a quota. In 1934 the Tydings-McDuffie Act was passed, limiting Filipino immigrants to an annual quota of 50 (Cordova, 1983).

FORMATION OF A SECOND GENERATION

Each Asian immigrant group worked its way into particular economic niches. All the groups except Asian Indians started out in contract labor in Hawaii, although most Chinese and Japanese soon moved off the plantations and into towns. On the Mainland, all the Asian groups worked in West Coast agriculture as day laborers following the crops. Starting in the late decades of the nineteenth century, many Chinese Americans were pushed out of agriculture, mining, and railroad building and settled in ghettos in Western cities. Some worked in industry, but most formed a tightly knit, separate ethnic economy in Chinatown (Lyman, 1974). The Japanese also moved out of the role of laborer on farms and in canneries and concentrated in small rural and urban entrepreneurship to a degree almost unprecedented among American ethnic groups. The Japanese on the West Coast formed vertical linkages connecting farmers, wholesalers, and retailers. In doing so they came to dominate the vegetable and flower industries around most West Coast cities (Bonacich & Modell, 1980).

A significant percentage of the small Korean population became small entrepreneurs, but the Koreans did not achieve the degree of community or of economic linkage that characterized the Chinese and Japanese. Far fewer members of the early Asian Indian and Filipino migrations made it out of the ranks of farm and factory worker and into small entrepreneurship.

In each of these communities a second generation grew up by the 1930s. It was tiny in the case of the Filipinos, Koreans, and Asian Indians. The Chinese American second generation was somewhat larger because there were so many more Chinese, although the percentage of Chinese who had children was very small. These Chinese Americans grew up in a ghettoized existence, in Chinatowns vibrant with ethnic life but largely cut off from the opportunities available to non-Asians (Wong, 1950).

The one Asian group to produce a significant second generation were the Japanese. Japanese Americans even introduced terminology—*Issei* for the immigrants and *Nisei* for their American-born children—to classify the generations. The Nisei were born mainly in the 1910s and 1920s and grew up only slightly less segregated than the Chinese Americans. More of them grew up in farm communities, but in most of those places, as in West Coast cities, they socialized mainly with other Nisei. They built a parallel social world, following the manners and clothing of Euro American teenagers in the 1930s, dancing and chewing gum and wearing bobby sox, but few of them were allowed to interact with the wider social world. Their economic opportunities, too, were circumscribed by their ethnicity. Despite an enviable record of academic achievement, only tiny numbers of Nisei found employment outside the ethnic economy during the Depression. It was not unusual to find a young man with a Stanford University master's degree in engineering washing carrots in a Los Angeles vegetable stand run by his uncle (Hosokawa, 1969; Kitagawa, 1974; Mori, 1985; Sone, 1953). Some Nisei resented the degree to which the Issei controlled their lives, and some of them formed an organization, the Japanese American Citizens League (JACL), to push for independence for their generation (Hosokawa, 1982; Spickard, 1983).

WORLD WAR II

World War II was a great watershed in the history of Asian American peoples. It brought an end to Chinese exclusion, although the immigration quota was still tiny. Many Filipinos served in the American war effort, and thereby earned U. S. citizenship.

But the major disaster of World War II for Asian Americans was the concentration camps in which Japanese Americans were incarcerated. Within hours after the war broke out in December 1941, federal agents swarmed into Japanese communities, arrested all the community's male leaders, and soon shipped them all off to prison camps for enemy aliens. None was ever found guilty of spying or sabotage, but that did not keep them from being denied due process of law (Daniels, 1972, 1981).

By midwinter, West Coast non-Japanese Americans were clamoring for the removal of all Japanese Americans from their midst. Part of this was racist hysteria induced by Japan's stunning successes in the war's early battles and non-Japanese Americans' inability to distinguish Japanese from Japanese American, citizen from alien, or loyal from disloyal. Part of it was the frank desire of some Westerners to appropriate the farms and businesses of their Japanese American neighbors. Against the objections of the government intelligence services, which insisted Japanese Americans were loyal, President Franklin Roosevelt signed the infamous Executive Order 9066, which allowed the West Coast army commander to prohibit anyone he wanted from his region (Commission on Wartime Relocation and Internment of Civilians, 1982; Daniels, 1975).

In short order, all 120,000 Japanese Americans who lived on the West Coast were rounded up and herded into barbed-wire enclosures, hastily converted from former racetracks and fairgrounds. Within months they were transferred to 10 "relocation centers"—the official government euphemism for prison camps—constructed by the army in the mountains, deserts, and swamps of the West and run by the civilian War Relocation Authority (WRA). There the Japanese Americans spent the bulk of the war surrounded by barbed wire (an electrified fence in one case) and guards armed with machine guns (Weglyn, 1976).

Conditions in the camps were Spartan at best. There was virtually no privacy. Families were split up or combined with other families. The government trusted the American-born Nisei slightly more than their Issei parents, so they dealt with the Nisei only and thereby further undermined the structures of family and community stability. In the camps the torch passed from the hands of the Issei generation, although the Nisei were not yet ready to pick it up (Kitagawa, 1974; Uchida, 1982).

Conflicts broke out in camp between accommodationists led by the JACL, which wanted to cooperate with the government at every turn in a desperate attempt to prove their loyalty, and others—Issei and Nisei— who insisted on a measure of dignity and civil rights. The accommodationists won in the short run, but the conflict created divisions that plague Japanese American communities to this day. Some camps existed fairly peacefully, but others witnessed mass meetings, strikes, riots, beatings, the intrusion of federal troops, and the incarceration and abuse of inmate resistance leaders. In the end, with the United States winning the war and Japanese American soldiers serving with distinction in both European and Pacific theaters, the government found itself embarrassed to be holding in jail more than 100,000 Americans, two-thirds of them citizens, none of them charged with any crime. In 1944 and 1945 the WRA started closing down the camps and trying to resettle the inmates, first in the East and Midwest, then back on the West Coast. At the war's end a few embittered Issei and Nisei gave up on the United States and went to Japan, while others tried to pick up the shreds of their prewar lives (Duus, 1987; Thomas, 1952; Thomas & Nishimoto, 1946).

Conspicuously absent from the camp episode were nearly all the Japanese in Hawaii, who remained free throughout the war. There, in the one place where their numbers were large enough (more than one-third of the islands' population) to have posed an actual security threat, they remained at liberty because they were in fact no threat and their work was essential to the war effort.

The costs of the concentration camps were enormous: for example, more than 200,000 worker-years lost to the war effort, Japanese American property losses ranging upwards from a half-billion dollars, the virtual destruction of Japanese communities, and the precipitous decline of the Issei generation. But equally great were the costs in terms of U. S. constitutional liberties. The Supreme Court let the incarceration stand; the inevitable implications have been: (a) that the liberties of U. S. citizenship are not guaranteed in wartime, even if there is no immediate military threat; and (b) that race and national origin are sufficient grounds for declaring someone a menace to society irrespective of his or her actual conduct. Only four and a half decades after the fact did the U. S. government get around to admitting that it had made a huge mistake and offering token compensation to those former inmates who were still alive in the late 1980s (Daniels, Taylor, & Kitano, 1986; Irons, 1983, 1989).

Following the war, the dispersed Japanese Americans faced the task of rebuilding. Some who had moved to midwestern and eastern cities remained there. Others went back to the West Coast and tried to reestablish their homes, businesses, and communities. Initially, European American opposition to the returning inmates was intense—even violent—in some places. The animosity faded quickly, but Japanese American communities never regained their prewar vigor. Churches reestablished themselves under Nisei leadership, but most of the other formerly Issei-dominated organizations remained in eclipse. The JACL, largely discredited by its collaboration during the war, did not establish itself as an organizer of community life. Most Nisei tried to blend into the mainstream of middle-class life as inconspicuously as possible. In the 1950s and 1960s, they pushed hard for educational and occupational mobility, and moved out of old Japanese neighborhoods into the suburbs. By 1970, outside of Hawaii and certain towns in Southern California, one would be hard-pressed to find two Japanese American families living next-door to each other anywhere in the United States. Japanese American communities and Japanese Americans as a group have yet to regain their prewar strength (Kitano, 1976).

One new factor among Asian Americans after the war was the arrival of a new wave of immigrants—"war brides," women married to GIs who had served in Asia as the United States maintained a major military presence there throughout the rest of the century. The largest number of Asian war brides were Japanese, but there were also Koreans, Chinese, Filipinos, and women from various parts of Southeast Asia.

For the most part, such women were not accepted in Asian communities until the 1970s and 1980s (Spickard, 1989).

NEW IMMIGRATION SINCE 1965

Immigration laws were passed in 1952, 1965, 1988, and 1990. The 1952 McCarran-Walter Act ended Asian exclusion, but granted only tiny, token quotas to people of Asian extraction. The 1965 Immigration Act was the most significant. It eliminated the restrictive Asian quotas and provided for 17,400 refugees to be admitted to the United States annually, along with 170,000 immigrants from the Eastern Hemisphere and 120,000 from the Western Hemisphere (Takaki, 1989). This resulted in the reorientation of U. S. immigration, with a flood of immigrants coming in every year since from Asia and Latin America. The leading countries sending Asian immigrants in the past 25 years have been China (including Hong Kong), the Philippines, India, Korea, and Vietnam, although significant numbers have come from every Asian nation (Reimers, 1985).

Total numbers of Asian Americans doubled between 1960 and 1970, then doubled again in the 1970s, and again in the 1980s. The largest Asian American ethnic groups in 1980 were (U.S. Bureau of the Census, 1991):

Chinese	806,040
Filipinos	774,652
Japanese	700,974
Asian Indians	361,531
Koreans	354,593
Vietnamese	261,729
Other Southeast Asians	130,659

The comparable numbers in 1990 were (U.S. Bureau of the Census, 1991):

Chinese	1,645,472
Filipinos	1,406,770
Japanese	847,562
Asian Indians	815,447
Koreans	798,849
Vietnamese	614,547
Other Southeast Asians	525,454

Where the earlier Asian immigrants had been mainly rural folk, this "second wave" of newcomers, as Ronald Takaki describes them, were more often professional people and city dwellers (Takaki, 1989). This was partly due to rapid urbanization in Asia, and partly due to the immigration law's preference for immigrants who had skills. Despite their professional backgrounds, these newcomers still had language and cultural barriers to overcome.

The new Chinese immigrants were the third-largest group after the Mexicans and the Filipinos. Takaki (1989) reports that the Chinese community went from 61% American-born in 1965 to 63% foreign-born in 1984, thus becoming mainly an immigrant community. With the anticipation of Hong Kong's conversion from British rule to Chinese Communist leadership in 1997, Hong Kong immigrants are greatly increasing in numbers, needs, and perhaps social problems, as they swell the populations of Chinatowns from New York to Houston to San Francisco to Honolulu.

The second wave of immigrants included very few Japanese—only 3% of the Asian immigrants between 1965 and 1984 (Takaki, 1989). Thus, by the latter date, the Japanese community was almost entirely native born, with community leadership passing into the hands of the Sansei (third) and Yonsei (fourth) generations.

The new Korean and Filipino immigrants, driven by repression at home and attracted by educational and economic opportunities in the United States, were generally college-educated people who brought their families with them. Between 1966 and 1970 there were 39,705 Filipinos admitted to the United States, and 65% had professional or technical skills (Takaki, 1989).

While the dominant motivation for most Asian immigrants continued to be economic betterment, some were impelled by more desperate forces. Several decades of war left much of Southeast Asia in ruins and plagued by chronic civil strife. Vietnamese, Cambodians, Hmong, Laotians, and others fled their homelands as refugees in the 1970s and 1980s. Some left on jumbo jets. But most had to survive torturous passages through jungles and across mountains or through pirate-infested waters in leaky boats, then to endure months and years in dreary refugee camps, in places like Thailand and Hong Kong, before a lucky few managed to secure entry to the United States (Freeman, 1989).

For some refugees, coming to the United States did not solve all their problems. In many cases it only added problems to their already complicated lives. For example, in 1979 there were clashes between Vietnamese and Euro American fishermen in Seabrook, Texas, on Galveston Bay. The Euro Americans complained that the Vietnamese were too successful and had unfair access to federal money. Threats were made by the Ku Klux Klan, shots were fired, Vietnamese boats were sunk, and the refugee fishermen were forced to flee (Knoll, 1982).

The Laotian refugees consist mainly of two different ethnic groups— Hmong and Mien people. Their escape from Laos to refugee camps in Thailand was difficult and traumatic. But adjustment difficulties also arose for those refugees who were able to settle in the United States. Adjustments from a rural, agricultural, non-technologically oriented environment in Laos to the fast-paced, computer-dominated environment anywhere in the United States were imposed upon all the refugees, some of whom did not survive this adjustment. The Hmong people, especially the men, have been plagued by mysterious, sudden, medically unexplainable deaths, which have struck scores of people. Theories about this sudden death syndrome range from unidentified gases used by the North Vietnamese during the Vietnam war to extreme stress placed upon the men because of poor adjustment to their new environment (Takaki, 1989).

One might assume that in the 1970s and 1980s difficulties and prejudices would be suffered mainly by the most recent newcomers to the United States, such as the Southeast Asian refugees. However, that was not the case. Prejudice, discrimination, and harassment plagued not only recent immigrants but also such older Asian groups as the Chinese and Japanese. In 1982, Vincent Chin, a 27-year-old Chinese American celebrating his impending marriage, was chased and clubbed to death with a baseball bat in Detroit by two Euro American men who had worked in the automobile industry. Not only was the beating outrageous, so was the men's defense at their trial: They pleaded guilty, but said that their act was in some way understandable because they mistook Chin for a Japanese American. That is, Japanese cars were hurting the sales of American cars, so the accused were out of work; therefore, it presumably would be okay for them to kill a Japanese American out of frustration. The confessed murderers did not do time in jail; they got off with 3 years' probation and a fine of $3,000 each plus court costs. Asian American groups and non-Asians who were concerned for the cause of justice protested, but to no avail (Chan, 1991).

Many of the problems of Asian peoples in the United States have been addressed by the Asian American movement. Beginning on West Coast university campuses in the late 1960s, in imitation of and solidarity

with African American, Latino, and Native American student movements, the Asian American movement blossomed in the 1970s and
1980s into a large number of initiatives: Asian American studies programs, legal aid societies, social service agencies, cultural organizations, and efforts at political organization (Gee, 1976).

One example from the 1980s was the movement for Japanese American redress. Most Japanese Americans had simply tried to lie low and
go about their lives after their World War II concentration camp experience. But in the late 1960s and 1970s, Sansei began investigating their
parents' past and reacting with outrage to the concentration camp
episode. By the late 1980s their legal and political campaigns had
resulted in new court decisions overturning the wartime cases used to
justify the incarceration, as well as congressional action to redress the
wartime wrongs (Daniels, Taylor, & Kitano, 1986; Hohri, 1984). In
1987 the U. S. government issued an official apology to the Japanese
Americans and agreed to pay each surviving internee $20,000 in token
compensation for their losses and the denial of their rights. For many
Japanese Americans the apology was the more meaningful event, since
no amount of money could compensate for the pain and humiliation they
had unjustly endured. In any case, it was not until 1989 that Congress
actually appropriated the money and began to compensate those who
had suffered.

No Asian ethnic group is immune from the ongoing racism and
discrimination in the United States today. All are still experiencing
incidents of prejudice and harassment at some level. For example, in
New York in May 1990, several years of accelerating animosities
resulted in a boycott of Korean grocery stores by their African American neighbors; a year later the tensions remained and some stores had
gone out of business. In academic institutions across the country racism
is still an ongoing issue. Many campuses witness complaints about the
rising number of Asian American students. At UCLA in May 1991, two
Vietnamese students woke up to find their doors vandalized with de-
rogatory and racial slurs, including "Viets go home" (Dong, 1991).

In part, such incidents reflect the growing myth that Asians are a kind
of "model minority"—talented, hard-working, uncomplaining, techni-
cally skilled people. In fact, the academic records and other achievements of many Asian Americans are extraordinary. But the achievements have been met with resentment by other Americans, and have
also masked enduring difficulties. Success has been very uneven, with
some groups and individuals much better suited to achievement than

others, and some unable to lift themselves out of poverty. Even skilled Asian Americans have complained of a "glass ceiling" in the business world—they are welcomed as technical specialists and may even become middle managers, but the top ranks of management remain closed to them (Kitano & Sue, 1973).

CONCLUSION

Four themes characterize the history of Asian American peoples: diversity, economic motives for migration, racist discrimination, and aggressive responses to that discrimination. This chapter looks at as many as nine distinctly different Asian American ethnic groups. They came to the United States for different reasons, at different times and by different means, from different geographical locations, speaking different languages, and they brought different cultures and values with them. They are not one people but several. Yet they have been seen by non-Asian Americans as an almost undifferentiable mass. This inability of non-Asian Americans to distinguish among Asians led to the anti-Chinese movement, later focusing its attentions on Japanese, Koreans, and Asian Indians. More recently, it led Vincent Chin's attackers to mistake him for Japanese, when he was neither Japanese nor Japanese American.

The primary motive for most Asian immigration throughout American history has been economic. Some people came from Korea or Vietnam or elsewhere as political refugees, and some revolutionary movements—Chinese, Indian, Korean, and Filipino—were plotted by exiles in the United States. But just as most nineteenth-century Chinese immigrants came to work, save money, and return to China, so most late-twentieth-century Asian immigrants also seek economic advancement.

Perhaps the most common thread uniting all these groups is their experience of racism and discrimination at the hands of Euro Americans. From the anti-Chinese riots in Wyoming in the 1880s to the widespread Japan-bashing of the 1980s and 1990s, acts of insensitivity, verbal attacks, and physical violence by non-Asians have characterized Asian American history. These experiences of racism and discrimination frequently focus on the differences of appearance, language, and customs between non-Asian Americans and various Asian peoples. But incidents have also been caused by jealousy, insecurity, and fear of competition on the part of non-Asians.

Throughout their history Asian Americans have been victims of discrimination, but they have seldom been passive victims. In the late nineteenth and early twentieth centuries, Chinese and Japanese immigrants hired the best lawyers in California and contested the exclusion acts, alien land laws, and other discriminatory legislation in the nation's highest courts (Fritz, 1980). When they could not overturn laws, they sought to evade their negative consequences by such measures as putting their land in the names of their American-born children. Frequently they presented themselves in an overtly deferential way, appropriate to their Asian cultural background, but their resistance was fierce nonetheless. The only major period of anti-Asian discrimination that went essentially unchallenged was the World War II imprisonment of Japanese Americans. That lack of challenge may be attributed to the overwhelming power of the U. S. government in wartime and to the removal of the Issei leaders in the war's first weeks (Spickard, 1983).

Since the rise of the Asian American movement in the late 1960s, resistance to oppression has become more vigorous. Not only in the movement for redress and in protests against specific acts of discrimination, but also in conventional party politics, Asian Americans are ever more active. Currently, Asian Americans represent the states of California and Hawaii in the U. S. Senate and House of Representatives. Moreover, there are Asian Americans who are major figures in the governments of all the West Coast states and of major Western cities.

Prejudice and discrimination remain. But this varied collection of Asian American peoples, by virtue of rapidly increasing numbers, economic achievement, and political assertiveness, has begun to emerge as a major force on the American scene.

REFERENCES

Armentrout-Ma, L. E. (1983). Urban Chinese at the Sinitic frontier: Social organizations in United States' Chinatowns, 1849-1898. *Modern Asian Studies, 17,* 107-135.

Bonacich, E., & Modell, J. (1980). *The economic basis of ethnic solidarity: Small business in the Japanese American community.* Berkeley: University of California Press.

Bulosan, C. (1973). *America is in the heart.* Seattle: University of Washington Press.

Chan, S. (1991). *Asian Americans: An interpretive history.* Boston: Twayne.

Chen, T. (1940). *Emigrant communities in South China.* New York: Institute of Pacific Relations.

Cheng, L., & Bonacich, E. (Eds.). (1984). *Labor immigration under capitalism: Asian workers in the United States before World War II.* Berkeley: University of California Press.

Chin, D., & Chin, A. (1973). *Uphill: The settlement and diffusion of the Chinese in Seattle, Washington*. Seattle: Shorey Bookstore.

Choy, B. (1979). *Koreans in America*. Chicago: Nelson-Hall.

Chu, Y. R. (1973). Chinese secret societies in America. *Asian Profile, 1*, 21-38.

Commission on Wartime Relocation and Internment of Civilians. (1982). *Personal justice denied*. Washington, DC: Government Printing Office.

Coolidge, M. R. (1909). *Chinese immigration*. New York: Holt.

Cordova, F. (1983). *Filipinos: Forgotten Asian Americans*. Dubuque, IA: Kendall/Hunt.

Daniels, R. (1968). *The politics of prejudice: The anti-Japanese movement in California and the struggle for Japanese exclusion*. New York: Atheneum.

Daniels, R. (1972). *Concentration camps U.S.A.: Japanese Americans and World War II*. New York: Holt, Rinehart & Winston.

Daniels, R. (1975). *The decision to relocate the Japanese Americans*. Philadelphia: Lippincott.

Daniels, R. (1981). *Concentration camps, North America: Japanese in the United States and Canada during World War II*. Melbourne, FL: Krieger.

Daniels, R. (1988). *Asian America: Chinese and Japanese in the United States since 1850*. Seattle: University of Washington Press.

Daniels, R., Taylor, S. C., & Kitano, H.H.L. (Eds.). (1986). *Japanese Americans: From relocation to redress*. Salt Lake City: University of Utah Press.

Dong, R. (1991, May 1). Racist graffiti spurs program reform. *UCLA Daily Bruin*, p. 1.

Duus, M. U. (1987). *Unlikely liberators: The men of the 100th and 442nd*. Honolulu: University of Hawaii Press.

Freeman, J. C. (1989). *Hearts of sorrow: Vietnamese American lives*. Palo Alto, CA: Stanford University Press.

Fritz, C. (1980). Bitter strength (*k'u-li*) and the constitution: The Chinese before the federal courts in California. *Historical Reporter, 1*, 2-15.

Gee, E. (Ed.). (1976). *Counterpoint: Perspectives on Asian America*. Los Angeles: UCLA Asian American Studies Center.

Hohri, W. M. (1984). *Repairing America: An account of the movement for Japanese-American redress*. Pullman: Washington State University Press.

Hosokawa, B. (1969). *Nisei: The quiet Americans*. New York: Morrow.

Hosokawa, B. (1982). *J.A.C.L. in quest of justice*. New York: Morrow.

Hoy, W. (1942). *The Chinese six companies*. San Francisco: Chinese Consolidated Benevolent Association.

Ichioka, Y. (1988). *The Issei: The world of the first generation Japanese immigrants, 1885-1924*. New York: Free Press.

Irons, P. (1983). *Justice at war: The story of the Japanese American internment cases*. New York: Oxford University Press.

Irons, P. (Ed.). (1989). *Justice delayed: The record of the Japanese American internment cases*. Middletown, CT: Wesleyan University Press.

Jensen, J. M. (1988). *Passage from India: Asian Indian immigrants in North America*. New Haven, CT: Yale University Press.

Karlin, J. A. (1948). The anti-Chinese outbreaks in Seattle, 1885-1887. *Pacific Northwest Quarterly, 39*, 103-130.

Kitagawa, D. (1974). *Issei and Nisei*. New York: Seabury Press.

Kitano, H.H.L. (1976). *Japanese Americans: The evolution of a subculture*. Englewood Cliffs, NJ: Prentice-Hall.

Kitano, H.H.L., & Sue, S. (1973). The model minorities. *Journal of Social Issues, 29*, 1-9.

Knoll, T. (1982). *Becoming Americans: Asian sojourners, immigrants, and refugees in the western United States.* Portland, OR: Coast to Coast Books.

Lai, H. M., Lim, G., & Yung, J. (1981). *Island: Poetry and history of Chinese Immigrants on Angel Island, 1910-1940.* San Francisco: Chinese Historical Society.

Lasker, B. (1969). *Filipino immigration.* New York: Arno Press/*The New York Times.*

Lee, R. H. (1978). *The growth and decline of Chinese communities in the Rocky Mountain region.* New York: Arno Press.

Leonard, K. (1982). Marriage and family life among early Asian Indian immigrants. In S. Chandrasekhar (Ed.), *From India to America* (pp. 72-75). LaJolla, CA: Population Review Publications.

Leonard, K. (1985). Punjabi farmers and California's alien land law. *Agricultural History, 59*, 550-561.

Li, P. S. (1980). Immigration laws and family patterns: Demographic changes among Chinese families in Canada, 1885-1971. *Canadian Ethnic Studies, 12*, 58-73.

Lyman, S. (1974). *Chinese Americans.* New York: Random House.

Lyu, K. K. (1976). Korean nationalist activities in Hawaii and America, 1901-1945. In E. Gee (Ed.), *Counterpoint: Perspectives on Asian America* (pp. 106-128). Los Angeles: UCLA Asian American Studies Center.

Mei, J. (1984). Socioeconomic origins of emigration: Guangdong to California, 1850-1882. In L. Cheng & E. Bonacich (Eds.), *Labor immigration under capitalism: Asian workers in the United States before World War II* (pp. 219-247). Berkeley: University of California Press.

Miyamoto, S. F. (1984). *Social solidarity among the Japanese in Seattle* (3rd ed.). Seattle: University of Washington Press.

Modell, J. (1977). *The economics and politics of racial accommodation: The Japanese of Los Angeles, 1900-1942.* Urbana: University of Illinois Press.

Mori, T. (1985). *Yokohama, California.* Seattle: University of Washington Press.

Moriyama, A. T. (1985). *Imingaisha: Japanese emigration companies and Hawaii.* Honolulu: University of Hawaii Press.

Nee, V. G., & Nee, B. D. (1973). *Longtime Californ': A documentary study of an American Chinatown.* New York: Pantheon.

Ogawa, D. (Ed.). (1978). *Kodomo no tame ni: For the sake of the children.* Honolulu: University of Hawaii Press.

Posadas, B. (1981). Crossed boundaries in interracial Chicago: Pilipino American families since 1925. *Amerasia Journal, 8*, 31-52.

Reimers, D. M. (1985). *Still the golden door: The third world comes to America.* New York: Columbia University Press.

Saloutos, T. (1956). *They remember America.* Berkeley: University of California Press.

Sandmeyer, E. C. (1973). *The anti-Chinese movement in California* (2nd ed.). Urbana: University of Illinois Press.

Sone, M. (1953). *Nisei daughter.* Boston: Little, Brown.

Spickard, P. R. (1983). The Nisei assume power: The Japanese American Citizens League, 1941-1942. *Pacific Historical Review, 52*, 147-174.

Spickard, P. R. (1989). *Mixed blood: Intermarriage and ethnic identity in twentieth-century America.* Madison: University of Wisconsin Press.

Sung, B. L. (1967). *Mountain of gold.* New York: Macmillan.

Takaki, R. (1989). *Strangers from a different shore: A history of Asian Americans.* Boston: Little, Brown.

Thomas, D. S. (1952). *The salvage.* Berkeley: University of California Press.

Thomas, D. S., & Nishimoto, R. S. (1946). *The spoilage.* Berkeley: University of California Press.

Uchida, Y. (1982). *Desert exile: The uprooting of a Japanese-American family.* Seattle: University of Washington Press.

Uchida, Y. (1987). *Picture bride.* New York: Simon & Schuster.

U. S. Bureau of the Census. (1991, June 12). Census bureau releases 1990 census counts on specific racial groups (press release).

Wakatsuki, Y. (1979). Japanese emigration to the United States, 1866-1924. *Perspectives in American History, 12,* 387-516.

Weglyn, M. (1976). *Years of infamy.* New York: Morrow.

Wong, J. S. (1950). *Fifth Chinese daughter.* New York: Harper.

Yung, J. (1977). A bowlful of tears: Chinese women immigrants on Angel Island. *Frontiers, 2,* 52-55.

Chapter 2

ASIAN CULTURAL COMMONALITIES: *A Comparison With Mainstream American Culture*

DOUGLAS K. CHUNG

There are profound differences between the value system of Asians and that of mainstream American culture. Since Asians share some cultural patterns and a sense of common identity, it is helpful for human service workers to understand this similar value system and the parallel problems and issues Asians face. The intent is not to deny the existence of differences among the various Asian ethnic groups, but rather to describe their common value system and compare it to that of the dominant culture. The approach presented is general because of the diversity between and within Asian ethnic groups.

The term *Asian culture* refers to the cultures of those countries from which Asians in the United States originated, cultures that were basically influenced by Confucianism, Buddhism, Hinduism, and Islam. A large number of Asians, recent arrivals in particular, are from countries that are within the areas influenced by Chinese culture; thus the emphasis is on East Asian, Confucian values. The roots of American culture, in contrast, are in the Greek philosophical tradition and culminate in Western philosophies, Western sciences, and Judeo-Christian values. The term *Euro Americans* refers to the dominant, white group in American society, which has been influenced primarily by the Western tradition.

ASIAN CULTURAL COMMONALITIES

What cultural traits and values do Asians hold in common? Scholars indicate a number of values, including filial piety, parent-child interaction in which communication flows essentially from parent to child, self-control and restraint in emotional expression, respect for authority, well-defined social roles and expectations, shame as a behavioral influence, middle position virtue, awareness of social milieu, fatalism, communal responsibility, inconspicuousness, high regard for the elderly, and the centrality of family relationships and responsibilities (Dhooper & Tran, 1986; Ho, 1976; Tsui & Schultz, 1985).

All these values are directly related to the fundamental value of harmony. Although typically the Asian family reflects the impact of Western familial values, such as a more egalitarian family role structure, nevertheless Asian values retain their influence on attitudes and behaviors. For example, even though the Asian individual may now choose a marital partner and a career, the individual belongs to a "group self" and not an "individual self," according to Ross-Sheriff and Meemeduma (1986) and Hirayama and Hirayama (1984).

WHAT ARE THE DIFFERENCES?

Hall (1983) espouses the dominance in today's world of two very different traditions. There is on the one hand the linear, externalized logic that began with the Greek philosophers and continues to be practiced in today's Western science. On the other hand, there are the inward-looking, highly disciplined Hindu, Buddhist, and Confucian philosophies, with Jen playing a prominent part. Each tradition works in radically different ways from the other to mold people and their natural environment. It is difficult, if not impossible, to understand another culture unless one knows one's own culture. In the following section, then, Asian cultural commonalities are defined and then compared to the dominant Euro American culture. The comparison will help professionals develop a culturally relevant practice by enhancing self-awareness and mutual understanding.

Cultural Context

Hall (1966, 1981, 1983) differentiates between what he calls high- and low-context cultures. Context here refers to the collection of social and cultural conditions that surround and influence the life of an individual, an organization, or a community. High-context cultures, such as traditional Chinese and Japanese, pay great attention to the surrounding circumstances or context of an event; thus, in interpersonal communication the elements of phrasing, tone, gestures, posture, social status, history, and social setting are all crucial to the meaning of the message. High-context cultures emphasize associations with people, and in them one's identity tends to be rooted in groups—family, culture, and employment.

On the other hand, in communication in a low-context culture, many of the surrounding circumstances are screened out and communication focuses more on objective facts and less on individuals. Euro Americans, according to Hall, fall in the medium low-context culture and their identity is rooted in the individual.

Worldview

A major difference between Asian culture and American culture is the individual's view of the world: Asians tend to be environment-centered while Euro Americans tend to be individual-centered.

A central feature of Asian philosophy is that of harmony between people and their environment, a theme that regularly appears in Asian art and literature. In traditional Chinese paintings, nature dominates the background and human beings are mere spots, expressing the greatness of nature, in contrast to the emphasis on the greatness of humanity in Western art. Asian art prescribes a person-and-environment relationship; the relative insignificance of human beings in the natural environment is an indication that in Asian culture, people realize their limitations and are willing to accept their limited life and its nature. This fatalistic attitude leads to a state of harmony with nature rather than conflict.

Similar to this concept is that of the unification of the person and God, a state in which the individual and nature become one and the individual acts to harmonize with his or her environment. In this environment-centered value system, the individual strives to resonate with the environment. Examples of the centrality of the value of harmony with the environment are in Japanese architecture and gardens.

The Chinese theory of Yin and Yang (negative and positive) has influenced many fields in China, including architecture, agricultural operations, medicine, and acupuncture—all of which seek to achieve harmony with the environment. In Yin-Yang theory, when harmony is achieved, one reaches the best condition for potential development. Failure to reach harmony violates the natural law, and if Yin and Yang do not reach a balance, sickness may result.

Asian culture was developed from and is still centered on an agricultural background, and people learned the principles of interaction and harmony with their natural and social environments. When the rules are changed, disharmony may result.

The principle of harmony with the environment was also extended to the social environment within the traditions of Confucianism, Buddhism, and Hinduism, and it was internalized as a part of the function of culture.

The art of living in these traditions encompasses not only trying to reach harmony with external and natural worlds but also being in sync with one's internal psychological state and in one's social relations. In Chinese society, the traditional social structure is based on five fundamental interpersonal relationships of Confucianism (Table 2.1): between superior and subordinate, between parent and child, between husband and wife, between brothers, and between friends. These relationships are arranged in a hierarchical order of position and status. Thus the structure of society is vertical, in contrast to the horizontal structure of American culture, and each individual has distinct obligations to the other in a particular relationship.

The first relationship, superior-subordinate, was originally the sovereign-minister relationship and required one's first loyalty to the ruler (which today means the government or one's superior on the job). In return, the ruler or employer takes care of subordinates' needs. Most of the other relationships require love, while others require protection, provision, loyalty, filial piety, and so on.

Confucianism prescribes family relationships and indicates the degree of intimacy and the social distance as well as the obligations within them. Anyone who is within this network is considered to be a part of the family; all others are outsiders. As a member of the family, one enjoys membership privileges such as trust, intimacy, and sharing. At the same time, one has family obligations, which include making contributions to the family (such as getting good grades, which enhance the family's reputation) and not creating problems. Related social institutions (schools or employers) become extensions of the family, and the same respect is required for elders and for authority. Self-control is expected as a means of maintaining social harmony.

Table 2.1
Five Relationships (Universal Obligations)

Social Roles and Relationships	Obligation
1. Ruler (Superior)	Protection and Provision
Subject (Subordinate)	Loyalty
2. Parent	Love and Protection
Child	Filial Piety
3. Husband	Provision and Protection
Wife	Love and Service
4. Siblings	Love and Respect
5. Friends	Trust and Righteousness

Harmony plays a critical role in influencing Asian behavior in various human interactions. Self-limits, shame, cooperation with the group, and embarrassment are natural products under this value system. Children are taught not to speak in front of elders and to apologize for disturbing the family. Self-expression, confrontation, and requests for promotion create difficulties for Asians who value the group and have had guilt and shame programmed into them throughout early childhood. Thus, Asian social scientists such as Ho (1976) warn that the conflict or confrontation approach, rather than helping Asian clients, may violate their cultural rules. Asian culture says, "It is good to have harmony and to be in sync with your environment." Harmony is what Asians, consciously or unconsciously seek and is evidenced by their behavior.

Euro American culture, in contrast, is highly individual-centered. A major theme of Western art is that man is the conqueror. Euro Americans are proud of how fast they can change their environment into highways and tall buildings; how fast their airplanes or cars can go; and how effectively their fertilizer increases agricultural production. They highly value self- or individual-expression and self- or individual-actualization; therefore, change and conflict are necessary to achieve their dreams. Self-expression as a means to actualization is taught as an important socialization theme from a very young age. The resulting individual-centeredness, with self-expression as the means of actualization, leads to a highly competitive society and to the development of a variety of technologies; social pressures and pollution are their natural by-products. American culture says, "This world is made for you, you are the manager. It is your job to do what you deem best."

Patterns of Association

Another major difference between the two cultural traditions lies in their patterns of association.

Collectivity Versus Individuality

Asians have a lot to lose if they fail because their identities are rooted in their families and groups. Thus the whole family or organization feels disgraced collectively when one of its members does something shameful. Likewise, when an Indochinese architect won the contest to design the Vietnam War Memorial, Asians collectively felt proud of her achievement.

A number of studies have concluded that the Japanese tend to place emphasis on the group somewhat at the expense of the individual, and that Euro Americans tend to emphasize the individual more than the group (Hirayama & Hirayama, 1984; Kurokawa, 1980; Reischauer, 1977; Zander, 1983). This emphasis on the group is also true of other Asian groups, such as Chinese, Koreans, Vietnamese, and Asian Indians. The family teaches children who belongs within each structure. Well-defined and interdependent roles promote a strong family commitment and cohesiveness, and a group-oriented identity of the child is shaped.

Hirayama and Hirayama (1984) state that the Japanese often refer to their own group as *uchino school* or *uchino company*. The literal meaning is "inside" and the term is synonymous with family or home. This concept accounts for the Japanese perception of their school or company as their own family, with the same intimacy and obligation to help their schoolmates or colleagues as their own family. Thus it is customary, for example, for subordinates to introduce their superiors directly by name, without using a title such as "Mr." or "President," the omission revealing that their sense of identity with their company is as intimate as with their own family.

High Commitment Versus Instant Relationship

Asian culture, having a group-rooted sense of identity, requires and develops a high level of commitment in social relationships. It is considered immoral for an Asian individual to act without due consideration of the family's welfare first. Mutuality is expected and taken for granted within family relationships, and lifelong employment commitment is expected as well. This commitment has led high-ranking government officers and even business leaders in China and Japan to commit suicide when they felt they had failed to fulfill their obligation to their rulers.

The characteristic of high commitment results in Asian enterprises wherein employees and employers work as a closed, big family, willingly making the extra effort to meet higher consumer expectations. Both employees and employers realize that an individual's fate is dependent upon the company's fate, and vice versa. Therefore, both management and labor are willing to go beyond their responsibilities and limit their individual needs.

On the other hand, the identity of Euro Americans is rooted in individual accomplishments. In order to achieve individual goals and dreams, Euro Americans treat human relationships on a conditional basis. The employees promote their own positions and well-being by moving to different organizations. The average American family moves every 3½ years. Employment relations also assume a conflict of interest between management and labor.

Another indicator of the individualistic orientation of Euro Americans is the high divorce rate: Fifty percent of recent marriages will end in divorce (Robertson, 1987). The instant relationship that begins and ends quickly is becoming the predominant form of social relationship in American society. The high-commitment relationship, which depends on trust and builds up slowly and becomes stable, is harder and harder to find. Asians may experience difficulties in relationships with Euro Americans due to differences in degree of commitment.

Process Versus Task Orientation

A third difference is in how people work, particularly in situations involving teamwork. Asians, generally speaking, tend to be process-oriented. They emphasize the working relationship and the group process. Euro Americans, on the other hand, are usually task-oriented, setting goals and objectives and determining the procedures to achieve them. They tend to move into the tasks immediately after setting the goal. Asians, however, will consider goals and procedures in terms of whether they would hurt people's feelings and relationships, thus slowing down decision-making.

Hierarchical Versus Egalitarian Structure

The fourth difference relates to one's perception of social structure. Asians tend to come from a hierarchical social structure, where authority is centralized and responsibility and leadership are at the top. The Asian who values harmony tends to behave submissively toward superiors and awaits instructions. Euro Americans, coming from an egalitarian environment in which social structure is decentralized, take more individual initiative. These differing attitudes are reflected in the responses of Asians and Euro Americans to new acquaintances. Most Asians look for the social status first in their personal encounters. When reading a business card, for example, they look at the title first, then the name, and interact according to their respective social positions.

Degree of Social Participation

A fifth difference relates to attitude toward social participation, particularly toward politics. One common criticism of Asians is that many are "indifferent" to American society. Many do not attend football games, fail to join political parties, and are not concerned with who wins in elections. Whenever discussing political issues, many Asians tend to avoid taking sides. This apparent indifference has a cultural and historical basis. The past 80 years have been a period of political instability in most of Asia. With every change in government, thousands of people died. It was not uncommon for Asian rulers to encourage public opinion only to identify their enemies and then do away with them.

Involvement in politics has thus been a life-or-death issue for many Asians. A Chinese saying is, "The wise man takes no sides." Many Asians learned from past experience to protect themselves and their families by keeping away from any conflict, not taking sides, and not joining political parties. Parents taught their children to avoid politics and never divulge opinions in public. Hence, the tendency for low social participation developed. Rather than "indifferent," perhaps a more accurate attitude might well be: "He wants to participate, but is afraid to get hurt." More recently, Kitano and Daniels (1988) note a small but growing number of Asians running for political office in the United States.

Interaction and Body Language

Body language is an important element of human interaction. Social norms, eye contact, the distance of interaction, and communication are significant components of interaction.

Social Norms

Human behavior patterns are the dependent variables of social norms. The author has devised the following Asian and Euro American Ten Commandments to explain the major beliefs, values, and social norms of both cultures.

Asian Ten Commandments (Chung, 1989)

(1) I am the Great Nature who feeds you, cares for you, and was with you originally. I am at your temporal and everlasting place.

(2) You may know me in various ways, in any place, and at any time.

(3) Do not put yourself in conflict with me in any situation.

(4) When you conflict with me, the punishment for your disobedience will be upon you, your children, and your grandchildren; but I lavish my love upon all people who love me and obey my commandments.

(5) Remember to observe my truth and rules day and night, when hot and cold, in all seasons, and in the mountains and oceans. Do your daily duties and regular work accordingly. Follow me by respecting my rules.

(6) Honor your ruler (your superior) and your parents; respect and love your spouse; love your brothers; treat your friends with trust and righteousness.

(7) Be polite and humble; respect your elders and love the young.

(8) Do not pursue your own good without considering me and others.

(9) Constantly examine and control yourself so you will not take advantage of others. Observe the principle of mutuality with me, in your work, and with others.

(10) When you obey my commandments, you will have learned truth, love, and freedom, and you shall enjoy peace and happiness. Otherwise, I respond to every action you make.

Euro American Ten Commandments

(1) I am the Great Nature full of potential for you to manage.

(2) You may explore me and change me to suit your progressive ambitions and materialistic goals.

(3) You can conquer me, change the world, and transcend your limitations through technology.

(4) When you conflict with me and feel limited, you must invent new technologies.

(5) Discover the principles through which I operate. By using these principles, you can change me to create a new reality.

(6) Honor yourself through maximum achievements and realize individual potential through independent actions.

(7) You must depend on yourself, maintain your self-confidence and self-pride, and reflect it in all your actions.

(8) Happiness is here and now achievable only by concentrating on your own interests and material possessions.

(9) You must constantly guard your own interests and remain cautious that others do not take advantage of you.

(10) When you obey my commandments, you shall receive the success and abundance of life. You will have control and power.

Eye Contact

Eye contact, the primary method an individual uses to judge one's surroundings varies greatly among cultures. In the helping context, where the therapist is perceived as an authority figure, Asian clients may behave submissively. Avoidance of eye contact between persons of higher social status is an Asian cultural norm and should not be misunderstood to indicate dishonesty or lack of confidence. Eye contact is significant among Asians because they take for granted the mutuality of their perceived social relations. For example, a Chinese graduate student came to me frustrated from an after-class conversation with her advisor. Her Euro American classmates interrupted them often during their conversation and made her wait. "Their conversation was nothing important," she said. I asked, "If so, why didn't you cut in?" She replied, "That would be impolite and embarrassing. My professor was supposed to know that I was waiting and needed help. I was there first."

Words carry more of the message for Euro Americans, who clearly and quickly verbalize their intentions. Asians may suffer frustrations in communication because of the assumption that "It need not be mentioned; everyone in the relationship knows it." Asians find it embarrassing to mention this "supposed-to-know" issue verbally. Both sides are often unaware of their different roles and expectations.

Interaction Distance

When Euro Americans meet, they introduce themselves and shake hands to show their goodwill and friendliness. Traditionally Asians bow to greet people and interact according to their social status, those with higher social positions receiving a lower and slower bow than others. The distance of interaction between strangers from different cultures illustrates the importance of space interaction. One person may pull the chair closer in order to be at ease; the other may increase the distance for the same reason. Euro Americans prefer the following ranges of distances, according to Hall (1980).

(1) Very close (3 to 6 inches) for top secret;
(2) Close (6 to 12 inches) for very confidential;
(3) Near (12 to 20 inches) for confidential;
(4) Neutral (20 to 36 inches) for personal subject matters;
(5) Neutral (4½ to 5 feet) for information of nonpersonal matter;
(6) Public distance (5½ to 8 feet) for public information/business conversation.

For Asians, the interaction distance depends upon the nature of the relationship. An insider, whether a friend or an employer, is in the extended-family circle. The preferred distance depends upon the degree of trust. Two close male friends, for example, may enjoy walking hand in hand, a behavior that should not be interpreted as homosexual. With an outsider or stranger, the public distance (5½ to 8 feet) is necessary for conversation.

In a professional relationship, it is suggested that the social worker sit first and allow the Asian client to set the interaction distance. It may take Asian clients longer than Euro Americans to build a trusting relationship, since most of their social relationships are slow to develop. It takes time and effort to move from being an outsider to an insider in the relationship circle. As members of an ethnic minority in the dominant society, Asians are more cautious in building relationships. Once they accept a new person, the conversational distance will be closer, and their body language will show they are much more at ease.

Communication

Communication is often a major barrier to a relationship between a client and a helping professional, particularly with Asians. Ryan and Smith (1986) report from their work with parents of developmentally disabled children that the scarcity of professionals who spoke their clients' language presented innumerable problems. The clients' biggest problem was simply not knowing what was happening. Wong, Shon, Lu, and Gaw (1983) stress that understanding Asian communication patterns, especially nonverbal communication, is a high priority. They add that most Western psychotherapies rely on verbal communication to express ideas and feelings, whereas Asian cultures frequently utilize nonverbal communication to express important messages. These messages may be misunderstood or not noticed by Euro American therapists.

In an earlier work, the author (1985) identified several factors that create communication problems between Asian and Euro American males that could probably be extended to Asian and Euro American females also. Communication barriers associated with Euro American males include prejudice, aggressive attitudes, impatience, ethnocentrism, jokes about Asians, and misinterpretation of Asian behaviors or messages. Communication barriers associated with Asians include small stature, clothing, accents, grammar, and tone of speech, all of which caused some Euro Americans to be impatient and even prejudiced.

People from the two cultures also have different patterns of communication. Asians, coming from a high-context culture, often rely on nonverbal communication, while Euro Americans rely more on words. Asians speak indirectly and insert key points at the end; Euro Americans communicate directly and place key points at the beginning. Asians' oral messages are more implicit and depend more on context (people and situations), while Euro Americans' verbal messages are explicit and less concerned with context. Asians treat communication as a way of engaging a person and consider it a social art; Euro Americans consider communication as a practical tool for exchanging information, ideas, and opinions and treat it as an individual right of self-expression.

Time

Americans have a monochronic attitude toward time (Hall, 1981) and often prefer to do one thing at a time. This preference requires either implicit or explicit scheduling. Several social factors keep most Euro Americans within monochronic forms. They consider time as a valuable commodity that can be measured, saved, spent, wasted, bought, and lost. Some like to schedule their time intensively, believing and expecting things to be done at a particular time. How to get things done effectively is their primary concern, and the surrounding circumstances are not as important. They attempt to do things quickly and expect to see immediate results. They set measurable objectives and evaluate the outcome in terms of effectiveness and efficiency. They separate the objectives into different periods with immediate, short-term, and long-term goals, so they can terminate a project should it not achieve its preset objectives. They expect extra pay for overtime work. They expect penalties for lateness and for failure to keep commitments.

In contrast, Asians usually do not schedule their time as strictly. Asians are often involved simultaneously in several activities, such as answering the phone, counting money, and handling incoming customers. They are satisfied with having a general guideline or plan and believe that everything has its own time. They anticipate unexpected needs and that the plan may have to change accordingly; the important thing is to get the work done without hurting people. These attitudes may explain why it is hard for the people in Korea, China, and the Philippines to have a "schedule for democracy" and to achieve a "timely" democratic society, as Americans expect. Because Asians' perceptions of issues are rooted in the past, they tend to change slowly, favoring social stability. Time itself does not belong to the individual only but also to others, the family, organizations, community, and even nature. This collective concern slows down their rate of change because they approach time from a process orientation.

From an Asian viewpoint, time springs from the self and is not imposed. In Zen training, for instance, the aim is to attune oneself to nature and to "eat when hungry and sleep when tired." On the other hand, as Ornstein (1975) describes, Euro Americans train their mind focusing on the left hemisphere of the cortex, the portion of the brain that deals with words and numbers and enhances the logical, bounded, linear functions. On the contrary the Asian goal, as seen in Zen meditation, is to empty the mind and eliminate consciousness of the self.

Law

In the United States, Hall (1981) points out, there is a government of laws, not of men. In most traditional Asian countries, however, the ruler often is the man. The administrator traditionally served as a societal parent, judging and punishing misbehavers. In Asian countries today, the judge wants to know who the culprit is, what his job is, whether he has any previous record, and what society's attitude is toward the case. In other words, the judge wants to understand the entire context both before and during the trial to assess the person as well as the situation as a whole. If robbery is the problem, the judge might give a serious punishment to "educate" both the robber and society, in order to maintain social morality. Much of the information used in an Asian court case would be judged irrelevant and considered unfair to the accused in an American court.

Again, this is a difference of cultural context. The high-context Asian court system brings in broad information and considers the related social situation in its judgment. The judge normally is supported by a highly centralized administration and by the public. The public believes that laws are made to secure wrongdoers and that a judge should use his power to balance human nature with sentiment, reason, and laws. The purpose of a trial is to provide a setting where the judge, supported by the government and the public, is able to control and punish offenders. At the same time, the trial also provides an opportunity for the accused to be publicly repentant for disrupting the social order.

In contrast, American laws are designed to operate apart from the rest of life. In court, lawyers may present only related critical evidence to prove or disprove criminal behavior. According to Hall (1981), the U. S. courts are the epitome of a low-context system:

> The common inadmissibility of contexting testimony, including hearsay, sets our courts apart and frequently makes them harsh, inhuman, and impersonal. . . . Only established facts, stripped of all contexting background data, are admissible as evidence. How many times has the reader heard, "Answer the question, Yes or No."

Both systems have their strengths and weaknesses. In the high-context system, the emphasis is on the collectivity; the low-context system focuses on individual rights. Asians, coming from a high-context system, often encounter difficulties in the low-context American system. They may perceive American law as cold, impersonal, unjust, and discriminatory. In Asia, the individual had the police, the judge, and the system to protect him. He reports to the police, just as a child reports to his parents.

In the United States, however, the victim of a crime must often go through a long, dehumanizing process. Asians often do not wish to humiliate themselves by undergoing this process and therefore may not report a crime. In addition, according to Ho (1976), fear and distrust of the U. S. justice system still linger today among the descendants of immigrants who were treated unfairly by earlier laws. When one reads about the lower crime rate in an Asian community in the United States, one must take such factors into account.

AN ASIAN VIEW OF CULTURAL DIFFERENCES

In 1978 a group of Vietnamese, after suffering cultural shock in the United States, drafted a list of cultural differences. The list, with additions, is an excellent summary of cultural differences from an Asian perspective.

EAST	WEST
We live in time.	We live in space.
We are always at rest.	We are always on the move.
We are passive.	We are aggressive.
We accept the world as it is.	We try to change it according to our blueprint.
We like to contemplate.	We like to act.
We live in peace with nature.	We try to impose our will on nature.
Religion is our first love.	Technology is our passion.
We delight to think about the meaning of life.	We delight in physics.
We believe in freedom of silence.	We believe in freedom of speech.
We lapse in meditation.	We strive for articulation.
We marry first, then love.	We love first, then marry.
Our marriage is the beginning of a love affair.	Our marriage is the happy end of a romance.
Love is an indissoluble bond.	Love is a contract.
Our love is mute.	Our love is vocal.
We try to conceal it from the world.	We delight in showing it to others.
Self-denial is a secret to our survival.	Self-assertiveness is the key to our success.
We are taught from the cradle to want less and less.	We are urged every day to want more and more.
We glorify austerity and renunciation.	We emphasize gracious living and enjoyment.
Poverty is to us a badge of spiritual elevation.	Poverty is to us a sign of degradation.
In the sunset years of life we renounce the world and prepare for the hereafter.	We retire to enjoy the fruits of our labor.

IMPLICATIONS FOR SOCIAL WORK PRACTICE

Asians in the United States must face many changes in cultural adaptation. They must assess the points of cultural conflict and the degree to which internal skills and knowledge have been acquired to achieve a balance of identity. The issue of dual perspective, as presented by Norton (1978), must be considered in any counseling or developmental project.

Whether pushed out of their old countries for economic or political reasons or pulled in by the host environment, Asians in the United States have sought political freedom and educational and economic opportunities. As an ethnic minority, they have been a largely silent group that often suffered from inequities in power and resource distribution. Certain cultural factors have enabled Asians to pull together for their survival and success; these factors sometimes cause adjustment problems and lead to personal, interpersonal, organizational, and social conflicts. It is important for social work professionals to understand these cultural factors and incorporate them in daily micro and macro practice.

How to reduce prejudice and prevent discrimination toward Asians, as well as how to help Asians handle these issues, are important questions for social work practice. Because Asians tend to be process-oriented and take longer to build personal relationships, a helping relationship should start with trust-building and be maintained on a steady and long-term basis.

Since Asians value harmony, they may tend to avoid any direct conflict with individuals, groups, organizations, and the host community. Therefore, attempts to use any conflict or confrontation approaches in the helping process may be counterproductive. Instead, the philosophies and methodologies of Confucius and Gandhi, which start with an attitude of sincerity and seek truth in a humanistic approach to deal with conflict, may be much more effective.

Mutual aid systems and the extended family are important indigenous systems for problem-solving and goal-achievement. Organizing interest groups, such as small business owners' clubs, golden age clubs, or computer education classes, is an effective way to help Asians help themselves. An individual's problem is a family problem. The individual who shares his personal problems with an outsider, such as a social worker, is considered to be a troublemaker in the family, unless the issue is raised by one of the extended-family members. Social workers need to work with an insider—particularly a respected, elderly member—to suggest the change, and thus avoid family resistance.

CONCLUSIONS

In this chapter a number of cultural commonalities and differences between Asian and Euro American cultures were discussed. We have taken only a brief look at a general picture, and we must allow for differences within each person and specific Asian group. People must be understood in the context of their personal life journey and their social environment. A helping technology can be developed, based on understanding differences between the two cultures and exploring the origins of conflicts and frustrations.

A useful concept in this regard is that of *culture competence*, defined by Cross (1988) as a set of congruent behaviors, attitudes, and policies in a system, agency, or professional that enable that system, agency, or professional to work effectively in cross-cultural situations. A culturally competent system of care acknowledges and incorporates at all levels the importance of culture, the assessment of cross-cultural relations, vigilance toward the dynamics that result from cultural differences, the expansion of cultural knowledge, and the adaptation of services to meet culturally unique needs.

The following three steps are essential for culturally competent social work practice: (a) gain a good understanding of one's own culture; (b) be aware of the client's culture; and (c) understand the cross-cultural dynamics involved in service processes.

REFERENCES

Chung, D. (1985, October). *Communication problems between Asian American and white males and its solutions.* Paper presented at the Eleventh SIETAR International Conference, San Antonio, Texas.

Chung, D. (1989, November). *A cultural competent social work practice for Asian Americans.* Paper presented at the Annual NASW Conference, San Francisco.

Cross, T. L. (1988). Services to minority populations: Cultural competence continuum. *Focal Point: The Bulletin of the Research and Training Center, 3*(1), 1-4.

Dhooper, S. S., & Tran, T. V. (1986, March). *Social work with Asian Americans.* Paper presented at the 32nd Annual Program Meeting, Council on Social Work Education, Miami, Florida.

Hall, E. T. (1966). *The hidden dimension*. Garden City, NY: Doubleday.

Hall, E. T. (1980). *The silent language*. Garden City, NY: Doubleday.

Hall, E. T. (1981). *Beyond culture*. Garden City, NY: Anchor.

Hall, E. T. (1983). *The dance of life*. Garden City, NY: Doubleday.

Hirayama, H., & Hirayama, K. K. (1984). Individuality vs. group identity: A comparison between Japan and the United States. *Journal of International and Comparative Social Welfare, 2*(12), 11-20.

Ho, M. K. (1976). Social work with Asian Americans. *Social Casework, 57*(3), 195-201.

Kitano, H., & Daniels, R. (1988). *Asian Americans: Emerging minorities*. Englewood Cliffs, NJ: Prentice-Hall.

Kurokawa, A. (1980). Value system and personality of Japanese in social work: From points of view of social relations and family relations. *Shakai Fukushi Kenkyu* (Social Welfare Studies), *26*.

Norton, D. G. (1978). *The dual perspective*. New York: Council on Social Work Education.

Ornstein, R. (1975). *The psychology of consciousness*. New York: Harcourt Brace Jovanovich.

Reischauer, E. (1977). *The Japanese*. Tokyo: Charles F. Tuttle.

Robertson, I. (1987). *Sociology*. New York: Worth.

Ross-Sheriff, F., & Meemeduma, P. (1986, March). *Sri Lankan adolescents living in the United States: The development of autonomy*. Paper presented at the 2nd Asian American Social Work Educators Association Symposium, Miami, Florida.

Ryan, A., & Smith, M. J. (1986, March). *A rationale for reconceptualizing social work tasks and skills for Asian American families*. Paper presented at the Annual Program Meeting, Council on Social Work Education, Miami, Florida.

Tsui, P., & Schultz, G. L. (1985). Failure of rapport: Why psychotherapeutic engagement fails in the treatment of Asian clients. *American Journal of Orthopsychiatry, 55*(4), 561-569.

Wong, N., Shon, S. P., Lu, F. G., & Gaw, A. C. (1983). *Asian and Pacific American patient issues in psychiatric residency training programs in mental health and people of color*. Washington, DC: Howard University Press.

Zander, A. (1983). The value of belonging to a group in Japan. *Small Group Behavior, 14*(1), 3-14.

Chapter 3

ADAPTATION AND INTEGRATION INTO AMERICAN SOCIETY: *Major Issues Affecting Asian Americans*

FARIYAL ROSS-SHERIFF

Asians come from many countries, each with its own language, culture, and experiences. These groups differ in terms of their historical background in the United States, number of years of residence in the United States, English language skills, and background in the country of origin, such as the level of urban experience, socioeconomic status, educational achievement, and religious affiliation. The early Asian immigrants, who came from Japan, China, Korea, and India as laborers, were subjected to exclusionary laws, oppressive working conditions, and discriminatory practices. Their experiences were very different from those who entered the United States after the Immigration Act of 1965 as professionals, students, or businessmen. Similarly, the adaptation experiences of refugees of one cohort group from one country, for example, South Vietnam, differed substantially from experiences of refugees from the same country but of a different cohort group (Forbes, 1985).

To understand Asian immigrants and their experiences with adaptation and integration into the American society, it is necessary to consider these experiences within the context of Asian immigration patterns, U. S. policies, political forces that have influenced past and current policy, and legislation relating to Asians, which was presented in Chapter 1.

COMMONALITY

Regardless of their history, national origin, settlement patterns, or status in the United States, all Asians share some critical common characteristics. These common characteristics are important in understanding the adaptation of Asians; however, these characteristics are not intended to be stereotypes that often are used to describe all Asian groups. Common characteristics that Asians share are high value on educational achievement, strong religious and cultural backgrounds, personal discipline, group orientation, and experiences of discrimination resulting from the negative perceptions of other Americans. Asians also recognize that the current political reality in the United States requires them to unite as a single interest group and to act collectively to advance their mutual interests. Understanding the common characteristics as well as the unique needs of each distinct group will enable social workers and voluntary organizations to facilitate the adaptation of Asians for harmonious living in American society.

ADAPTATION TO AMERICAN SOCIETY

Adaptation refers to strategies for dealing with the process of acculturation to the host society and the long-term outcome of acculturation (Berry, 1988). At the individual level, adaptation is "the process in which immigrants modify their behaviors and attitudes in order to maintain and improve their life conditions compatible with the new environment" (Hurh & Kim, 1984, p. 35). For an immigrant community, adaptation to a new society is a process of coping with the social, cultural, and ecological setting of the host society and becoming comfortable in the new environment.

The level of differences in ethnic-group characteristics and host-society characteristics results in acculturative stress and related adaptation problems. For example, Asian groups that have distinctly different cultural characteristics and worldviews from those of the host society are likely to experience severe stress and mental health problems. Those Asian groups that have viable ethnic social supports, through which they give one another assistance, experience less stress and less negative mental health consequences than those who do not have such social support. Prejudices, discriminatory acts, and policies of the host society also are listed among other group factors that are associated with levels of acculturation stress (Berry, Kalin, & Taylor, 1977; Berry & Kim, 1988; Forbes, 1985).

Because of the distinct differences in observable cultural aspects, such as food preferences, choice of clothing, patterns of residence, language skills, and speech patterns, most Asian groups experience acculturative stress and the resulting adaptation problems upon entry into American society. Other distinct characteristics that separate Asians from the predominantly Euro American population are their race and skin color, distinguishing characteristics that Park (1913) has referred to as their "racial uniform."

Cultural characteristics that are distinctly different from those of the host society result in interfamily and intrafamily conflicts among Asian immigrants and influence their adaptation to American institutions. For example, peers often ridicule some Asian children and adolescents at school (Ross-Sheriff, 1985) because their "lunch is smelly"; they "talk funny"; their clothing, which is selected by their parents, reflects "poor taste"; and they look like "Chinks"—a reference to Chinese, Japanese, and Korean children (Takaki, 1989). Parent-child relationships, resourcefulness of families to respond to such ethnic slurs, and sensitivity of teachers and other significant adults in educational institutions influence the responses of children. They also influence children's sense of self, their feelings about their family members, friendship patterns, and educational outcomes.

Similarly, in the workplace, especially upon entry into the job market, many Asian immigrants face discrimination because of their dress, speech patterns, and cultural patterns of relationships. Throughout their history, different waves of Asians have struggled in various ways to adapt to the norms and expectations of the host society. Although few research studies of Asian immigrant adaptation exist, descriptive information from diaries, letters, newspapers, ethnic journals, and biographies has provided insight into the adaptation processes and outcomes. These include individual struggles to conform, feelings of marginality, group efforts to support each other, organization of clubs and support networks, and political pressures, including eruption of ethnic violence in times of stress (Hurh & Kim, 1984; Hurh, Kim, & Kim, 1979; Takaki, 1989). The following example illustrates both one young Asian Indian's experience with stress and the resultant adaptation outcome.

Leela perceived that she was not hired for a job, although she was highly qualified, because of her dress, hair style, and accent. After four unsuccessful interviews, her cousin advised her to get a new haircut and wear Western clothing. Leela feared social rejection and cultural ambivalence and experienced an identity crisis. She made the decision to cut her hair and buy Western clothing; but she moved to another town, where she had a friend, because she was embarrassed by her decisions. In the process, she isolated herself from relatives and support networks.

The nature of the adaptive actions and outcomes depends on personal and group experiences. Individual efforts, ethnic institutional development, primary group affiliation, and intergroup relations are different levels at which adaptation can be facilitated. Four possible outcomes of adaptation of Asian to America are (a) assimilation, (b) integration, (c) separation, and (d) marginalization (Berry, 1984; Cox, 1987). Although adaptation outcomes are on a continuum rather than in discrete categories, they are presented here separately for the purposes of describing a model. The model of adaptation of Asians considers two important factors. The first factor relates to the maintenance and development of the ethnic and cultural distinctiveness of the culture of origin in the pluralistic host society. The second factor pertains to the value placed on the cultural practices of the host society and interethnic relationships with members from the larger host society. An individual or group's decisions on the two factors influence adaptation outcome (Figure 3.1).

Assimilation implies a loss of identity of the Asian culture of origin in the process of acquiring the values and behaviors of American culture. None of the Asian groups has assimilated entirely into American society; however, a few individuals from all groups consider themselves completely Americanized and a part of the White Anglo-Saxon Protestant (WASP) gemeinschaft.

Integration outcome refers to the maintenance of a significant part of the identity of the Asian culture of origin while having effective interethnic contact through active participation in American society. Almost all Asian groups have developed ethnic community organizations and mutual support networks to maintain their distinct identity while they also participate in the various structures of American society.

Separation refers to the establishment of separate sets of institutions in America for social interactions, in many cases even for specific subgroups within Asian communities. This pattern is most commonly observed through the establishment of enclaves—for example, "Chinatown," "Little Tokyo," and "Little Saigon."

		Value given to maintenance of cultural practices of society of origin	
		Higher	Lower
Value given to relationship with other groups in host society, and cultural practices of the host society	Higher	Integration	Assimilation
	Lower	Separation	Marginalization

Figure 3.1. Adaptation Options for Asian Immigrants.

Marginalization, the least observed outcome, is characterized by a loss of identity of the Asian culture of origin as well as a striking out against American society. This group includes some living in poverty or facing serious problems of family breakdown, delinquency, and alienation. Included in this group are young Southeast Asian refugees and recent immigrants from Hong Kong, mainland China, and the Philippines who are involved in gangs, substance abuse, crime and delinquency, school dropout, teenage pregnancy, prostitution, and commerce in drugs (Morales, 1989; Murase, 1989; Takaki, 1989). This group, though small, is likely to increase and require social work prevention and intervention programs and services.

Historically, integration and separation have been the normative options for adaptation of Asians. With geographic and social mobility, many Asian groups have integrated into American society. They have managed to maintain the cultural integrity of their Asian group of origin and have responded to the acculturative pressures of American society to become an integral part of the society. Some refer to them as "hyphenated Americans" for example, Chinese-Americans. Those who have settled in Asian ethnic enclaves have recreated many structures of their society of origin, such as business practices, language and religious educational programs, and recreational programs (B.Wong, 1987). They are able to maintain their culture and traditions.

The critical characteristics of the Asian culture of origin that remain for generations, for both the integrated Asian groups and those in ethnic enclaves, are aspects of the Asian self that arise from the Asian worldview. To provide relevant services for all groups of Asians, social workers and human services providers must understand the worldview and the concept of self of Asians.

WORLDVIEW AND CONCEPT OF SELF

Worldview is defined as the ways in which people "perceive relationships to nature, other people, institutions, and objects" (English, 1984). A person's worldview denotes his or her psychological orientation to life. It determines how the individual thinks, behaves, makes decisions, analyzes events, and conducts social relationships. A person's worldview shapes both the normative and expressive context of social relationships and can provide insight to help human services professionals plan effective programs and services.

A person's or cultural group's worldview is influenced by a religious and philosophical orientation to life and the concept of self. Unlike the Western mode of thinking, in which science and religion, natural and supernatural, mind and body are viewed dichotomously, the Asians' thinking typically orders and understands their world in indivisible terms. The worldviews of Asian cultural groups are similar, especially among the South, Southeast, and East Asian cultures whose Hindu, Buddhist, Confucian, and Islamic cultural traditions share common roots. A code of conduct or *adab* is clearly defined for all age groups and for all relationships (Metcalf, 1984). A "middle way" governs daily life, with an emphasis on good deeds and on balance between the secular and religious elements. An example of one specific Asian religion, Confucianism, and its impact on social relationships and a day-to-day code of conduct for its followers is presented in Chapter 7.

Asian cultures emphasize significant values such as family/kin responsibilities, obligations and filial piety, hierarchical order in carrying out responsibilities, sensitivity to the feelings of others, respect, loyalty, and righteousness. Group needs are emphasized over individual needs, and value is placed on appropriate behavior for all occasions.

Group pressures are applied to elicit appropriate behavior. Discipline techniques invoking shame, guilt, and avoidance of embarrassment lead toward conformity to the code.

Asians place great emphasis on responsibilities and obligations for giving and receiving support. The hierarchical order for responsibilities and obligations, from the highest priority to the least, was described in Chapter 2. Within this support process, kinship relations are extended to close friends and co-workers, who are addressed with kinship terms such as brother, sister, uncle, aunt, son, or daughter.

Asians' worldview influences their concept of self. The Asian concept of self is best explained in contrast with the Western concept of self, as presented by Roland (1984, 1988), who compared Asian Indians and the Japanese with Americans. He found that the group/familial Asian concept of self contrasted sharply with the highly individuated Western/American concept of self. Roland suggested that the differences between the Asian and American selves can be conceptualized as differing gestalts of the integration of the three self subcomponents: (a) individual self, (b) familial self, and (c) transcendental self.

The *individual* self is what most Western cultures equate with self: the personalized self that is free to develop within certain boundaries. The *familial* self emphasizes the symbiotic linkage between the individual and his family and the rights, responsibilities, and obligations of family members toward each other. Family needs are more important than individual needs, and loyalty toward and cooperation with family members is expected. In addition, family status and respectability are valued greatly. The *transcendental* self is a metaphysical concept of self that identifies people's relationship to the infinite universe. The Asian self exists as an integrated gestalt in which the familial self predominates and its impact is observed most clearly through daily relationships; the transcendental self exists but is not overtly presented, with the individual self being least emphasized. In contrast, the American self gestalt is characterized by dominance of the individual self, with some influence of the familial self or transcendental self (Roland, 1984, 1988).

For individuals of Asian descent, the self exists in the sense of the position the person occupies within a system of interpersonal and intergroup relationships in the family and community. The individual in social interactions represents the family or the ethnic or religious group and is not free to conduct relationships in a totally individuated way. Social relationships between nonfamily members often are contained and guarded.

Among family members, the familial self has "relatively open ego boundaries, and there is relatively little private psychological space around the self" (Roland, 1984, p. 176). During the socialization process in the early years of life, dependency on the family is reinforced. Group dependency is encouraged in relationships that develop between the child, the mother, and the members of the extended family. Family members anticipate and meet children's needs without verbal requests; nonverbal cues are sufficient to indicate need. This type of socialization is in marked contrast to Western socialization, which stresses verbal and direct cues and attempts to lead toward independence. Instead it fosters family and group commitment as well as interdependency to achieve goals. Thus, helping professionals must consider family and group factors and cultural sensitivities in intervention or support, even for those individuals not living within a family for adaptation to life in America.

With migration to the United States, the Asian concept of self changes as a result of participation in American society. Yet, many culturally distinct characteristics of self, which are the essence of the continuity of psychological, social, and self-understanding, endure over generations (De Vos, 1980). The concept of self of Asians—the way they think, feel, organize meaning, conduct relationships, and expect to be treated—remains distinct and influences resulting adaptation outcomes in the United States.

ADAPTATION OUTCOMES

The success of adaptation of immigrant communities is usually assessed through structural and economic measures and in terms of social stability. Structural measures include residential patterns (segregation versus assimilation) and participation in the cliques, clubs, and institutions of the host society at a primary level (Gordon, 1964, 1975). Economic measures relate to income, participation in the labor force, and employment rates and achievements in educational and occupational pursuits. Social stability is assessed through mental health status, cultural identity, and overall feelings of well-being.

The adaptation pattern for first-generation Asians has been one in which "certain aspects of the new American culture and relations with the host society are added on to the traditional culture and social networks without replacing or modifying any part of the old"; this has been referred to as adhesive adaptation (Hurh & Kim, 1984, p. 35). Adhesive adaptation is a limited form of pluralism. Because of racial visibility and ethnic segregation against people of color in the American social structure, it has been argued that even second- and third-generation Asian groups such as the Chinese and Japanese, who have achieved educational, economic, and occupational parity with the dominant American population, will continue to experience modified forms of adhesive adaptation (Hurh & Kim, 1984; Kitano, 1976).

Residential Patterns

One form of adaptation associated with Asians is the pattern of settling in an ethnic enclave upon arrival in the new country. Debates center around the role of ethnic enclaves in facilitating the adaptation of Asians to American society. In his study of Chinese garment factories in New York, B. Wong (1987) argued that enclaves are a successful form of adaptation in that they provide economic opportunities and social mobility. For those Asians with limited English language skills, capital, and urban experience, enclaves provide jobs and a stable environment for family life during acculturation into the host society. For the entrepreneurs, enclaves provide opportunities to initiate close-knit small businesses and to generate capital, using family resources or culturally specific institutions, such as "rotating credit associations," as well as a cheap labor supply. Enclaves also provide a set of customers with similar needs and interests.

Other analysts have associated enclaves with low income and cultural isolation (Nee & Sanders, 1985). Still others view economic enterprises within enclaves as transitory businesses with apathetic workers (Piore, 1973) and unscrupulous businessmen who exploit their co-nationals (Bonacich, 1973). Regardless of their position on enclaves, researchers tend to agree that proximity of work and residence and social interactions within enclaves perpetuate ethnicity and provide resources as well as the social environment to support the high educational attainments associated with children of Asian groups (Hurh & Kim, 1984).

Many Asian refugees and immigrants, including a number of Koreans, Chinese, and Southeast Asians, work or start businesses in low-rent areas in inner-city neighborhoods. These immigrants pull together family resources and work long hours to run successful businesses. They have been both credited for revitalizing poor inner-city neighborhoods and blamed in the popular press for creating tensions between ethnic groups, such as the African Americans and Koreans.

However, not all Asian families have been spared the current problems faced by the larger society. Unemployment, overcrowding, and juvenile delinquency are prevalent in most enclaves and inner-city neighborhoods where Asians have settled. Whether in the enclaves or in inner cities, Asian families—specifically the refugees and recent immigrant families living in poverty and with high amounts of stress— are experiencing increasing intergenerational conflicts between parents and children and among peer groups, resulting in gang affiliation, drug use, and delinquency. Similarly, Amerasian children who have grown up without the family care and support also are experiencing difficulties in the United States. This Asian population is likely to increase and continue to experience severe stress and mental health problems.

A related problem experienced by Asians is residential segregation. A study (Langberg & Farley, 1985) on the residential segregation of Asians in 1980 indicated that the Vietnamese are the most highly segregated group, and the Japanese the least segregated. The Vietnamese came as refugees with little preparation for an orderly migration, many with limited language skills and orientation to life in the United States. Their need for institutional and cultural support is likely to be greater than for other groups that have immigrated to the United States for occupational reasons or for family reunification. The Japanese, on the other hand, have the smallest proportion of foreign-born population (28%), resemble the middle-class Euro Americans in socioeconomic status, were forced to collectively relocate in concentration camps during World War II, and today are the least segregated.

Another pattern of Asian settlement is residence in ethnically diverse neighborhoods. Three distinct groups among Asians who have settled in more ethnically diverse neighborhoods are (a) immigrants who arrived after 1965 from urban backgrounds and have reached high educational, occupational, and income levels; (b) owners of small businesses and workers outside ethnic enclaves; and (c) the second- and third-generation immigrants sometimes referred to as the "elites." This third group includes highly successful scientists, engineers, business executives, doctors, lawyers, and college professors who are middle- and upper-middle-class Chinese, Japanese, Asian Indians, Koreans, and Filipinos. Many among this elite group are accepted by the larger American society and have integrated into the American upper-middle class because of their prestigious positions and high income. Their life style, their dress, and some of their patterns of relationships are not very different from those of their American neighbors, business partners, and colleagues. In addition, their children attend leading universities.

Despite their economic, academic, and occupational achievements and their ownership of homes in good to affluent neighborhoods, many Asians living in scattered areas experience discrimination. Even a large number of this group, who have integrated structurally into American society, choose to interact socially with, and depend on support from, other Asians with similar cultural, religious, or national backgrounds. Within this residential pattern, few live in close proximity to each other to make possible ethnic-based support for critical groups such as the elderly, unemployed women, or youths. They find themselves isolated, and many of them turn to enclaves and ethnic organizations for social interaction and support.

Economic Patterns and Achievement

Socioeconomic achievements of Asians have received a great deal of attention. There is widespread belief that Asians have made significant socioeconomic gains since World War II (Nee & Sanders, 1985; Peterson, 1971). Despite a history of discrimination, some Asians have achieved parity with Euro Americans (Sowell, 1981). Many Asian refugee and immigrant groups, for example South Vietnamese and Korean families, have surpassed their Euro American counterparts in labor-force participation and economic achievement within 10 years of arrival in the United States (Chiswick, 1980; Forbes, 1985; Simon, 1989).

Hirschman and Wong (1984) suggested that the socioeconomic achievement of Asians is a result of their educational attainment. Cultural as well as structural explanations have been provided for the educational achievement of Asians. For example, obligation to an interdependent family unit, socialization and support, and high expectations are often provided as cultural explanations for their successes. Other explanations include the changing economic conditions of the expanding market economy since World War II, and the formation of organizations to deal with discrimination.

The successes of Asians were greatly exaggerated in the mass media during the 1980s. For example, two popular television news programs aired special segments on the success of Asians in 1986. In 1987 a television magazine-format program presented a glowing report of the academic achievements of Asians. In addition, leading news magazines published lead articles, cover stories, and sections on the achievements of Asians or their success stories ("America's Super Minority," 1986; "Asian Americans: A Model Minority," 1982; "Asian Americans: Are They Making the Grade?" 1984; Bell, 1985; "The Changing Face of America," 1985). Asians have been called the "model minority" and "super minority." They also have been compared with and pitted against other ethnic groups in the United States.

However, an analysis of the achievements of Asians in the income and occupational arena often is incomplete because it does not include all relevant variables. For example, higher family income among Asians relates to the presence of more workers per family, rather than higher income per worker (Cabezas & Kawaguchi, 1988). These analyses of select Asian groups, such as the Japanese and Asian Indians, do not reflect structural problems faced by most of them who are absent in top management and top administration. Takaki (1989) refers to this pattern as being "characterized by a 'glass ceiling'—a barrier through which top management positions can only be seen, but not reached, by Asian Americans" (p. 476) .

The middle- and lower-middle-class Asians, who are less successful than the business people and the elite, encounter social and economic discrimination. Despite hard work, many have not been able to achieve occupational upward mobility. The United States Equal Employment Opportunity Commission (1988) has revealed discriminatory patterns of low employment for Asians in all occupations in private industry, except service work. As a result of discrimination in private industry and in the public sector at the city, state, and federal levels, young Asians have formed organizations to advance their cause through political processes (Kuo, 1982).

Overall, Asians have made educational, economic, occupational, and political gains. The myth of the "model minority" has opened windows of opportunities for Asians who are considered intelligent and hard-working. The myth also has resulted in efforts to close doors by attempting to set quotas on the numbers of Asians entering institutions of higher learning. Few Asians have integrated totally into American society. Segregation decreases as social class rises; however, at all levels of income, education, and social class, there is some degree of residual segregation. Racial and cultural background, rather than levels of achievement (Langberg & Farley, 1985), continue to influence the adaptation of Asians.

Social Stability

Asians, like other groups of immigrants, can achieve social stability through adjustment to American society by learning what is expected, participating in its institutions, identifying with the larger American society, and contributing to the host society. Ethnic community organizations have served as intermediaries between the Asian immigrant groups and American society. Informal support networks, specifically the familial support networks, play an important role in the adjustment and social well-being of Asian immigrants (Meemeduma, 1988). Formal organizations, including religious institutions and business and self-help organizations, generally referred to as Mutual Assistance Associations, serve as a core for ethnic organizations. They are social or cultural in nature and not only provide social, emotional, and spiritual support, but also offer education, employment, and other services.

Several studies of Asians reported on the significance of the above organizations. For example, Stanford Research Institute International (1983) found that support offered by ethnic community organizations was crucial to the adjustment of Southeast Asian refugees. Ross-Sheriff and Nanji (1991) described both the establishment of and the role of Muslim community organizations at the local, regional, and national levels in the development of Muslim identity of Indo-Pakistani youths and in the establishment of support networks for the elderly. W. Kuo (1979) and C. Kuo (1982) referred to the historical role of ethnic organizations in the integration of the Chinese and Japanese in American society.

Despite the support of family, friends, co-nationals, and ethnic community organizations, some Asian families experience stress and related psychosocial consequences. Asians have been affected by discrimination and prejudice as well as the ills of society at the group, family, and individual levels. At the group level, Berry (1988) has described the acculturative stress and related mental health problems of Southeast Asian refugees. Dhooper (1986) has discussed the effects of discrimination on Asian Indians: emotional outrage, stress, and related psychological consequences. Asian university students have expressed their outrage by using Chinatowns as battlegrounds from which they have demonstrated their opposition to policies that exclude Asians from the labor market, political participation, and adequate services (Wong, 1982).

At the family and individual levels, women, adolescents, and elderly people have experienced the highest levels of stress and related mental health problems. Acculturation stresses among adolescents, women, and elderly people lead to low self-esteem, low levels of productivity, psychosomatic illnesses, and even to self-destructive or antisocial behavior.

Adolescents are of vital concern to Asians because they represent the future. However, for them, the stresses of their minority status and the pressure to live in and perform well in at least three cultures—(a) Asian culture of the families of origin, (b) American culture in the institutions in which they are expected to excel, and (c) popular culture they relate to through their peers—are confounded and multiplied by the inherent stresses of adolescence. As a visible ethnic minority, they face the more complex task of developing self-identity while simultaneously resolving conflicts among the cultural values that compete for their allegiance. The problem is further compounded emotionally for those immigrant youths whose parents, grandparents, or other relatives are unsuccessful by the economic and social standards of either culture.

Asian women generally bring substantial strengths to the family through defined role responsibilities for nurturing and cultural preservation skills and entrepreneurial expertise. These assets are essential for cultural continuity and for the socialization of other family members.

Yet, Asian women themselves typically face difficult obstacles, including service needs, such as the need of those who enter the job market for child care services; male-female role changes that often strain family bonds; cultural barriers, imposed by the ethnic culture of origin, which inhibit women's assumption of leadership roles; and cultural barriers to social-support networks in the adopted homeland, which result in low levels of social interaction and consequently, low self-esteem, especially for those who are separated from their extended families.

Asian women experience stress because of family conflicts resulting from: (a) work overload when they attempt to sustain all the functions of homemaking in addition to working outside the home; (b) expectations that women, as primary caretakers of young children, will lead in the resolution of children's acculturation problems; (c) pressures to resolve conflicting demands from within the family for change or constancy in cultural practices such as dress, food, and social interactions; and (d) conflicting attitudes of self and of family members toward the women's role as wage earners—often seen as a necessary but culturally undesirable feature of life in the United States. Although their adaptations to out-of-home employment may be smooth, immigrant women's adaptations within the family and within their ethnic group create enormous stress.

The Asian elderly are at risk from both increased physiological vulnerability and dependency on others. They face the risk of psychological distress in their adjustment to the United States because they have had not only the most to lose in leaving their countries but also the least to gain in their new lives. For many, their loss of identity and self-worth is compounded by their increased isolation in the United States.

CRITICAL ISSUES

Public confusion and resistance to Asians and other people of color persist throughout the United States. There is concern about whether these people of color will be able to integrate into the American society the way Europeans have or whether they will polarize neighborhoods linguistically and culturally. These fears result in anti-Asian sentiments and sometimes in violence, making it difficult to develop harmonious relationships between Asians and other Americans. However, the prevailing view is that the new Asian immigrants and refugees, like their co-nationals who have resided in the United States for several generations, will succeed economically, socially, and politically at the expense of established communities (Schwartz, 1985).

Contrary to economic analysis (Borjas, 1989; Simon, 1989), many Americans believe that Asian refugees and immigrants are taking away their businesses and jobs. Those Asian immigrants and refugees who work at low wages in the service industry are accused of depressing wage rates and utilizing social welfare and income-maintenance services that are much needed for non-immigrant, low-income Americans. The fear is expressed that, through their hard work, long hours, cultural practices, and family ties, Asians are acquiring businesses and accumulating wealth at a faster pace than their indigenous counterparts. Many of these businesses are in ethnic neighborhoods and in inner-city locations vacated by Euro Americans. The role of Asians in reviving inner-city businesses has not gone unnoticed, but some people feel that they are exploiting the minority poor without making a significant contribution to the community within which they are embedded. On the other hand, there are those who argue that Asians, some recent immigrants as well as long-term residents, have contributed significantly to technological and entrepreneurial activities leading to economic growth and employment possibilities for all other U. S. residents.

Prejudice against Asians is also based on the resentment of the academic and economic success of the group. Rather than admiring or emulating the characteristics of hard work, self-discipline, family cohesiveness, achievement orientation, and respect for education associated with Asians, some Americans convince themselves that Asians must somehow be dishonest and need to be punished. Such convictions perpetuate hostility and acts of racism that have been directed toward the group historically and that continue to affect the adaptation patterns of Asians in the United States.

Thus, there are those Americans who resent Asians and oppose the admission of any Asian refugees or immigrants to the United States. On the other hand, others support Asian refugees, like other refugees, on humanitarian and economic grounds, and value the ethnic diversity within the American society. Many recognize the positive impact of the immigrants and thus promote the presence of Asians. Such contradictory views result in conflicting attitudes toward Asians as well as a lack of consensus regarding policies toward Asian immigrants and refugees. Despite the conflicting public opinions, Asians continue to immigrate to the United States in large numbers.

CONCLUSIONS

Knowledge, awareness, and understanding about diverse Asian groups are required for both Asians and other Americans to facilitate Asian integration into American society and to dispel myths related to Asians. Research knowledge, rather than fears based on observations of a few, should guide policy and human relations. Similarly, social work services and programs, whether for the newly arrived young families or for established elderly Asian groups, should be guided by an understanding of cultural practices and traditions of diverse Asian groups. Like all other ethnic groups, Asians experience the stresses of life. Service delivery models based on an understanding of cultural background, history, and specific life experiences are more likely to meet the needs of new immigrants as well as established Asians.

Individual Asian families and Asian communities with common religious, linguistic, or cultural backgrounds must provide support so that Asians can become productive citizens. Service providers must empower Asian populations to chart their life course. The host society must provide enabling environments and supports not only to help

Asians adapt to life in the United States, but also to facilitate their contributions to society. Otherwise, as indicated through Takaki's (1989) historical analysis, Asians may remain "strangers from a different shore." It is through building bridges, rather than erecting fences, that the host society can facilitate Asian integration into the United States and make it possible for immigrants to become contributing members in their adopted homeland.

REFERENCES

America's super minority. (1986, November, 26). *Fortune*, pp. 148-165.

Asian Americans: "A model minority." (1982, December 6). *Newsweek*, pp. 40-51.

Asian Americans: Are they making the grade? (1984, April 2). *U. S. News and World Report*, pp. 41-47.

Bell, D. (1985, July 15 & 22). The triumph of Asian Americans: America's greatest success story. *New Republic*, pp. 24-31.

Berry, J. W. (1984). Cultural relations in plural societies: Alternatives to segregation and their sociopsychological implications. In N. Miller & M. Brewer (Eds.), *Groups in contact* (pp. 11-27). New York: Academic Press.

Berry, J. W. (1988). *Understanding the process of acculturation for primary prevention.* Minneapolis: Technical Assistance Center, University of Minnesota.

Berry, J. W., Kalin, R., & Taylor, D. M. (1977). *Multiculturalism and ethnic attitudes in Canada.* Ottawa: Government of Canada.

Berry, J. W., & Kim, U. (1988). Acculturation and mental health. In P. Dasen, J. W. Berry, & N. Sartorius (Eds.), *Health and cross-cultural psychology: Towards application* (pp. 207-236). London: Sage.

Bonacich, E. (1973). A theory of middleman minorities. *American Sociological Review, 38,* 583-594.

Borjas, G. (1989). *Friends or strangers: The impact of immigrants on the U. S. economy.* New York: Basic Books.

Cabezas, A., & Kawaguchi, G. (1988). Empirical evidence for continuing Asian American income inequity: The human capital model and labor market segmentation. In G. Y. Okihiro et al. (Eds.), *Reflections on shattered windows: Promises and prospects for Asian American studies* (pp. 148, 154). Pullman: Washington State University Press.

The changing face of America [Special immigration issue]. (1985, July 8). *Time*, pp. 24-101.

Chiswick, B. (1980). Immigrants' earnings patterns by sex, race and ethnic groupings. *Monthly Labor Review, 103,* 22-25.

Cox, D. (1987). *Migration and welfare, an Australian perspective.* Englewood Cliffs, NJ: Prentice-Hall.

De Vos, G. (1980). Identity problems in migrant minorities: A psychocultural comparative approach applied to Korean and Japanese. In R. Bryce-Laporte (Ed.), *Sourcebook on the new immigration: Implications for the United States and the international community* (pp. 321-328). New Brunswick, NJ: Transaction Books.

Dhooper, S. (1986, March). *Social work with Asian Americans.* Paper presented at the 32nd Annual Program Meeting of the Council on Social Work Education, Miami, Florida.

English, R. A. (1984). *The challenge of mental health: Minorities and their world views.* Austin: Hogg Foundation for Mental Health, The University of Texas, Austin.

Forbes, S. (1985). *Adaptation and integration of recent refugees to the United States.* Washington, DC: The Refugee Policy Group.

Gordon, M. (1964). *Assimilation in American life.* New York: Oxford University Press.

Gordon, M. (1975). Toward a general theory of racial and ethnic group relations. In N. Glazer & D. Moynihan (Eds.), *Ethnicity: Theory and experience* (pp. 84-110). Cambridge, MA: Harvard University Press.

Hirschman, C., & Wong, M. (1984). Socioeconomic gains of Asian Americans, Blacks and Hispanics: 1960-1976. *American Journal of Sociology, 90*, 584-607.

Hurh, W., & Kim, K. (1984). *Korean immigrants in America: A structural analysis of ethnic confinement and adhesive adaptation.* Cranbury, NJ: Associated University Press.

Hurh, W., Kim, H., & Kim, K. (1979). *Assimilation patterns of immigrants in the United States: A case study of Korean immigrants in the Chicago area.* Washington, DC: University Press of America.

Kitano, H. (1976). *Japanese Americans: The evolution of a subculture.* Englewood Cliffs, NJ: Prentice-Hall.

Kuo, C. (1982). Perceptions of assimilation among the Chinese in the United States. *Research in Race and Ethnic Relations, 3*, 127-143.

Kuo, W. (1979). On the study of Asian Americans: Its current state and agenda. *The Sociological Quarterly, 20*, 279-290.

Langberg, M., & Farley, R. (1985). Residential segregation of Asian Americans in 1980. *Sociology and Social Research, 70*, 71-75.

Meemeduma, P. (1988). *The support networks of Sri Lankan women living in the United States: A study of settlement and adaptation.* Unpublished doctoral dissertation, Howard University.

Metcalf, B. (1984). Introduction. In B. Metcalf (Ed.). *Moral conduct and authority: The place of adab in South Asian Islam* (pp. 1-23). Berkeley: University of California Press.

Morales, R. (1989). *Filipino street gangs.* Unpublished manuscript.

Murase, K. (1989). *Ethnic minority social work mental health clinical training programs: Assessing the post-planning for the future Asian Pacific Americans.* A report prepared for the National Institutes of Mental Health.

Nee, V., & Sanders, J. (1985). The road to parity: Determinants of the socioeconomic attainments of Asian Americans. *Ethnic and Racial Studies, 8*, 75-93.

Park, R. (1913). Racial assimilation in secondary groups with particular reference to the Negro. *Paper and proceedings of the Eighth Annual Meeting of the American Sociological Society* (Vol. 8). Chicago, 1914, 71.

Peterson, W. (1971). *Japanese Americans: Oppression and success.* New York: Random House.

Piore, M. (1973). *The role of immigration in industrial growth: A case study of the origins and character of Puerto Rican migration to Boston* (Working paper 112). Cambridge: Department of Economics, MIT.

Roland, A. (1984). The self in India and America: Toward a psychoanalysis of social and cultural contexts. In V. Kavolis (Ed.), *Design of selfhood* (pp. 170-194). London: Associated University Press.

Roland, A. (1988). In search of self in India and Japan: Toward a cross-cultural psychology. Princeton, NJ: Princeton University Press.

Ross-Sheriff, F. (1985, July). Ismaili youth: In transition. *American Ismaili*, 36-40.

Ross-Sheriff, F., & Nanji, A. (1991). Islamic identity, family and community: The case of the Nizari Ismaili Muslims. In E. Waugh, S. Abu-Laden, & R. Qureshi (Eds.), *Muslim families in North America* (pp. 101-118). Edmonton: The University of Alberta Press.

Schwartz, D. F. (1985). *Immigration and refugees: Issues, politic and democratic pluralism*. Paper presented at the National Immigration, Refugee and Citizenship Forum, Washington, D. C.

Simon, J. (1989). *The economic consequences of immigration*. Cambridge, MA: Basil Blackwell.

Sowell, T. (1981). *Ethnic America*. New York: Basic Books.

Stanford Research Institute International. (1983). *Southeast Asian refugee resettlement at the local level: The role of ethnic community and the nature of the refugee impact*. Palo Alto, CA: Author.

Takaki, R. (1989). *Strangers from a different shore: A history of Asian Americans*. Waltham, MA: Little, Brown.

U. S. Equal Employment Opportunity Commission Report, (1988, May 13). Summary in L. Harrison, U. S. finds few Asians in management. *Asian Week*, 1.

Wong, B. (1987). The role of ethnicity in enclave enterprises: A study of the Chinese garment factories in New York City. *Human Organizations, 46*(2), 120-130.

Wong, M. (1982). The cost of being Chinese, Japanese, and Filipino in the United States, 1960, 1970, and 1976. *Pacific Sociological Review, 25*, 59-78.

Part II

MICRO-LEVEL INTERVENTION PRACTICES AND PROGRAMS

KENJI MURASE

Part I presented an introduction to the histories and cultures of Asian Americans and their adaptation in the American society. Part II will consider social work practice and service delivery programs with respect to Asians from the perspective of micro intervention in the United States. As the references cited indicate, there has been increasing attention in the social work literature to issues of concern to ethnic minority communities. Much of this literature reflects a renewed focus on ethnic cultural issues in social work practice. While attention to the vital role of culture in both the manifestations of behavioral dysfunction and their treatment is welcome, it is necessary to emphasize that the responsible use of cultural knowledge requires sensitivity and care.

The importance of ethnic and cultural variables for understanding an individual remains dependent upon the level of cultural sensitivity of the social worker, whose store of cultural knowledge serves as a general field against which the individual or client group is viewed. The social worker must possess adequate information about history, cultural values, norms of conduct, language patterns, nonverbal behavior, family structures and functions, and how such factors are mediated or transformed by the client's environment.

In addition to recognizing the immense variability of behavior across cultures, within the individual and within cultures, between individuals and across time and space, the social worker must be aware that each individual manifests a unique cultural and developmental synthesis in personal behavior.

In considering the comparative influence of Asian cultures vis-à-vis the dominant American culture, there are a variety of perspectives from which to view cultural interaction, including: (a) the trans-cultural perspective, where Asian cultures cross over and interact with the dominant Euro American culture;

(b) the cross-cultural perspective, where there is movement from one side (Asian culture) to the other (Euro American culture) and then a passing across; (c) the para-cultural perspective of a side-by-side comparison of the two cultural worlds for immigrants and refugees, and for first-, second-, and third-generation American born; (d) the meta-cultural perspective of focus on the similarities and differences between Asian cultures and other minority cultures; and (e) the pan-cultural perspective, which seeks out the universal and common elements of all cultures. Failure of the social worker to recognize the variability of cultural interaction and its expression can result in a counterproductive form of benign ethnic stereotyping.

The chapters that follow in Part II delineate the complexities of social work practice with Asian Americans and offer specific guidelines to facilitate effective responses to their problems and needs. Noreen Mokuau and Jon Matsuoka address the often raised issue of the appropriateness of theories derived from Western psychology in practice with Asian Americans in "The Appropriateness of Personality Theories for Social Work With Asian Americans." They identify the central problems that arise in cross-cultural practice and encounters, and they explicate the multiple factors that must be taken into account in resolving therapeutic issues. Case illustrations serve to provide specificity to concepts that may otherwise remain elusive abstractions difficult to apply in practice.

To fully understand any ethnic group, it is axiomatic to say that one must understand the history of that group. Judith Shepherd's chapter, "Vietnamese Women Immigrants and Refugees in the United States: Historical Perspectives on Casework," underscores the importance of a historical perspective, in terms of not only the chronology of historical events and their effects, but also the cultural-historical influences that continue to persist in their lives. In addition, the application of historical perspectives is illustrated by Shepherd's assessment of problems presented in four cases of women from Vietnam.

Much of the social work literature on ethnic minorities points to the unavailability of social services and their relevance to and utilization by minority communities. Considerably less attention has been directed to how ethnic minority communities have responded to the problems of service availability, relevance, and utilization. In "Models of Service Delivery in Asian American Communities," I report on the experiences of Asian Americans in developing their own community-based services in response to the unavailability or inappropriateness of services in their communities. Particularly instructive to other ethnic communities is the formulation of the processes by which Asian American communities have initiated and maintained their community-based services.

The authors hope that the concepts and principles of practice discussed in this section will be useful to social workers in micro-level intervention with Asian Americans.

Chapter 4

THE APPROPRIATENESS OF PERSONALITY THEORIES FOR SOCIAL WORK WITH ASIAN AMERICANS

NOREEN MOKUAU
JON MATSUOKA

Social casework, the earliest defined method of social work, reflects a diversity of theories and approaches. The more formal schools of thought include the psychosocial, problem-solving, and functional approaches. These approaches represent open systems of thought that are subject to change with the incorporation of new ideas and data. As such, they continually draw upon a broad range of behavioral science theories, with theories of personality and counseling being the most predominant. Theories of personality that have heavily influenced social work practice might be conceptualized as comprising three major groups: psychodynamic, existential-humanistic, and the cognitive-behavioral schools.

In working with Asians, social workers must be cognizant of these three major groups of personality theories and how they may be appropriately used with this clientele. A study on utilization rates of these three approaches suggests that they can be appropriately used with Asian clients (Mokuau-Matsushima, Tashima, & Murase, 1982). In this study, the utilization rates of psychodynamic, existential-humanistic, and cognitive-behavioral approaches were assessed for 347 Asian and Pacific Islander practitioners throughout the United States working with Asian clients. The results showed that the cognitive-behavioral modality was frequently ("almost always" or "usually") used by 46% of the practitioners, and the existential-humanistic (or phenomenological) approach by 38%, and the psychodynamic approach by 32%. When comparing the mean scores for these three approaches, it was discovered that there is a comparable utilization of the approaches, with some preference for the cognitive-behavioral approach.

This chapter will examine the concepts and processes underlying the psychodynamic, the existential-humanistic, and the cognitive-behavioral approaches and will extrapolate some ideas that are relevant and appropriate for practice with Asian clients. It will also examine assessment issues and explore the utility and appropriateness of assessment concepts for working with this population. The relevance of such a discussion is predicated on an understanding of the development of Asian worldviews.

ASIAN WORLDVIEWS

The formation of a worldview in a multicultural situation is complex in that the individual adopts and modifies cultural tradition in order to accommodate new forms of learning. Acculturation, or the "process of learning a culture different from the one in which a person was originally raised," as described by Berelson and Steiner (1964), addresses a complicated interplay of many variables. These variables include periods of immigration, geography and ethnic communities, generational differences, and the social effects of racism and prejudice. The periods in which various Asian groups emigrated to the United States may have influenced the development of their worldviews. Kitano (1974) suggested "continual contact" as one element that facilitates acculturation. This means that persons living in the United States for longer periods of time receive more exposure and contact with the American culture and are inclined to be more acculturated than persons without such experience. The historical literature documents the experiences of the Chinese, Japanese, and Filipino immigrant groups in the pre-1930s period and the Koreans and Southeast refugees in the post-1965 period. Following the "continual contact" line of reasoning, one might conclude that the Japanese, Chinese, and Filipinos are more acculturated than more recently arrived immigrant groups.

A second variable that is likely to affect the development of a unique worldview relates to area of residence and a strong identification with others within one's ethnic group. In a comparative study of Japanese in Hawaii and on the continental United States, Suzuki and Yamashiro (1980) found that different environments affected the degree of transmission of ethnic values from one generation to another. The development of an ethnic identity or worldview is contingent upon the social milieu in which an individual is raised. For example, it is logical to assume that Japanese who reside in ethnic-dominated geographic settings, such as Hawaii, will have different socialization experiences from those Japanese residing in predominantly white communities in the continental United States. Those who live in predominantly white communities are subject to a different system of reinforcement and do not readily benefit from its institutions and cultural processes.

A third variable concerns the generational differences that may exist between those persons who belong to first-, second-, third-, and fourth-generational families in the United States. Several reports indicate that there are psychological and behavioral changes in persons of different generations, and there is an increasing trend among the younger generation to adopt norms of the host culture (Connor, 1977; Ishisaka & Takagi, 1982; Masuda, Hasegawa, & Matsumoto, 1973). Interestingly, these studies report that while the younger generations may be more acculturated than the older generations, there is an ongoing attempt to preserve and promote pride in one's cultural heritage.

The presence of racism and prejudice also affects the development of one's worldview. Institutional racism and prejudice tend to impede the acculturation process and strengthen cultural traditions. Lee (1952) comments:

> [Acculturation] is usually prevented largely through the historical restrictions imposed by the majority of society. When one is thwarted from sharing equally in the goods of society, one tends to adopt temporary frames of security by means of substitute satisfaction. This often manifests itself in the strengthening of ties already established within a membership group.

The racial discrimination and prejudice directed at the pre-1930 immigration groups were perceived to be more overt and severe than for the post-1965 immigration groups. While this may be true, in part, it is more important to recognize that racism is a chronic problem in our society and it affects all Asians.

An understanding of the formation of Asian worldviews provides the foundation for examining the interface of culture and personality theories. Psychodynamic, existential-humanistic, and cognitive-behavioral theories will be discussed in terms of their relevance to Asian issues and concerns.

PSYCHODYNAMIC APPROACHES

The concepts and processes defined in the psychodynamic approaches have great import for working with Asians. However, it must be emphasized that the degree of their relevance is predicated on a merging of the concepts and processes of the approaches with the cultural worldviews and lifestyle practices of the clientele. Psychodynamic theories derive from the works of Sigmund Freud and the Neo-Freudians and ego psychologists such as Otto Rank, Carl Jung, Erik Erikson, and Alfred Adler. The Freudian view of human nature is deterministic, with an emphasis on unconscious factors, psychosexual stages of development, significant others from one's childhood, and psychic energy. The Neo-Freudians extended orthodox Freudian theory and emphasized sociocultural factors that affect personality development, psychosocial stages of development, and interpersonal relations. These Neo-Freudians identified the importance of understanding one's development and interaction with the environment. In a generalized manner, several of the ideas found in the psychodynamic approaches appear to be congruent with Asian worldviews and life-style practices.

One of the strongest propositions underlying several of the Neo-Freudians' approaches relates to the influence of a sociocultural environment on the development of the personality. For example, Adler suggests that happiness and success are largely derived from a social connectedness, and that since we are a part of a society, we cannot be understood in isolation from the social context (Corey, 1986). Furthermore, if this sense of belonging is not fulfilled, anxiety and dysfunctional behavior will occur. When working with Asian clients, it would be useful to keep in mind those sociocultural factors that may have influenced the development of personality. For example, institutionalized forms of racism and prejudice in mental health, education, employment, and so on, have impacted on Asians' perceptions of themselves as well as their relationships with significant others and society at large. Problematic behavior may be understood in terms of these sociocultural factors, but it is also significant to recognize that it may be the sociocultural factors that precipitate the problems. It is important for practitioners to recognize whether ethnic minority membership is a dominant factor in dysfunctional behavior or whether the difficulties are characterologic in nature.

The emphasis in the Neo-Freudian approaches on social connectedness is also reaffirmed in the psychoanalytic principle pertaining to role relationships. According to this viewpoint, relationships with significant others from one's past are critical to the understanding and resolution of dysfunctional behavior in the present. Especially important are one's relationships with one's parents. In the Asian culture, there is a strong emphasis on family systems and the identification of specific roles and proper relationships among family members. Within the family context, it is important to be respectful of the hierarchical nature of role relationships and the reverence attributed to ancestors, older family members, and males. Cultural tradition places ancestors and male elders and parents at the top of the hierarchy. Thus, if the social worker is dealing with a multigenerational Asian family in a clearly hierarchical structure, it may be advisable to approach the grandfather first and than proceed downward (Ho, 1987).

The importance of role relationships is reflected in a specific method of therapy in Japanese culture called Naikan therapy, in which dysfunction in the present is believed to be the consequence of unhealthy relationships with significant others from the past. Efforts to reduce the problems of the present include meditating on significant relationships of the past, and being able to "transfer" that learning onto relationships of the "here-and-now."

In addition to noting psychodynamic concepts that may be appropriate, practitioners should also identify methods that may have relevance. For example, the Jungian method of "sandbox therapy" is potentially useful for working with Asian clients who are unable to articulate their emotional concerns. Sandbox therapy allows for these individuals to find expression and insight through the symbolic use of toy figures in a sandbox and allows the practitioner, through interpretative means, to redirect the client and facilitate discussion. There appears to be a resurgence of Jungian methods of practice, which are appropriate for adults and children.

Case Illustration: Susan A. is a second-generation Chinese American who entered treatment because of severe depression resulting from marital problems. Susan is emotionally reserved and has difficulty articulating her problems. In utilizing sandbox therapy, the practitioner was able to determine that Susan's marital problems stemmed from a feeling of inadequacy and isolation from her husband. Susan's placement of two dolls, identified as self and spouse, in the sandbox, was always divided by another toy object, such as a tree, building, or car, and sometimes by a mound of sand. The size and significance of the dividing toy object helped to reflect Susan's current state of thinking. Identification of the client's problem was an important step in this situation.

EXISTENTIAL-HUMANISTIC APPROACHES

The concepts and processes of existential-humanistic approaches have value and relevance for Asian clients. Postulated by theorists such as Carl Rogers, Rollo May, Abraham Maslow, and Frederick Perls, this group of theories emphasizes the client's potential for self-direction in determination of a "creative self." The self is a basic construct that is typically defined as "the individual's dynamic organization of concepts, values, goals, and ideals which determine the ways in which he/she should behave" (Shostrom & Brammer, 1952). According to this perspective, human beings have a capacity for self-awareness in which the greater the awareness, the greater the possibilities for freedom (Corey, 1986). This capacity for self-awareness is directly related to a social base in which the search for self is done in context of one's environment, and most significantly, in context of one's relationship to others.

This proposition on self-awareness can contribute to an understanding of and practice with Asians today. Asians represent unique personalities with a commonality in culture. By understanding the cultural and social dynamics that shape the development of the "self," the practitioner will be able to raise issues that can be the impetus for further self-exploration and development. For example, many third- and fourth-generation Asians today experience identity conflicts related to a merging of "traditional" values with "contemporary/Western" values. For these Asians, a pride in cultural values and a desire to have the freedom to incorporate different values are not always compatible, and this sometimes precipitates questions about "how ethnic" one really is. While the challenge to one's cultural roots may have dysfunctional consequences for the individual and his or her family, it may also be the opportunity to develop a greater capacity for self-awareness. Existentialism provides the vehicle in which this kind of opportunity may be offered.

Existential-humanistic theories maintain that the quality of the practitioner-client relationship is the substance of the helping process. Corey (1986) states that the growth force of the client is released in terms of a living and authentic relationship with the practitioner. This relationship is characterized as nondirective and equalitarian, with an emphasis on self-disclosure. Such an approach may be inappropriate for Asians who adhere to traditional cultural values, such as a belief in hierarchical and role relationships and emotional reticence, and who prefer active direction from the practitioner. However, it would be appropriate for Asians who value opposing beliefs. It is important that practitioners be accustomed to viewing Asians as a heterogenous group with diverse worldviews and life-style practices, and be prepared to find the best match of practice theory with the client's circumstances.

Case Illustration: An elderly first-generation Filipino woman sought bereavement counseling from a practitioner. Her husband died unexpectedly, and the woman felt that there was much unfinished business between her husband and herself. She had wished to express her feelings of love and happiness for their time together, but was experiencing guilt and remorse because she had not had the time to do so. In borrowing from existential thought, the practitioner suggested that the woman role-play and speak to her husband as if he were still alive. Utilizing her creative self, the woman was able to communicate to her husband her previously unexpressed feelings, and at the same time, project her perceptions of his reactions. This process reflected a respect for the importance of role relationships and, at the same time, provided the woman with an opportunity to self-disclose to her husband in the safety of a practitioner's office. In doing the role-play, the woman experienced a sense of comfort and relief, and was better able to establish a healthy closure to the situation.

COGNITIVE-BEHAVIORAL APPROACHES

Cognitive-behavioral theories offer an orientation to problem conceptualization and treatment that can be applied to Asians. An assumption shared by many theorists is that basic cognitive-behavioral principles apply to all persons despite their sociocultural background. Few theorists, however, have attempted to merge cognitive-behavioral concepts with the cultural characteristics of non-Western societies.

Higginbotham and Tanaka-Matsumi (1981) have written one of the few articles that examine the feasibility of cognitive-behavioral approaches for clinical work with Asian populations. They suggest that basic cognitive-behavioral principles can be modified according to the cultural variables of any group. For example, they contend that the concept of reinforcement is inherent to all people, although forms of reinforcement will vary according to learning histories and values. What may serve to reinforce behaviors in one culture may not be effective in another because of cultural variations of importance, yet the basic notion of reinforcement applies.

Characteristics of a cognitive-behavioral approach include: (a) a focus upon variables that precede and maintain problem behaviors, (b) an emphasis upon quantification, and (c) the specification of aberrant cognitions that contribute to problematic conditions.

Prior to administering a behavior change program, it is imperative to focus upon antecedent and maintaining variables. A precise behavioral definition and identification of behaviors and relevant environmental factors will enable the therapist to have a more comprehensive understanding of the problem. An accurate conceptualization of the problem will allow the practitioner to design an appropriate intervention program. In cross-cultural work it is essential for the practitioner to have a broad understanding of the normative behaviors and subtle interpersonal dynamics occurring in the culture that the client represents. Without such knowledge, the practitioner may be prone to bias, errors, or incomplete assessments, which will have detrimental effects upon the intervention program.

In the context of the client's world, the practitioner can then identify both antecedent conditions to the problem and the psychological and emotional significance these events represent. The practitioner must also determine whether the ascribed causative attributes of those events are primary, or if new factors have replaced or compounded the original ones. For example, in the case of depression, the mood of the client may have had aversive effects upon his or her friends. This network of friends, which previously served as a primary source of social support, becomes alienated from the client. Having lost such support, the client's depression becomes compounded and aggravated.

Within the cognitive-behavioral model, it is often desirable to know the frequency and duration of problem thoughts and behaviors. The quantification of data not only allows the practitioner to determine a baseline, but also helps the client attend to and identify target behaviors and events. This form of self-monitoring at the very least sensitizes the client to the frequency of problematic behaviors. From an evaluation standpoint, the effectiveness of treatment can be determined by comparing initial baseline rates with post-intervention rates. Inferences can be made about the effectiveness of the intervention, based upon the margin of change.

The cognitive-behavioral model also ascribes importance to internal events and examines the way an individual processes information. Negative moods and feelings are frequently attributed to dysfunctional or aberrant cognitions that have long-term sustaining properties. A crucial cognitive characteristic relates to how information is perceived, interpreted, and remembered. For example, a person with a negative self-concept is prone to be systematically biased against oneself.

Cognitive factors must also be considered within the context of one's culture. Differential value systems account for cultural variations in morality, propriety, and belief systems. These factors serve as guidelines for interpreting events and behaviors. Problems often occur when practitioners, encapsulated in their own culture, misinterpret the motives and attitudes of clients from a different culture. Without some understanding of the clients' cultural system, the practitioner may regard their thoughts and beliefs as illogical and invalid. Often these thoughts and beliefs are based on a highly refined system of protocols and custom. The response cost for deviation may be severe.

Case Illustration: Phuc is a 21-year-old first-generation Vietnamese experiencing depression over the recent breakup with her boyfriend. Her symptoms included frequent crying spells, insomnia, and negative ruminations related to her self-image. During the assessment phase the practitioner examined these symptoms and the conditions surrounding them. For example, the practitioner found out that the client was most likely to experience crying spells during the evening hours, when she was accustomed to spending time with her ex-boyfriend. She would cry consistently each day during this time for as long as an hour. Combined with this pattern were her negative thoughts concerning herself and the consequences on her family. She blamed herself for the breakup and believed that she would never find another boyfriend.

Intervention included the development of activity schedules to fill the time void left by the breakup. Instead of pondering the loss of her boyfriend, the client was instructed to identify and actively participate in enjoyable activities. Cognitive techniques were employed to challenge the irrational beliefs about "never being involved in a relationship again." The practitioner also focused on cultural issues surrounding the significance of this type of relationship. In Vietnam, dating was rare, and a relationship of this type would be viewed as a precursor to marriage. Themes of shame and guilt were pervasive in this case, inasmuch as the client felt that she had "failed" to meet cultural expectations of marriage. Thus, much of the cognitive-behavioral work involved dealing with reasonable expectations for the future.

It is hoped that the above discussion of the psychodynamic, existential-humanistic, and cognitive-behavioral approaches provide a perspective for the application of these typically "Western" approaches to practice with Asian clients. The task is to selectively utilize those concepts and processes that are compatible with the cultural and social circumstances of the client. A part of this selection task is to pay attention to the accuracy and sensitivity of assessment tools and procedures. The definitions of deviance, normality, and abnormality vary significantly between cultures. Based on these definitions, a culture structures certain ways of dealing with problems. Practitioners working with Asian clients need to evaluate the relevant cultural issues related to the utility and appropriateness of assessment systems.

ASSESSMENT ISSUES

Asian Americans experiencing psychological difficulties have historically been subject to a universal approach to assessment and diagnosis. The assumptions made about their symptomatology have often resulted in the misdiagnosis of individuals. Because personality structures vary across cultures, it is logical to assume that there are corresponding differences in the expression of mental disorders. For example, among Asians, a primary pattern is the tendency to express symptoms via somatization (Sue & Morishima, 1982). Personality patterns may also influence how psychological difficulties are manifested by virtue of temperament styles, cognitive and physiological coping patterns, and general personality orientations (Marsella, 1979).

Currently, diagnostic systems do not usually provide essential data regarding sociocultural conditions under which symptoms are acquired and labeled. This lack of attention or value placed on cultural factors points to a general lack of cultural sensitivity in the mental health field. Consequently, assessment and diagnostic procedures may fail in their attempt to reliably address cultural factors. Murase (1973) discusses assessment problems encountered by the practitioner in work with Asians and states the need to be able to differentiate cultural paranoia from real pathology, cultural resistance from depressive withdrawal, and traditional family needs from abnormal dependency.

Inadequate assessment concepts and procedures are exacerbated by the cultural barriers between the practitioner and the client. These barriers include: (a) the culturally encapsulated practitioner, (b) cultural stereotyping, and (c) countertransference.

Culturally Encapsulated Practitioners

The development and maintenance of mental health services is derived from a Euro American base. Consequently, practitioners may interpret ethnic minority group experiences from this orientation. "Counselors who force their notions of healthy and normal onto persons who do not share the worker's value assumptions have, through cultural naivete, cognitive rigidity, or misunderstanding, become tools of their own dominant political, social and economic systems" (Pedersen, Lonner, & Draguns, 1976). Various studies have pointed to the operation of cultural biases on the part of therapists in diagnostic evaluations of Asians (Hsu, Tseng, Ashton, McDermott, & Char, 1985; Li-Repac, 1980; Wampold, Casas, & Atkinson, 1981).

Cultural Stereotyping

Somewhat antithetical to the practitioner encapsulation phenomenon is the barrier of cultural stereotyping. According to Atkinson, Morten, and Sue (1979), stereotyping is a major problem of practice, which may be defined as rigid preconceptions that are applied to all members of a group, or to an individual over a period of time, regardless of individual variations. Common examples of cultural stereotyping of Asians are: (a) they are model minorities, (b) they are good at mathematics and sciences, and (c) they are less proficient at interpersonal communication. Cultural stereotyping may be manifested in two detrimental effects:

practitioners who have preconceived notions about minority group members may act upon their beliefs, and ethnic minority members may actually come to believe these stereotypes about themselves.

Countertransference

Countertransference refers to the practitioner's reacting to the client as he or she had reacted to someone from the past (Greenson, 1964). Mendes (1977) suggests that countertransference represents practitioners' preconceived conscious and unconscious standards upon which judgments are based. These standards and ideas may present themselves as distortions of reality and, ultimately, misinterpretations of clinical data. Wyatt, Strayer, and Lobitz (1976) advocate that it is important for practitioners to acknowledge racial feelings and attitudes that they bring to any interview. A specific example of countertransference is a situation in which a practitioner projects onto an Asian client attitudes or feelings influenced by childhood memories. In this reaction, the practitioner may be overzealous in attempting to help the client, and normal interactions may be inhibited.

In summary, efforts to reduce the inadequacy of assessment systems and the barriers operating between the practitioner and the Asian client depend on the practitioner's being able to: (a) identify the range of values in a client's cultural group, (b) compare his or her values and assumptive framework with the client's in a nonjudgmental way, and (c) develop assessment procedures that are congruent with the client's worldview and also compatible with the practitioner's values and beliefs.

CONCLUSIONS

Asians are a heterogenous people with varying worldviews and life-style practices. Historically, these groups have been diagnosed and treated according to personality theories and practice models that often conflict with their cultural perspectives. However, in recent times there has been some effort to make social work practice more accountable to Asians. One way to enhance accountability is to examine widely used personality theories and practice methods and identify those components that have greatest relevance and adaptability to this population. The importance attached to these efforts derives from the increasing recognition that Asians are entitled to culturally appropriate diagnosis and treatment. The initiative to find the "match" of theoretical approach with the needs of the Asian clientele is an ongoing responsibility of all social workers committed to cross-cultural practice.

Reading: A Case Study

The radical shift from one culture to another may have resulted in the loss of traditional age-related roles that members of a family occupied. These roles become critical in terms of how individuals view themselves. For Asian American individuals self-image can be construed as an aggregate of experiences related to performance in an individual's several social roles. Among particular populations, like Southeast Asian refugees, the process of evacuation and resettlement may have resulted in the displacement of the multiplicity of social roles occupied by the refugees prior to evacuation. The process of a cultural transition is likely to predispose individuals and families to role loss and disintegration.

Breakdown in family discipline due to a cultural conflict is illustrated in the case of Trinh, a 17-year-old Vietnamese female. Trinh was born in Vietnam and emigrated to America at the age of 4. Her father was an American retired from the military who married her Vietnamese mother and went to work for an American business in Vietnam. When Trinh was 3 years old her father died of natural causes. Soon afterwards she and her mother were evacuated from Vietnam and were allowed to resettle in America. Trinh had difficulty remembering the period surrounding evacuation and resettlement. It was generally a time of great fear and apprehension. A few years after their arrival, her mother met and married another Vietnamese refugee who was an ex-soldier. They gave birth to two more children: a boy, then age 8, and a girl, then age 6. Trinh reported getting along very well with her siblings, although her relationship with her stepfather has never been very close.

Trinh resided in an area that lacked a concentrated population of Vietnamese. Because of the lack of an ethnic community, reinforcement for appropriate Vietnamese behavior was not available for her family. The reinforcement loss and the loss of various role patterns, which would ordinarily give her a strong definitive role as a Vietnamese adolescent, left her in a confused, ambiguous, and depressive state.

In Vietnamese culture, there was greater emphasis on achieving one's identity and sense of worth through close relationship with family adults and being a member of an established lineage and extended family system. However, the disruption and separation of many families, coupled with exposure and socialization in an age-segregated society, had increased the importance and influence of peers.

In school, she felt a need to identify more and more with American age-mates and she found American customs to be very attractive. She became a member of a clique of friends, which permitted her to keep up with the fads and fashions in clothes, personal grooming, music, and interpersonal behavior. With the heightened importance of the peer group came the increased pressure for conformity. To keep up with her peers, she felt pressure to have a boyfriend. Her parents objected to her choice of friends, her behavior, and her keeping late hours. When they discovered their daughter's boyfriend had no intention of marrying her, they forbade her to see him. In customary Vietnamese practice, all contacts between young men and women are viewed as preliminaries to marriage. Dating for recreation is very uncommon and it is inconsistent with traditional Vietnamese values.

Trinh refused to obey her parents and continued to see her boyfriend away from home without her parents' knowledge. When her mother found out, she shamed Trinh in the worst way a Vietnamese mother could shame her daughter. She told her that she "must pick her eyes out, for she has shamed herself, her family, and her people." When Trinh told her peers about this, they referred her to the Child Protective Services. The social worker at Child Protective Services misinterpreted the symbolic gesture of her mother as an assault with a knife and felt that Trinh's safety and welfare were endangered. He offered her a foster home. Because Trinh desired more freedom from her restrictive parents, she accepted the social worker's offer.

This case serves as an example of an adolescent who began to experience difficulties due to the rapidity at which she was able to Americanize. This kind of adjustment can occur and carries with it some difficulties in functioning for all parties.

Intervention

Trinh remained in the foster home until a bilingual and bicultural social worker was assigned to the case. The social worker immediately recognized the event preceding Trinh's removal as a "figure of expression" and returned her to her family home. The social worker, however, became aware of the severity of the family's problems and prescribed treatment involving Trinh on an individual basis and the entire family in terms of family therapy.

The events surrounding Trinh's early childhood had severe consequences, which exacerbated her current developmental issues associated with the ambiguity of adolescence. Her earliest memories reflected vague, yet very fond feelings toward her "real" father. He, in many ways, epitomized the strong American image. His death was extremely traumatic and it seemed to set off a whole series of negative experiences related to family disruption and instability. She never had the opportunity to appropriately terminate any of her early childhood relationships. With the onslaught of Communist forces, Trinh and her mother had been forced to leave their homeland in fear of persecution. In the mass confusion of evacuation, they had no sense of who might be able to evacuate and who might be left behind. As a result, she left behind her grandparents, uncles, aunts, and cousins whom she was not psychologically prepared to leave and whom she can never hope to see again. This sense of loss at such a critical period in her development was viewed as extremely traumatic.

Much of individual therapy was based on reminiscing about the past and analyzing her current feelings associated with those experiences. Trinh's feelings of guilt and depression over lost loved ones needed to be treated before the social worker was able to move ahead to other concerns. She experienced a degree of guilt, which could be best described as "survivor guilt." She wondered why she was so fortunate to live in such an affluent society when her relatives in Vietnam were forced to live under such oppressive conditions. The treatment focus was on reliving, analyzing, and working through the events contributing to her feelings of guilt and depression. The therapeutic objective was to allow her to accept the conditions or aim toward a reconceptualization of the self-blame. From there she was encouraged to move away from the stressful events and the associated thoughts. Reminiscing about her natural father, with the support of her mother, allowed her to grieve his death for the first time. The process of grieving brought with it a degree of self-awareness and a connection with her past. It also brought her closer to her mother, who was able to provide support and reconcile her own unresolved feelings from the past.

Family therapy focused on the dynamics between members. The primary source of conflict was between Trinh and her stepfather. She felt that her stepfather never really liked her because she wasn't of "his blood." He, on the other hand, felt that she never accepted him because he didn't measure up to the image she held of her natural father. He felt she resented him for taking away her mother's affection and because he was Vietnamese, not American. Once these assumptions were openly expressed, a better understanding was reached between family members.

Trinh generally felt neglected by her parents, who were working long hours to generate enough income to meet survival needs. This may in part explain her acting-out or withdrawn behavior from her family. In this case, therapy was aimed at reintegrating her into the family system so that she felt as though she was a contributing member. A reconciliation with her past allowed Trinh to accept her ethnic heritage and identify and assume, to a certain degree, traditional role behaviors. Family members were taught techniques in contingency management in order to reward each other for desirable behaviors, as defined by mutual agreement. Recreational activities were also planned for the family when the parents had free time to spend with their children.

To address the problems related to her new behaviors and peer group, Trinh was generally encouraged to develop a broader set of bicultural behaviors. That is, she could be "American" outside of the home and maintain Vietnamese behaviors while among her family. She would therefore have access to understanding both worlds and would be able to react to new situations in an appropriate way. She would maintain as much of the native culture as possible, but learn skills necessary to function in the American society. Her parents, at one point bewildered by this process of acculturation, had to be reminded that their American-socialized children may have ideas and interests that might not coincide with their own. Particular issues, such as Trinh's having a boyfriend, were presented as age-appropriate behaviors in the American culture.

This case illustrates the types of problems encountered by Asians who are faced with the task of finding reliable alignments between old and new cultures. Particular treatment technologies can be appropriately applied to facilitate this process. As demonstrated, other techniques have universal qualities that can be effectively streamlined according to the cultural traits of individuals and families. The practitioner in this case employed psychodynamic techniques to enable Trinh to resolve past conflicts; existential techniques were used to allow her to examine her past in relation to her current life and to develop self-awareness; and cognitive-behavioral techniques were used to encourage family support and expand her behavioral repertoire. To the extent that all of these goals were achieved, treatment was considered successful.

REFERENCES

Atkinson, D. R., Morten, G., & Sue, D. W. (Eds.). (1979). *Counseling American minorities, a cross cultural perspective*. Dubuque, IA: Brown.

Berelson, B., & Steiner, G. (1964). *Human behavior*. New York: Harcourt, Brace, and World.

Connor, J. W. (1977). *Tradition and change in three generations of Japanese Americans*. Chicago: Nelson-Hall.

Corey, G. (1986). *Theory and practice of counseling and psychotherapy*. Monterey, CA: Brooks/Cole.

Greenson, R. (1964). *Technique and practice of psychoanalysis*. New York: International Universities Press.

Higginbotham, H. N., & Tanaka-Matsumi, J. (1981). Behavioral approaches to counseling across cultures. In P. B. Pedersen, J. Draguns, W. Lonner, & J. Trimble (Eds.), *Counseling across cultures*. Honolulu: University Press of Hawaii.

Ho, M. K. (1987). *Family therapy with ethnic minorities*. Newbury Park, CA: Sage.

Hsu, J., Tseng, W. S., Ashton, G., McDermott, J. F., & Char, W. (1985). Family interaction patterns among Japanese Americans and Caucasian families in Hawaii. *American Journal of Psychiatry, 142*, 577-581.

Ishisaka, H., & Takagi, C. (1982). Social work with Asian- and Pacific-Americans. In. J. Green (Ed.), *Cultural awareness in the human services*. Englewood Cliffs, NJ: Prentice-Hall.

Kitano, H.H.L. (1974). *Race relations*. Englewood Cliffs, NJ: Prentice-Hall.

Lee, R. H. (1952). Chinese immigration and population changes since 1940. *Sociology and Social Research, 41*, 195-202.

Li-Repac, D. (1980). Cultural influences on clinical perceptions—a comparison between Caucasian and Chinese American therapists. *Journal of Cross Cultural Psychology, 11*, 327-342.

Marsella, A. (1979). Cross-cultural studies of mental disorders. In A. Marsella, R. G. Tharp, & T. J. Ciborowski (Eds.), *Perspectives on cross-cultural psychology* (pp. 233-262). Troy, MO: Academic Press.

Masuda, M., Hasegawa, S. R., & Matsumoto, M. (1973). The ethnic identity questionnaire—a comparison of three Japanese age groups in Tachikawa, Japan, Honolulu, and Seattle. *Journal of Cross Cultural Psychology, 4*, 229-245.

Mendes, H. A. (1977). Countertransferences and counter-culture clients. *Social Casework, 58*(3), 159-163.

Mokuau-Matsushima, N. M., Tashima, N., & Murase, K. (1982). *Mental health treatment modalities of Pacific Asian American practitioners*. CA: Pacific Asian Mental Health Research Project.

Murase, K. (Ed.). (1973). *Asian American task force report: Problems and issues in social work education*. New York: Council on Social Work Education.

Pedersen, P., Lonner, W., & Draguns, J. (Eds.). (1976). *Counseling across cultures*. Honolulu: University Press of Hawaii.

Shostrom, E. L., & Brammer, L. M. (1952). *The dynamics of the counseling process*. New York: McGraw-Hill.

Sue, S., & Morishima, J. K. (1982). *The mental health of Asian Americans*. San Francisco: Jossey-Bass.

Suzuki, L., & Yamashiro, C. (1980). *A study of the attitudes of third generation Japanese Americans in Hawaii and the mainland.* Unpublished master's thesis, University of California at Los Angeles.

Wampold, B. E., Casas, J. M., & Atkinson, D. R. (1981). Ethnic bias in counseling: An information processing approach. *Journal of Counseling Psychology, 28*(6), 498-503.

Wyatt, G. E., Strayer, R. G., & Lobitz, W. C. (1976). Issues in the treatment of sexually dysfunctioning couples of Afro-American descent. *Psychotherapy: Theory, Research and Practice, 13*, 44-50.

Chapter 5

VIETNAMESE WOMEN IMMIGRANTS AND REFUGEES IN THE UNITED STATES: Historical Perspectives on Casework

JUDITH SHEPHERD

This chapter explores the conditions of individual Vietnamese refugee and immigrant women's pre- and post-immigration experience for relevance to social work interventions. Rindner (1985) notes the growing recognition among people working with refugees that refugee women are a group "at risk" within an already vulnerable population. Furthermore, Rindner indicates that three-fourths of the world's refugees are women, and that there is a lack of programs to meet refugee women's needs. She suggests that policymakers at every level of the refugee field do not fully understand the nature and scope of the situation facing these refugee women.

This chapter, based on a study I conducted of a purposive sample of 30 Vietnamese refugee and immigrant women from Los Angeles and Northern California, introduces those historical perspectives that aid social workers in making more culturally appropriate assessments of Vietnamese women clients. The majority of the women came from middle-class backgrounds, and their length of residence in the United States ranged from 4 months to 16 years. Excerpts from 4 out of 30 interviews will be used to illustrate how knowledge of Vietnamese history and culture can enable social workers to make sensitive assessments and responses to female client needs. Two of the respondents cited in this report emigrated to the United States prior to the overthrow of the South Vietnamese government by North Vietnam in 1975. These women are considered immigrants. The other two women whose experiences are partially described in this chapter left their country after this event, under duress, and are thus considered refugees.

Social workers help both immigrant and refugee women. However, they may find that refugee women rather than immigrant women present more urgent needs and require their priority attention. Many of the acute problems refugee women face are related to physical health and mental health. For example, the United States Catholic Conference (1985) notes that, of the mothers who arrived from Vietnam through the Orderly Departure Program (a joint Vietnam–U. S. government-sponsored program begun in 1979 that allows coordinated resettlement of Amerasian children and their Vietnamese mothers), 20% suffer serious medical problems. Similarly, Vietnamese mothers with young Amerasian children tend to have more serious mental health problems than those with older children. Women who escaped from Vietnam by boat face severe psychological problems, particularly as consequences of abduction and rape. Burton's 1983 study, of two Vietnamese women who were raped by Thai pirates while fleeing Vietnam, illustrates how painful the experience is for refugee women and how few interventions exist to ameliorate the effects of rape. Female children who were raped while escaping Vietnam are an equally vulnerable population psychologically. Schroeder-Dao's (1985) study documents the extreme negative effects of rape on young children for all family members who might have witnessed such an event.

Despite the less extenuating political, social, and economic conditions under which women left Vietnam prior to 1975, those who immigrated to the United States during this period are likely to make increasing demands on the caseloads of social workers. Since many of these women have lived in the United States for at least a decade, they may experience divorce, generational conflict with children, unemployment, problems related to aging, and complex intercultural issues. Because immigrant women share the linguistic, cultural, and historical background of refugee women, social workers will need to employ the same sensitivities to both groups of women. Practitioners especially need knowledge and understanding of immigrant and refugee women's experiences before leaving Vietnam to provide the best possible services to this population.

THE USE OF HISTORICAL PERSPECTIVES
IN CASEWORK

The Elite Interviewing Technique developed by Dexter (1970) was employed to elicit contextual data for social workers about the lives of four excerpted illustrative cases of Vietnamese women both in Vietnam and the United States. Elite interviewing assumes that the respondent, rather than the interviewer, is the expert (or "elite") in terms of defining the variable in question. In this case the variable was "immigrant experience." After the four interviews had been transcribed, each was analyzed, using one or more "historical perspectives" to provide a context in which to view coping behaviors and cultural factors that affect the Vietnamese family. By putting a particular issue concerning resettlement in a historical perspective, the social worker may understand how current feelings, emotions, attitudes, and behaviors are related to the client's past.

To do so, however, social workers must acquaint themselves with the history of women from Vietnam. The majority of books on Vietnamese history tend to focus on military, economic, and political issues. By and large, these works exclude specific references to women. For example, Karnow's (1983) highly acclaimed reference book, *Vietnam: A History*, does not list "women" in its index. FitzGerald's (1972) *Fire in the Lake* remains one of the most useful books to gain a sense of Vietnamese women's past. FitzGerald examines important cultural and religious groups like Confucianism, *Cao Dai, Hoa Hoa*, and Catholicism in addition to the more global political and military events that are part of Vietnam's history. Her insights into Vietnam's culture are particularly useful in trying to understand women's historical role in the family.

Gough (1978), Marr (1981), Chi (1980), and Eisen (1984) have written books containing historical information on Vietnamese women. In *Vietnamese Tradition on Trial*, for example, Marr devotes one chapter to the subject of women, based on his research of numerous Vietnamese and Chinese texts. He points to their ability through the ages to maintain a relatively high status despite the effects of various colonist efforts to denigrate their position. In a discussion of Neo-Confucianism's impact of Vietnamese women, Marr states:

Vietnamese mandarins and scholars—all male—had nurtured and refined a clear system of oppression for Vietnamese women. While this varied

according to class, all women were to some degree affected. Coming into
the twentieth century, Vietnamese women had ample reason to protest.
That they were able to do so effectively, however, was in part due to the
fact that they had never been fully cowed, and that men had never treated
them entirely as chattel. (p. 198)

The position of Vietnamese women historically is stated in a slightly
different way by Chi:

The most distinctive characteristic of the Vietnamese culture in comparison with other East Asian cultures is the active role of the women in the
Vietnamese society. In theory, a Vietnamese female is supposed to be as
submissive to male authority as her Chinese sisters. However, there is a
great difference between theory and practice. (p. 29)

Both these authors and Eisen note the tradition of independence and
resilience of Vietnamese women, citing the successful campaign of the
famous Truong sisters against Chinese forces during the Bronze age as
an example.

The two writers who have focused exclusively on the importance of
history for Vietnamese women are Eisen and Gough. Eisen's work,
Women and Revolution in Vietnam (1984), is a landmark piece on the
history of Vietnamese women. It describes the triumph of Vietnamese
women since the 1940s over such obstacles as illiteracy, polygamy, and
unfair labor practices, especially while struggling with the cultural,
legal, and military impositions of the Chinese, Japanese, French, and
American occupations. Both Eisen and Gough have documented the
historical incidents and trends that have affected Vietnamese women
since the turn of the century. In no other literature are the effects on
women of slave labor, enforced prostitution, and ecological damage
described in such detail. Eisen also describes research on the physical
problems women have sustained as a result of war.

Three specific historical perspectives or paradigms emerge from the
literature as helpful in evaluating interview material from Vietnamese
women immigrants and refugees. These may be classified as (a) a
cultural-historical perspective, (b) a chronological-historical perspective, and (c) a historical-effects perspective. Optimally it would be
desirable for all three perspectives to be utilized. However, in any given
case this may not be possible; therefore, the circumstances advanta-
geous for the use of a particular perspective will be indicated.

EVALUATING A SOCIAL WORK INTERVIEW
USING A CULTURAL-HISTORICAL PERSPECTIVE

The cultural-historical perspective requires social workers to be familiar with the philosophical, religious, and cultural issues that have affected Vietnam's institutions, ranging from the nuclear and extended family to the broadest unit of national government. The works of FitzGerald (1972) and Thuy (1976) are good beginning resources to understand the complexity of Vietnam's cultural institutions. Learning about the historical differences between the cultural heritages of Vietnam, Thailand, Cambodia, and Laos would provide further valuable information. The lasting influence that Chinese Confucianism had on Vietnam, as opposed to the strong Buddhist influence in the surrounding countries, is one example of historical information to better understand Vietnamese female clients. Confucianism may have as much relevance to immigrant and refugee women today as it did in the past.

Historians agree that Confucianism's impact on Vietnamese society began with China's attempt to subjugate Vietnam in the first century, a period that lasted roughly 1,000 years (Chu, 1985; Eisen, 1984; FitzGerald, 1972; Gough, 1978; Marr, 1981; Thuy, 1976). The Confucian legacy from China had a profound impact on all the major institutions in Vietnam, including the family, where Vietnamese women traditionally have had the most influence. Historians differ on the degree to which women have been negatively affected by Confucianism. Eisen and Gough regard it as one of the most oppressing forces on Vietnamese women, interpreting Confucian patriarchy as having eliminated women's access to education, property ownership, and authority over children. Confucianism is also blamed for providing the historical rationale for such practices as concubinage, female infanticide, footbinding, and unequal division of labor between the sexes.

On the other hand, some assert that certain aspects of Confucianism may have contributed to positive social development among Vietnamese immigrant and refugee women. Thuy (1976), for example, discusses some of the behaviors assigned by Confucianism over a woman's lifetime. In the Confucian ideal, *công* (versatile ability in the home), *dung* (subtle beauty), *ngôn* (soft speech), and *hạnh* (gentle behavior) should be present from the time of a woman's birth until her death.

Another dimension of Confucianism is *phúc dục*, which describes the broader institutionalization of Vietnamese women's deferential roles. According to Sloat (1977):

Phúc duc refers to the accumulation of family strength through generations and accomplishments of the past. However, its achievement is
primarily the responsibility of the women. She must be self-effacing,
trustworthy, hardworking and moral. If she is not, her family can be
destroyed for generations to come. (p. 40)

Attributes like *công* and *phúc dục* may account for findings like those
in a study (Ferguson, 1984) of 60 successfully resettled refugee families,
which found that only 2% of the married women had worked outside
their home in Vietnam; in contrast, in the United States only 6% of the
women were full-time homemakers. Women who had learned to sew
in Vietnam, as part of the accomplishments of upper- and middle-class
females, turned their talents into cash income for the first time in their
lives. Many managed to build successful small businesses shortly after
their arrival in the United States.

While sheer economic necessity could be a major explanatory factor,
cultural-historical factors like *công* and *phúc dục* might also account
for women's motivation and success in the American labor force. Social
workers who attempt to apply a cultural-historical perspective that
includes Confucianism to the cases of immigrant and refugee women
would be well advised to look at the positive as well as negative
historical effects of the institution in question.

The cultural-historical perspective will probably be the least used
because of the enormous investment of time required to read and
reflect upon Vietnam's cultural-historical institutions. Nonetheless, it
offers social workers one of the richest contexts in which to view
information about resettlement.

EVALUATING A SOCIAL WORK INTERVIEW
USING A CHRONOLOGICAL-HISTORICAL
PERSPECTIVE

This perspective consists of familiarity with major historical events
and dates ranging from the 1940s to the present. The following chronology is derived mainly from Karnow (1983). Social workers who are
aware of significant events and dates may better understand the interview material obtained from Vietnamese women. For example, one or
more of these events that may be unfamiliar to practitioners could be of
paramount importance to a client.

1940 Japan occupies Indochina, but leaves French colonial administration intact.

1941 Viet Minh formed to fight Japan and France.

1945 Japan surrenders to Allies in World War II. Ho Chi Minh declares Vietnamese independence.

1946 Viet Minh struggle with the French begins.

1954 Geneva agreement ends war with France. Provisional demarcation line set at the 17th parallel.

1957 Communist insurgency begins in South Vietnam.

1962 American advisers are increased to assist President Diem in his fight against the Communists.

1963 President Diem assassinated.

1968 Tet Offensive—massive destruction of South Vietnamese cities and countryside.

1969 President Nixon begins withdrawing U. S. troops.

1975 Communist forces take over South Vietnam government.

1975 Vietnam starts to repress its ethnic Chinese population, invades Laos and then Cambodia.

1979 Orderly Departure Program begins, repatriating unwanted Amerasian children and their mothers to the United States.

1986 Orderly Departure Program suspended.

1988 Orderly Departure Program resumed. Beginning of Vietnamese troop withdrawal from Cambodia.

EVALUATING A SOCIAL WORK INTERVIEW USING A HISTORICAL-EFFECTS PERSPECTIVE

The final model, the historical-effects perspective, is one that may be highly beneficial to social workers in the fields of physical health and mental health. Eisen (1984) describes the effects of ecocide, separation of family members, rape, prostitution, drug addiction, and reproductive problems from the standpoint of women during the French and American occupations of Vietnam. Immigrant as well as refugee women have invariably felt their historical effects. It would not be unusual for social workers to encounter these events in descriptions of their clients' lives.

Ecocide

More than 43% of South Vietnam's plantations and orchards were destroyed during the 1970s. Essential irrigation networks were bombed.

The countryside was systematically defoliated, particularly by spraying the chemical Agent Orange at the ratio of 6 pounds per person in 1975.

Separation of Family Members Along Political Lines

The 1954 Geneva Accords divided Vietnam into North and South at the 17th parallel. One provision of the Accords specified that those who fought with the Viet Minh in the South would regroup in North Vietnam when the country reunified 2 years later. The thousands of families that separated, expecting to meet 2 years later, were unable to reunite because the Accords were not honored.

Rape

Rape was a prevalent form of military exercise in rural areas. Eisen (1984) notes that few, if any, villages were spared such practice.

Prostitution

While prostitution was considered an illegal activity, as many as a half-million prostitutes may have existed at the height of the U. S. troop occupation. Eisen states: "As the GIs left Vietnam, the prostitutes remained trapped in a cycle of heroin addiction, poverty and self-hatred. Probably a majority were infected with venereal disease. Their Amerasian children, although loved, became reminders of their degraded past" (p. 46).

Drug Addiction

Eisen reports a 400% increase in heroin available in Vietnam between 1964 and 1970. In 1975 official documents obtained by Eisen reported as many as 150,000 heroin addicts in Saigon. Other drug use and addiction rates are unknown. It is not known how many addicts were women.

Reproductive Disabilities

Due to the use of defoliants, many babies have been born with birth defects. Eisen reports an interview with a North Vietnamese doctor who said:

> They [the couples] have been waiting so long for reunification—then the newborn baby dies because of serious genetic mutations resulting from one of the parent's exposure to defoliants. . . .

The evidence of miscarriage rose dramatically in the 1960s and 1970s. It climbed from 1 percent in the mid-1950s to 20 percent in 1976. Cervical cancer also saw an increase during this period. (p. 37)

While any of the three historical perspectives may be used to facilitate the assessment phase of casework, a combination of perspectives may yield the most relevant information. For example, the chronological-historical and historical-effects perspectives may be used as a list against which to check clients' comments that appear to be out of context, or are not associated with events that are familiar to the social worker. The cultural-historical perspective will provide social workers with a cultural context in which to view all other client material, especially cultural conflicts that arise for Vietnamese women in the host country.

In the following section three different historical perspectives are applied to the interview material of two immigrant women and two refugee women. Analyzing interview materials from these perspectives illustrates the way in which historical information can clarify the varied needs of immigrant and refugee women, and thus aid the social worker in intervention.

CASE STUDIES OF TWO IMMIGRANTS: KATHERINE AND LI

Katherine arrived in the United States in 1970 when she was in her early twenties. She was the daughter of a university professor who sometimes served as an unofficial adviser to the South Vietnamese government. Her life was circumscribed by Confucian ideals regarding femininity and by a sense of deprivation from sagging economic conditions and a lowered standard of living that began when her Saigon-based family took in displaced relatives from the countryside.

In 1970 Katherine's father's life was threatened because of his close relationship to the then-president of Vietnam. A cultural-historical perspective is helpful while assessing the confusion Katherine faced when she was suddenly told she would be sent overseas. Confucianism comes to mind when Katherine discusses her place vis-à-vis her brothers in the family, and the impact of a former legal system that permitted concubines:

My family decided to send me away, although they had never talked about that before. My brothers were always destined to go overseas to study. But for a girl, they never thought I'd need to do that. I'd just stay at home with my mother and support her and go to the university.

Katherine's extended family in Saigon consisted of several women who were legal concubines of Katherine's grandfather until laws made illegal this Confucian practice. The children of these arrangements were particularly jeopardized by the change in living standards. When talking about her grandfather's third wife, Katherine notes: "She was no longer official. They [the other wives] all became mistresses. That's how we inherited a lot of our extended family."

Use of the historical-effects perspective helps the social worker understand Katherine's description of how family separations and the prostitution of a relative affected her adolescence in Saigon. Regarding family separations, Katherine relates the story of a recently arrived refugee aunt and her separation from her husband who was a Communist in the North:

Now she finds her husband alive. He is in Ho Chi Minh City and is a fervent Communist who does not know he has a wife in America . . . a wife who has lived in Saigon all these years and then to America, and in a way deserted her country.

About the effect of prostitution Katherine noted:

I remember being very friendly with three women who were not really related to me by blood but who were part of the extended family . . . found out later that [one] worked, for want of a better word, as a prostitute. But she was very ashamed. With me she was very different. She was worried she wouldn't have any place to stay.

Katherine didn't know what had happened to this cousin. The last she heard, the cousin was still in Vietnam.

Katherine's history prior to her emigration gives us an understanding not only of Katherine, but also of her female relatives and what they might have experienced in the late 1960s. The cultural-historical perspective enables us to relate to expectations that were placed upon her as a woman, expectations that were frustrated, thwarted, and undercut by a host of events. The sudden erasing of centuries-old concubinage laws left some of her aunts with no legal status within the family. The lack of self-esteem of some immigrant women in the host country may be due to this kind of historical factor. If Eisen were to have examined this material, she might have seen Katherine's relative the prostitute as an unwilling victim, but Katherine's views of prostitution appear to be more generous. The historical perspectives employed enable one to identify the special Vietnamese heritage Katherine brought to the United States.

From the chronological-historical perspective, the quality of life of Katherine's family declined significantly after the Tet Offensive in 1968. A new era of poverty began for the extended family.

The second Vietnamese immigrant case is Li, who emigrated to the United States in 1975 shortly before the collapse of the Vietnam government. She imparts vivid descriptions of the Japanese and French troops who occupied the village her family lived in, not far from Ho Chi Minh City, while she was a child.

The cultural-historical perspective is useful in gaining an overall understanding of how the war affected Li. Although much of Li's education was within the Catholic school system, it was her grandmother's experience as a psychic, based on her belief in reincarnation and other Buddhist tenets, that gave Li the strength to cope with the vicissitudes of war. As Li related:

> And then my family's Buddhist. And my grandmother is against Catholic. So I have many talks with her about religious issues. She said she believes in reincarnation theory. . . . I have a chance to be very close to her, talk to her. I come home every weekend and be with her and stay almost all summer with her. Just to talk and discuss about philosophy of life, about reincarnation theory. . . . And that gave me a strong belief to let me survive during the war, and survive 10 years in the United States.

When Saigon fell, Li was shocked. She had not anticipated that the same American forces for whom she had once served as a translator would abandon the South Vietnamese people. Understanding such an event may explain some of the ambivalence encountered in immigrants' and refugees' views of their country. Li related: "So, all the Vietnamese still are angry at the Americans. But they can't say anything . . . if the destiny mean lose, it's gonna lose . . . doesn't matter what you do. So it's another kind of explanation just for your peace of mind."

For many Vietnamese women who went to Ho Chi Minh City from rural areas as the war intensified, the Tet or New Year Offensive was a chronological event of major importance. Li recalled: "The Communists attack the Vietnamese, South Vietnamese and Americans both. . . . And they were shooting not even one mile from my house. . . . Some bombs drop before my house; some drop behind, but didn't hit my house."

Such historical information may lead to a greater understanding of post-traumatic stress, a syndrome that both refugees and immigrants can re-experience in the host country. Li relates the hardship on families of this fighting: "The indirect effect of the Vietnamese war is so big, especially on women, because many women became widows. And they have a whole bunch of children to feed. And not many jobs available."

The historical-effects perspective is helpful when listening to Li describe how the war alienated people in the country from their environment. Ecocide is recalled when she states: "Under President Diem, there was a project we called Hamlet . . . the idea is to get together in one small hamlet; small village . . . that uproot people like my grandmother who have to move her house into the hamlet."

Historical effects are recalled again when she describes how old houses were destroyed, and trees cut down, to discourage Communists who might use them as hiding places:

> [A]nd that really damaged the land . . . every house in the village would have a pond around the house, for using water. We don't have running water in the village . . . and around the pond people grow bamboo thatch to protect the water in the pond so it doesn't evaporate during summer. It's very hot. It's very hot. And the government make them cut down this bamboo. So the pond expose to the sun, the water evaporate . . . fish die. You lack of drinking water.

This information gives us insight into the different life-styles women and their families might have had to give up in order to repatriate to the United States. As these women recount their life stories, social workers become aware of larger cultural and historical differences between Vietnam and the United States. Once social workers can divide the historical content of the Vietnamese clients' pre-immigration experience into distinct categories like cultural-historical variables and environmental or ecological factors, they may be able to help the clients work through their emotions and difficulties in some depth.

CASE STUDIES OF TWO REFUGEES: TU AND HANH

Tu is a Vietnamese refugee of ethnic Chinese descent who faced discrimination from the Communist government because of her ancestry. Tu taught high school in the Chinese community for many years before finally escaping to the United States in 1982. A social worker who knows that the government began to persecute its Chinese-Vietnamese population in 1975 could more readily understand Tu's past and present. The consequences of this event led to Tu's need—and that of many other Chinese-Vietnamese women—to flee Vietnam. Tu notes: "In 1979 when the conflict between mainland China and Vietnam began, I was teaching. The Chinese government said that Chinese-Vietnamese are our people. So they have something they asked us to sign, whether you are Vietnamese, we could never get out of the country."

Eisen's (1984) notion of ecocide in the historical-effects paradigm gives us added insight into the ways in which women like Tu experienced the physical destruction of the city. In rural areas it may have been more common to relate to destruction of irrigation ditches and rice fields because of unretrieved bombs, mines, and other ammunition embedded in the soil. But Tu had this to say about the new government's approach to the problem of ecocide:

> They [the Communists] had all the students and teachers to work for them. "Clean the street! The theater . . ." and all that kind of work. It was very sad. We told our students to clean the streets. A lot of grenades were still embedded in the streets and a lot of students died because of that. One teacher would have 10 or 20 students . . . we cannot control or supervise all of them. A lot of students died like that.

The continuous fighting and turmoil surrounding Tu's life explain another significant point about Tu and other refugee women. This may be general historical information about marital status and the importance of the extended family.

> I was grown up in that country for more than 20 years. How can I forget that? I cannot. During the years, years of war, a lot of people fight in Vietnam. Maybe that's why I'm still single. Some people like us ask, what happens if we marry? When we marry there will be no children. Who

knows whether they will come back or not. No one in my family got married in Vietnam. We have only one brother out of nine children.

Social workers may note a tendency among refugee women to prefer extended family arrangements over those of marriage. Thus, in the case of Tu, we see how the effects of ecocide and the stresses of war in general contributed to the decision of many Vietnamese women to remain single. This information alerts social workers to a distinction they may want to make between the resettlement of ethnic Chinese-Vietnamese and Vietnamese women.

The second refugee case is Hanh. Hanh, 44, fled Vietnam with her family immediately after the fall of Saigon. Hanh's formative years were influenced by attendance at an American missionary school. Her bilingualism and adjustment to American customs may be a reflection of this experience. She described how hard life was for women with families during the war. Hanh supplemented her husband's meager income as an army officer by working as a translator for the RAND Corporation. She found working and raising two children difficult, but was determined to help her family gain some financial stability. She managed to help the family achieve a degree of comfort by 1975, but the United States' total withdrawal ruined any chances she had of staying in Vietnam to enjoy what she had earned. Having escaped penniless with her family, she said:

> I feel like I have always been taking care of myself and my family; I feel like I never had a break. Sometimes it's a problem with the family when I'm angry, it comes out. Coming here, you have to start all over again from zero. I worked so hard to build a family and to establish us, to buy a home, a car.

The influence of Confucianism and the importance of knowing the cultural-historical perspective may be seen in another of Hanh's statements:

> Thinking back, I would say that it's from our culture that our women are the way we are . . . so strong, and accommodating and persistent. We are ingrained with thoughts like, when you're in the family you obey your father. When you're married, if your husband will go into the cave of the dragon, you have to follow him. So whatever it takes to support your husband and family, you do.

Hanh's oral history was replete with examples of how certain Vietnamese attitudes toward women and their need to persevere were compatible with American ideals of hard work and profit. The Confucian ethic of *công* and *phúc đức* is again recalled. The cultural-historical perspective as it relates to *phúc đức* and *công* and the chronological perspective interacted to explain, on one hand, how proud Hanh was of the tremendous strides she has made in her career, while on the other hand she felt that the move to the United States added further stress on her role as a woman. Hanh not only recounted the pressures attributed to marital life according to Vietnamese custom, but also the pressures of a new marital system in the United States—one that stresses the importance of dual wage earners. Although she had worked in Vietnam out of sheer necessity, she considered it contrary to the ideal for Vietnamese women.

With this perspective in mind, social workers begin to understand how traditional Vietnamese social values combine with new sociopsychological pressures. Hanh's case was illuminated by using the historical perspectives mentioned above, but in any work with Vietnamese women refugees and immigrants, the practitioner is cautioned to remember that each client is unique. For example, the impact of the Tet Offensive may have been minimal for Hanh, but considerably more complex for another client.

CONCLUSIONS

Interviews with Katherine, Li, Tu, and Hanh have been analyzed from a cultural-historical, a chronological-historical, and a historical-effects framework to gain a realistic understanding of the unique issues Vietnamese women face in coming to the United States. It has been suggested that a historical perspective of the Vietnamese woman client can best be used in the assessment phase of the intervention process to gain a clear picture of how the woman's cultural heritage impinges upon her immigration experience. In addition, practitioners who apply historical perspectives with Hmong, Lao, Meo, and Cambodian women clients may likewise increase their understanding of these women and enhance intervention.

REFERENCES

Burton, E. (1983). *Surviving the flight of horror: The story of refugee women.* Washington, DC: Indochina Project, Center for International Policy.

Chi, N. (1980). Vietnam: Culture of war. In L. E. Tepper (Ed.), *Southeast Asian exodus: From tradition to resettlement*. Ottawa: Canadian Asian Studies Association.

Chu, J. (1985). Southeast Asian women: In transition. In A. Spero, *In America and in need: Immigrant, refugee and entrant women* (pp. 40-50). Washington, DC: American Association of Community and Junior Colleges.

Dexter, L. A. (1970). *Elite and specialized interviewing*. Evanston, IL: Northwestern University Press.

Eisen, A. (1984). *Women and revolution in Vietnam*. London: Zed Books.

Ferguson, B. (1984). *Successful refugee resettlement: Vietnamese values, beliefs and strategies*. Unpublished doctoral dissertation, University of California, Berkeley.

FitzGerald, F. (1972). *Fire in the lake*. Boston: Little, Brown. [Reprinted. (1989). New York: Vintage.]

Gough, K. (1978). *Ten times more beautiful: The rebuilding of Vietnam*. Vancouver: Monthly Review Press.

Karnow, S. (1983). *Vietnam: A history*. New York: Viking.

Marr, D. (1981). *Vietnamese tradition on trial, 1920-1945*. Berkeley: University of California Press.

Rindner, N. (1985, May 24). Refugee women: A forgotten majority. *Refugee Reports, 6*(5). Washington, DC: American Council for Nationalities Service.

Schroeder-Dao, T-K. (1985). *Study of rape victims among the refugees on Pulau Bidong Island: An experience in counselling women refugee "boat people."* Washington, DC: American Council for Nationalities Service.

Sloat, W. H. (1977, March 26). *Adaptation of recent Vietnamese immigres to the American experience: A psycho-cultural approach*. Paper presented at the annual meeting of the Association of Asian Studies, New York.

Thuy, V. (1976). *Getting to know the Vietnamese and their culture*. New York: Ungar.

United States Catholic Conference (1985). *In our father's land: Vietnamese Amerasians in the United States* (Executive Summary). Washington, DC: Author.

Chapter 6

MODELS OF SERVICE DELIVERY IN ASIAN AMERICAN COMMUNITIES

KENJI MURASE

INTRODUCTION

This chapter is based on an exploratory study of 49 Asian community-based agencies that are delivering mental health and mental health-related services in four cities on the West Coast—Los Angeles, San Diego, San Francisco, and Seattle. The study was undertaken in response to findings of previous research, which have documented a pervasive pattern of differential treatment, based on race and ethnicity, in mental health services to Asian and other ethnic minority communities (Sue & Morishima, 1982). The study objective was to identify and define the response of Asians to mental health and mental health-related needs by developing alternative models of service delivery that address the problems of denial, inaccessibility, and inappropriateness of services to members of their communities.

Agencies serving Asian communities in Los Angeles, San Diego, San Francisco, and Seattle were selected on the basis of information elicited from knowledgeable sources. Data was then collected by means of personal interviews with agency directors and by perusal of agency reports and other documents. The information collected was essentially

AUTHOR'S NOTE: This study was supported by Grant MH32148, National Institute of Mental Health, Department of Health and Human Services.

exploratory-descriptive in nature, and no attempt was made to quantify the data since the sample of agencies was too small to permit useful statistical analysis or generalizations. Therefore, the findings of this study are largely tentative and impressionistic. Nevertheless, it is my hope that the questions and issues raised by this study will stimulate further research.

The chapter begins with a brief review of problems in service delivery encountered by Asian communities. Their response to such problems will then be analyzed in terms of the organizational structures and functions of programs developed in Asian communities. The functions of these programs are presented in terms of two broad categories: direct and indirect services. *Direct services* are services to individuals, families and groups, consisting of both preventive and treatment services at primary, secondary, and tertiary levels. *Indirect services* are services to organizations and the community at large, consisting of planning, coordination, advocacy, community organization, and related macro-practice activities. The analysis of the organizational structures of these programs differentiates patterns of uniformity in terms of the variety of ethnic populations served and the variety of services provided, ranging from single-ethnic, single-service structures to multi-ethnic, multi-services organizations. The chapter then concludes with an analysis of the processes of program development carried out by Asian communities and an identification of issues for further research.

INEQUITIES IN SERVICE DELIVERY

Essentially, the problem addressed by this study is the problem of inequities in the delivery of services to Asian populations. For example, it has been found that diagnosis becomes less accurate and disposition nonspecific as the sociocultural differences increase between the therapist and the client (Gross, Herbert, & Knatterud, 1969). Therapists' attitudes and recommendations for treatment are frequently influenced by the clients' ethnicity. Furthermore, Euro Americans are more likely to be seen by psychiatrists and non-Euro Americans by paraprofessionals (Sue, McKinney, Allen, & Hall, 1974). Patients of insight-oriented therapy are more likely to be Euro Americans than non-Euro Americans.

In general, non-Euro American patients tend to receive "qualitatively inferior" or "less preferred" forms of treatment (Yamamoto, James, & Palley, 1968). A study of 40 randomly selected Chinese patients carried by an after-care program in San Francisco found that their average stay in a state hospital was 17 years, and the nature of the treatment most often received was chemotherapy (Wang & Louie, 1979). In this country, there appears to be a two-class system of mental health care, in which the uninsured, non-Euro American patients with chronic and more severe diagnoses (organic brain syndrome, schizophrenia, alcoholism) predominate in public institutions (state and county mental hospitals, Veterans Administration hospitals, and community mental health centers) while better-insured, Euro American patients with less severe, acute disorders occupy private institutions (Goldman, Sharfstein, & Frank, 1980).

It is not surprising that a commonly recurring problem among Asians is premature termination of treatment or underutilization of services. Sue's study (Sue & McKinney, 1975) in Seattle showed that over a 3-year period, the dropout rate of Asian patients was 52%, or almost twice that of Euro American patients. Moreover, although Asians comprised 2.4% of the population in Seattle, they represented only 0.7% of the patient population. In Los Angeles County, where Asians represented close to 4% of the population in 1971, they constituted less than 1% of the patient population in the county mental health system (Hatanaka, Watanabe, & Ono, 1975). In San Francisco, where the Chinese comprise 29% of the catchment area of the Northeast Mental Health Center, they represent a mere 10% of the patients served. For the city as a whole, at a time when the Chinese were 10% of the population, they made up only 2% of the patients served (San Francisco Community Mental Health Services, 1977).

RESPONSE TO THE PROBLEM

As will be shown by this study, the response of Asian communities to the problems identified above has been to develop community-based mental health service programs located in their own communities, with bilingual/bicultural staff, and governed by their own representatives. When visible, culturally relevant services are provided, there is a significant response among Asian clients. For example, the number of Asians utilizing a single Asian community-based program in Seattle in one year was approximately equal to the total numbers of Asians utilizing a sum of 18 other community mental health centers over a 3-year period (Sue & McKinney, 1975).

After the establishment of an Asian community-based mental health center in San Francisco, more Asian patients were seen by the center in the first 3 months of its operation than were seen by traditional mental health programs in the previous 5 years (Wong, 1978). In addition, this center had the lowest no-show rate for first appointments of all comparable outpatient centers. Ninety percent of all clients who called for services showed up for their first appointment. In Oakland, an Asian community-based mental health program saw 131 Chinese in the first year of operation, in contrast to 3 Chinese out of a total of 500 seen in a central outpatient facility (True, 1975). The presence of a comprehensive, accessible, and ethnically appropriate community-based service in Los Angeles resulted in a 200% increase in the utilization rate of Asian clients over a 3-year period (Hatanaka et al., 1975). These are but a few examples of the validity and effectiveness of Asian community-based mental health services that have previously been cited in the research literature.

SERVICES PROVIDED BY ASIAN COMMUNITY-BASED PROGRAMS

This study compiled an inventory of the mental health and mental health-related services provided by Asian community-based programs in Los Angeles, San Diego, San Francisco, and Seattle. The information collected reveals an impressive array of services, both direct and indirect (Yoshioka, Tashima, & Chew, 1981). Direct service functions address both prevention and treatment of mental health and mental health-related problems at primary, secondary, and tertiary levels.

Primary prevention typically addresses the elimination of the causes of a disorder by reducing risk factors (stressors) and thereby reducing the occurrence or rate of new cases of the problem. This study found that primary prevention in Asian communities consists of programs that focus on education, advocacy, networking, social support systems, ethnic identity and pride, and preservation of ethnic traditions and values.

The *secondary* level of prevention is invoked after the earliest identification of symptoms to prevent the disorder from becoming more serious or chronic, and the focus is on early casefinding and treatment. In Asian communities, secondary prevention is shown by this study to be carried out by community-based programs that provide culturally and linguistically appropriate individual and group therapy, marital counseling, juvenile diversion, crisis intervention, day treatment, drug-abuse programs, and related services.

Tertiary prevention involves the rehabilitation of chronically symptomatic individuals and the use of maintaining and correcting therapies to minimize the resulting disability. At this level, the data show that programs in Asian communities are largely limited to services to the aged in specialized facilities that provide a culturally and linguistically appropriate environment.

Treatment services are also classified in terms of primary, secondary, and tertiary levels of intensity of care. At the primary level, treatment services in Asian communities were found to be provided by community-based health and mental health services and by primary care practitioners. Secondary treatment services are provided in community hospitals and centers. Tertiary treatment services are more limited in scope, generally confined to specialized hospitals and residential treatment facilities.

Direct Services

Based on data collected from the 49 Asian community-based agencies, the following classification was derived of direct services offered to Asian individuals, families, and groups.

Information and Referral Services

This is a basic service that all agencies provide. Certain agencies, however, specialize in information and referral functions. An example is the county-funded Asian Community Service Center in Los Angeles, which is unique in providing services to all Asian communities on a county-wide basis.

Case Advocacy, Case Management, Networking Services

These are highly individualized case-by-case services that involve matching individual clients with community resources, following up with agencies to which clients are referred, and coordinating or networking with the services of the various agencies involved in an individual case. These services are provided by most Asian community-based agencies to some degree.

Counseling and Treatment Services

These include individual and group therapy, marital counseling, crisis intervention, day treatment, and related services. Examples of agencies that provide the full range of counseling and treatment services are the Asian Counseling and Treatment Center in Los Angeles, the Pacific/Asian Preventive Program in San Diego, the Richmond Area Multi-Service Center in San Francisco, and the Asian Counseling and Referral Service in Seattle.

Health Services

This category includes health screening, primary health care, family planning, nutrition, hot meals, and home health care. Examples are the Asian Women's Health Project in Los Angeles, which specializes in family planning; Operation Samahan in San Diego, which specializes in health services to the Filipino community; On Lok Senior Health Services in San Francisco, which provides services to the functionally dependent elderly; and the International District Community Health Clinic in Seattle.

Drug Abuse Services

These include residential programs and preventive education. The Asian American Drug Abuse Program in Los Angeles is one agency that provides a full complement of services, including outpatient care, a therapeutic residential unit, and extensive preventive education.

Protective Services

This category includes child abuse and battered women. The Pan Asian Parent Education Project in San Diego is a child abuse prevention program designed to assist Asian parents with child-rearing and acculturation problems.

Vocational Rehabilitation Services

These refer to services for the physically challenged (disabled). The Asian Rehabilitation Services in Los Angeles provide a comprehensive program of counseling, job training, and placement for such clients. The agency is unique in its production unit, which generates 90% of the agency's budget through subcontracts for electronic parts and a packaging service.

Youth Services

Services for Asian American Youth in Los Angeles were established to serve Asian youth from economically disadvantaged backgrounds, as well as recent immigrant youth who encounter problems of discrimination, language barriers, unemployment, and alienation.

Housing Services

The International District Improvement Association in Seattle has probably done more than any other single agency to improve housing conditions for Asians. Originally founded in 1969 as part of the Model Cities Program to attack physical decay, deterioration, and human service need, the Association has been responsible for renovating three hotels, securing 300 units for low-income residents, taking the lead in the enforcement of housing code violations, and generally mobilizing the community to preserve existing housing and develop new housing.

Employment Services

This category includes career counseling, job training and placement, job development, and English as a second language (ESL) classes. Most of the services to Southeast Asian refugees fall into this category. The Center for Southeast Asian Refugee Resettlement in San Francisco, with a staff of 42, provides a comprehensive program of employment counseling, training, placement, and job development.

Immigration and Legal Assistance

Most agencies involved with immigrant families provide immigration and legal services. The West Bay Filipino Multi-Service Corporation in San Francisco maintains an immigration specialist in the lobby of the Immigration and Naturalization Service to handle immigration problems on-site.

Refugee Resettlement Services

This includes most of the services described above. Agencies specializing in services to refugees include the Indochinese Health Intervention Program in San Francisco; the Indochinese Refugee Service Center, funded by Los Angeles County, which coordinates all county Southeast Asian refugee services; the Pacific Asian American Center in Santa Ana, Orange County, which has the highest concentration of Southeast Asian refugees nationally; and the Indochinese Service Center in San Diego, whose 31-member staff performs the important role of coordinating services among existing agencies.

Indirect Services

Data collected from Asian agencies providing indirect services showed the following categories of services were provided to organizations and groups.

Planning, Coordination, and Advocacy

Generally, these organizations are councils or federations consisting of member organizations. The Asian Pacific Planning Council of Los Angeles is an agency membership organization, established to advocate, inform, and educate the public on issues pertaining to the Asian community. For example, the Asian Pacific Planning Council was instrumental in efforts that resulted in United Way membership for an Asian community resource development program and in continued funding by Los Angeles County for services such as the Asian/Pacific Counseling and Treatment Center and the Asian Community Services Center.

Consultation and Technical Assistance

This category includes grant writing, organizational development, management, economic development, and resource development. The Asian Community Service Center, funded by Los Angeles County, works with community groups in organizational and community development. For example, its Filipino Community Development Aide organized a Council of Filipino Organizations, and the Thai Community Development Aide was instrumental in developing the Thai Community Service Center, in addition to helping to organize the only Thai newspaper in the city. The Asian American Voluntary Action Center in Los Angeles, funded by the United Way, provides technical assistance to community groups and has an active program for the recruitment and placement of volunteers in agencies that need assistance with projects or activities. One such project is the Little Tokyo Food Coop, which is funded by the City Department of Community Development.

Organizational Structures

The study of 49 Asian community-based agencies found a variety of patterns of organizational structures developed to deliver the range of services described above. The diversity of structural patterns can be categorized in terms of (a) the variety of ethnic populations served, and (b) the variety of services provided.

Single-Ethnic, Single-Service

In increasing order of complexity, at one extreme is the single-ethnic, single-service agency. An example would be the Korean American Mental Health Service Center in Los Angeles, which specializes in mental health services to a single ethnic group. Another example would be Operation Samahan in San Diego, which specializes in outpatient health care to the Filipinos.

Single-Ethnic, Multi-Service

More common is an agency that is targeted to one ethnic community but provides multiple services. Examples of this would be the China-town Social Service Center and the Samoan Service Center in Los Angeles; the Chinese Social Service Center in San Diego; the Korean Community Service Center and the West Bay Filipino Multi-Service Corporation in San Francisco; and the Chinese Information and Service Center in Seattle.

Multi-Ethnic, Single-Service

Another structural variation is the agency that provides a specialized service to a multi-ethnic clientele. An example would be the Asian American Drug Abuse Program in Los Angeles whose clients come from a range of ethnic groups, which fall into the following categories: African (50%), Asian (25%), Hispanic (12.5%) and Euro American (12.5%). On Lok Senior Health Service in San Francisco provides comprehensive health care to functionally dependent Chinese, Filipino, and Euro American elderly in the Chinatown/North Beach area of San Francisco. At the International District Community Health Clinic in Seattle, 90% of the patients are Asian; of these, 30% are Chinese, 29% Southeast Asian, 27% Filipino, 7% Korean, and 4% Japanese.

Multi-Ethnic, Multi-Service

At the opposite end of this spectrum is the multi-ethnic, multi-service agency. While requiring a highly complex organizational structure, it is probably the most cost-effective form of service delivery. An example is the Union of Pan Asian Communities (UPAC) in San Diego. UPAC recently purchased a building to house most of its nine different programs and 81 employees. The projects under UPAC auspices include the following:

> Pan Asian Senior Services, for Korean, Filipino, Chinese, Japanese, Samoan, and Guamanian elderly;
>
> Indochinese Service Center, for refugee health and social services;
>
> Indochinese Community Health and Education Project, to provide cultural awareness training for mental health providers and training for Southeast Asian community workers;
>
> Pacific Asian Preventive Program, a mental health service program;
>
> Pan Asian Parent Education Project, a preventive child abuse program;
>
> Indochinese Youth Corps, with a focus on cultural conflicts and identity issues for Southeast Asian youth and youth leadership training in community relations to reduce tensions in the multicultural neighborhoods where they live;
>
> Multi Cultural Nutrition Program, to serve ethnic meals to seven ethnic elderly groups; and,
>
> Pacific/Asian and Latino Training Center, to train paraprofessional and natural helpers to function in mainstream mental health programs.

Another successful multi-ethnic, multi-service program is the Asian Counseling and Referral Services in Seattle, with four major program components and a staff of 36 persons. Its program components include: mental health services; social services focusing on advocacy, case management and networking services; community education involving workshops on health, family development, sexuality, drug abuse, stress reduction, and parenting skills; and information and referral services through a highly developed network of community resources.

Funding Patterns

Funding for Asian community-based programs, as found by this study, comes from a diversity of sources. Public funding from federal, state, and local sources makes up the largest part of the budget of agencies included in this study.

Federal funding sources include:
- Administration of Aging (senior citizen center, nutrition programs)
- Community Services Administration (community action programs)
- Comprehensive Employment and Training Act
- Law Enforcement Assistance Administration (youth programs)
- National Center on Child Abuse and Neglect
- National Institute of Drug Abuse
- National Institute of Mental Health
- Office of Education, Title IX Program
- Volunteers in Service to America (information and referral programs)

State funding sources include:
- California State Department of Health Services
- California State Department of Mental Health
- California State Department of Social Services
- Title XX, Indochinese Refugee Assistance Program
- California Youth Authority
- Short-Doyle Act (mental health services)

Local city and county funding sources include:
- Area Agency on Aging
- City Community Development Block Grant Program
- City Department of Human Resources (Seattle)
- County Department of Community Development
- County Drug Abuse Program
- County General Purpose Funds
- County Revenue Sharing
- Model Cities Program (Seattle)

Private funding sources include:
- Catholic Social Service
- Church World Service
- Episcopal-Church Center Coalition for Human Needs
- Foundations

- Presbyterian Council
- United Methodist Church
- United Way

Most community-based agencies must also raise supplemental funds through various internal fund-raising efforts. These include fees for services, consultations, donations, fund-raisers, and for-profit enterprises.

CHARACTERISTICS OF SUCCESSFUL MENTAL HEALTH SERVICES

In the course of this study, a number of characteristics of successful mental health service delivery programs for Asian communities were identified. The research literature has established that there is tremendous diversity among Asians (Endo, Sue, & Wagner, 1980). However, there are also certain basic similarities that Asian community-based agencies have recognized. These similarities include: (a) strong family relationships, (b) respect for parental and other authority, (c) respect for traditional values and practices, and (d) primacy of the collectivity over the individual.

These characteristics have been translated into programmatic terms in mental health services (Kitano & Matsushima, 1981). For example, members of the family become part of the therapy team, and the therapist's role becomes that of an authority figure. To be effective with Asian clients, the therapist must be prepared to make adaptations of the usual stance taken with Euro American-oriented patients. Instead of being neutral, nondirective, nonjudgmental, and noncritical, the therapist may need to be more assertive, directive, and authoritarian.

The literature indicates that group work can be done successfully with Asians if attention is given to practical considerations for the pre-group phase and group interaction phase (Ho, 1984). For example, Ho (1984) espouses structured, concrete goals when working with Asian groups as well as a modified group approach (Ho, 1976; Lee, Juan, & Hom, 1984), which conforms to the family or friendship network structure. The literature also indicates strategies and leadership characteristics (Chu & Sue, 1984; Corey, 1990; Kaneshige, 1973; Lee et al., 1984), which have been found useful when working with Asian groups.

Depending upon the degree of acculturation, Asian clients tend to seek symptomatic relief through short-term treatment. They are not receptive to long-term treatment directed to uncovering and resolving underlying conflicts. In short, they are accustomed to the medical, as opposed to the psychotherapeutic, model. The concept of time-limited therapy over a period of perhaps 2 or 3 months for the reduction of symptoms seems preferred, with subsequent treatment subject to negotiation if necessary. Typically, the presenting mental health problem of Asian clients tends to be described in somatic terms as a physical complaint. The expectation is that the problem must be treated medically, with pills or injections. It is striking that all of the health care service programs for Asian communities report a high frequency of physical complaints that have a heavy psychological underlay.

Ideally, therefore, physical and mental health services should be integrated so that the patient who comes in with a psychologically induced physical complaint can be evaluated and treated in the same setting. The most successful example of such integration is seen in the South Cove Community Health Center of Boston (Gaw, 1975). The Center is part of a complex that also includes an elementary school, a swimming pool and gym, an auditorium, a little City Hall staffed by representatives of major city departments, a day-care center, and a 160-unit high-rise apartment for the elderly.

The Center functions as a one-stop neighborhood service center that serves as a "second home" for many Chinese families. For instance, a mother may take her child to school, see a physician or social worker, attend English classes, visit in-laws nearby, and go shopping, all at the same location. The child may stay after school to participate in such activities as swimming, basketball, arts and crafts, ballet class, or Chinese dancing. A full range of health care, including pediatric, adult medicine, eye, dental, and OB/GYN services, performs a case-finding function for the mental health clinic.

PROCESS OF PROGRAM DEVELOPMENT

This study also examined the program development processes that led to the establishment of Asian community-based programs. The data revealed certain distinct processes, which may constitute a set of guidelines or principles for community groups to consider in their program planning, such as the following.

Mobilization of Community Support

Most of the programs came into being only after mobilization and demonstration of community support. Without concrete evidence of widespread and sustained community support, it is doubtful that any Asian community-based program would have received the initial funding to establish itself.

Impacting the Local Political System

Invariably, where local city or county funding was necessary, the founders of Asian community programs had to learn how to impact the local political system effectively. Frequently, this meant years spent in cultivating political support, appearing repeatedly before public hearings, organizing letter-writing campaigns, and the endless monitoring of the slow and tortuous progress of an application or proposal through the bureaucratic maze.

In many instances, nothing decisive happened until an Asian representative was appointed or elected to a Community Advisory Board or governing body whose support was critical in the decision-making process. For example, Asian Community Counseling Services in Sacramento functioned for 4 years as basically an advocacy organization with information and referral services. Only when one of its own members was elected to the County Mental Health Advisory Board did the agency receive funding for expansion into direct services.

Incremental Growth

Most Asian community-based agencies also grew incrementally, that is, bit by bit, in a slow and often painful process of adding components or spinning off new projects, only as the necessary resources became available. Many agencies began as advocacy organizations, which provided basic information and referral services and expanded into community outreach. At this point, many discovered that services were nonexistent or underutilized. They then demonstrated that there was sufficient need to justify their taking on a direct service function. The names of some of the agencies clearly point to their advocacy origins. Examples of this are East Bay Japanese for Action in Berkeley, currently a multi-service agency for Japanese elderly, and Asian Americans for Community Involvement in San Jose, a multi-ethnic, multi-service agency.

Utilization of Existing Resources

Propelled by the desire to gain recognition and autonomy, community groups can overlook the fact that there are often existing resources that can be supplemented or built upon to provide the specialized bilingual/bicultural service needed. Services to Asian communities could be extended through a contractual arrangement with an existing agency. The use of an existing agency's physical facilities and administrative structure can result in considerable savings.

Existing resources available within the Asian community itself also include technical expertise in such organizational and program functions as needs assessment studies, grant writing, fiscal management, management information systems, and program evaluation. Asian community-based agencies have established an impressive record for competent management and fiscal responsibility, largely through the utilization of expertise within their own communities.

Diversification of Funding Base

Most successful Asian community-based programs do not rely upon a single source of funding; rather, they try to diversify their funding base. This assures continuity of funding should any one source be terminated. With the continued decrease in public funding, agencies must consider developing for-profit enterprises to generate supplemental income.

Coalition Building

In most cities, Asians would constitute a relatively insignificant force if each distinct ethnic community acted independently. Collective action as a Pan-Asian American united front is likely to enhance visibility and impact upon the larger community. The success of such programs as the Union of Pan Asian American communities in San Diego, the Asian Pacific Planning Council in Los Angeles, the Richmond Area Multi-Services Center in San Francisco, and the International District Improvement Association in Seattle clearly derives from their multi-ethnic support base.

PROGRAM DEVELOPMENT ISSUES FOR THE FUTURE

An assessment of the data collected from this study points to several distinct problem areas in Asian communities that will require new or expanded programmatic responses in the future. They appear to cluster around problems related to immigrant and refugee families, the elderly, and the severely mentally ill.

Immigrant and Refugee Families

By far the greatest utilizers of services in Asian communities are immigrant and refugee families. Their numbers are likely to continue to grow in the future, and there will be an increasing demand for services in Asian communities to meet their needs. Immigrant and refugee families face severe stresses in the process of moving to a new country; they must cope with culture shock and the forces of acculturation. The disruptions in the continuity of family life create enormous pressures that destabilize normal family relations and individual role performance. As the acculturation process takes place, there are increasing intergenerational tensions and alienation between parents and children. Children are influenced by the values of their peer culture and reject the traditional values of their families. Their internal conflicts are then often acted out in gang affiliation, drug use, and delinquency. Their parents, reacting in accustomed ways, often resort to physical punishment and sanctions that are not accepted by the larger society.

Refugee children often have serious problems of physical health related to malnutrition, anemia, and parasitosis, in addition to severe behavioral and emotional problems (Carlin, 1986). The consequences of the trauma of wartime, their perilous escape on the high seas, and the prolonged periods of deprivation in the refugee camps take their toll in manifestations of nightmares, fear, guilt, and acting-out behavior. Special problems of adaptation and integration are faced by Amerasian children who are raised in the streets without the care and support of families. This population will undoubtedly make special demands on mental health and other related services because few existing organizations are equipped to meet the extraordinary needs of a group about which very little is known.

The Elderly

Among the Chinese, Japanese, and Korean communities is a rapidly growing aging population with problems stemming from alienation and isolation, illness, and the need for long-term care. Traditionally, Asians have placed a high value on the status of the aged, and every effort was made by families to care for the elderly in their own homes rather than in nursing homes. However, due to changing life styles, economic circumstances, and the erosion of traditional values among Asians, it is becoming more and more difficult to care for the aged in their own homes. Increasingly, in-home supportive services, as well as long-term care facilities, will be required.

Severe Mental Illness

Severe mental illness is increasingly prevalent among recent Chinese immigrants and Southeast Asian refugees (Gong-Guy, 1987). Acute states of depression are related to stresses common to all refugee experiences: loss and grief; disrupted family relationships; social isolation; status inconsistencies; prolonged, severe, and repetitive trauma; culture shock; and acculturation stresses. Clinical depression is also found in other Asian groups and is frequently seen in adolescents who attempt suicide or have suicidal ideation (Lee, 1985).

Post-traumatic stress disorder is found particularly among Cambodian refugees who are survivors of a genocidal experience. Their symptoms include recurring and intrusive memories of traumatic events, recurring nightmares and dreams, sudden acting or feeling as if the traumatic event were happening in the present, suffering intense distress at exposure to symbolic or similar events, feeling acute shame or survivor guilt and rage at the perpetrators of the traumatic event (Kinzie, Fredrickson, Rath, Fleck, & Karls, 1984).

Schizophrenia is frequently found among Chinese immigrants from the Asian mainland who have been isolated or separated from relatives for prolonged periods of time (Tsai, Teng, & Sue, 1981). Without their extended family network, they have had to cope with the stresses of integration by themselves. Because of the stigma of mental illness in the Asian community, the problem of schizophrenia and other aberrant behavior tends to be concealed and not brought to public attention until an acute crisis occurs. By this time, the patient's condition is so advanced that confinement to an inpatient facility becomes necessary and long-term care is required. Included in this population are an increasing number of Southeast Asian refugees and recent immigrants from Korea who are unable to cope with the stresses of their migration experience and the acculturation process in this country.

PROBLEMS AND ISSUES FOR FURTHER RESEARCH

This study represents a beginning attempt to delineate the scope and characteristics of social services provided by community-based organizations in Asian communities. Much further investigation is needed to clarify issues raised by this study. Such an investigation might include the following:

- Analysis of the relationship among such structural or institutional variables as racism, cultural diversity, and social change, and their consequences for the quality of life of Asians.
- Study of the role of informal and natural support networks in the help-seeking patterns of Asians; how such networks are mechanisms for identifying persons requiring services and for facilitating access to and utilization of services.
- Study of family structures and cultural behavior, such as the nature and consequences of traditional and modern life-styles, developmental cycles, socialization processes, social values, and culture-specific influence processes unique to particular Asian groups.
- Study of stress and the specific processes that create, mediate, and reduce stress among Asians, and whether techniques of stress reduction are similarly used by Asians as compared with other Americans.
- The applicability of traditional role models of intervention and the exploration of alternative modes of intervention for use with Asians, with particular attention to group as opposed to one-on-one therapeutic modalities.
- Defining culturally relevant modes of social service delivery to Asian clients, integrating indigenous or culturally derived and sanctioned practices.

CONCLUSIONS

In conclusion, while inequities exist in the delivery of services to Asian communities, this study has identified a variety of successful Asian community-based programs that provide alternative models for replication. These programs reflect enormous vitality and creativity in responding to diverse community problems and needs. They are contributing significantly to enhance the quality of life of Asians, particularly the most vulnerable at-risk population—immigrants and refugees. Reviewing and learning from this experience of program planning and program development in Asian communities is an important step toward improvement and expansion of services to Asian and other Americans and their communities in the future.

REFERENCES

Carlin, J. E. (1986). Child and adolescent refugees: Psychiatric assessment and treatment. In C. L. Williams & J. Westermeyer (Eds.), *Refugee mental health in resettlement countries* (pp. 131-139). Washington, DC: Hemisphere.

Chu, J., & Sue, S. (1984). Asian/Pacific-Americans and group practice. In L. E. Davis (Ed.), *Ethnicity in social group work practice* (pp. 23-36). New York: Haworth.

Corey, G. (1990). *Theory and practice of group counseling.* Belmont, CA: Brooks/Cole.

Endo, R., Sue, S., & Wagner, N. (Eds.). (1980). *Asian Americans: Social and psychological perspectives* (Vol. 2). Palo Alto, CA: Science and Behavior Books.

Gaw, A. (1975). An integrated approach in the delivery of health care to a Chinese community in America: The Boston experience. In A. Kleinman (Ed.), *Medicine in Chinese cultures* (pp. 327-350). Washington, DC: Government Printing Office.

Goldman, H. H., Sharfstein, S., & Frank, R. G. (1980). *Equity and parity in psychiatric care.* Unpublished manuscript, National Institute of Mental Health.

Gong-Guy, E. (1987). *The California Southeast Asian mental health needs assessment.* Oakland, CA: Asian Community Mental Health Services.

Gross, H., Herbert, M. R., & Knatterud, G. L. (1969). The effects of race and sex on the variation of diagnosis and disposition in a psychiatric emergency room. *Journal of Nervous and Mental Diseases, 148*(6), 638-642.

Hatanaka, H. K., Watanabe, B. Y., & Ono, S. (1975). The utilization of mental health services in the Los Angeles area. In W. H. Ishikawa & N. H. Archer (Eds.), *Service delivery in Pan Asian communities* (pp. 33-39). San Diego: Pacific Asian Coalition.

Ho, M. K. (1976). Social work with Asian Americans. *Social Casework, 57,* 195-201.

Ho, M. K. (1984). Social group work with Asian/Pacific-Americans. In L. E. Davis (Ed.), *Ethnicity in social group work practice* (pp. 49-61). New York: Haworth.

Kaneshige, E. (1973). Cultural factors in group counseling and interaction. *Personnel and Guidance Journal, 51*(6), 407-412.

Kinzie, J. D., Fredrickson, R. H., Rath, B., Fleck, J., & Karls, W. (1984). Post traumatic stress disorder among survivors of Cambodian concentration camps. *American Journal of Psychiatry, 141,* 645-650.

Kitano, H. L., & Matsushima, N. (1981). Counseling Asian Americans. In P. B. Pedersen, J. G. Draguns, W. J. Lonner, & J. T. Trimble (Eds.), *Counseling across cultures* (pp. 163-180). Honolulu: University of Hawaii Press.

Lee, E. (1985). In-patient psychiatric services for Southeast Asian refugees. In T. C. Owan (Ed.), *Southeast Asian mental health: Treatment, prevention, services, training and research* (pp. 307-327) (DHHS Publication No. ADM 85-1399). Washington, DC: Government Printing Office.

Lee, P. C., Juan, G., & Hom, A. B. (1984). Group work practice with Asian clients: A sociocultural approach. In L. E. Davis (Ed.), *Ethnicity in social group work practice* (pp. 37-48). New York: Haworth.

San Francisco Community Mental Health Services, Bureau of Research (1977). *Annual report*. San Francisco: Department of Public Health.

Sue, S., & McKinney, H. (1975). Asian Americans in the community mental health care system. *American Journal of Orthopsychiatry, 45*(1), 111-118.

Sue, S., McKinney, H., Allen, D., & Hall, J. (1974). Delivery of community mental health services to black and white clients. *Journal of Consulting and Clinical Psychology, 42*, 794-801.

Sue, S., & Morishima, J. (1982). *The mental health of Asian Americans*. San Francisco: Jossey-Bass.

True, R. H. (1975). Mental health services in a Chinese American community. In W. H. Ishikawa & N. H. Archer (Eds.), *Service delivery in Pan-Asian communities*. San Diego: Pacific Asian Coalition.

Tsai, M., Teng, L. N., & Sue, S. (1981). Mental health status of Chinese in the United States. In A. Kleinman & T. Lin (Eds.), *Normal and abnormal behavior in Chinese culture* (pp. 291-310). Boston: Reidel.

Wang, I. S., & Louie, W. (1979). *The Chinatown after-care program: A report on a selected group of Chinese patients and their state hospital experience*. San Francisco: Department of Public Health.

Wong, H. (1978). Community mental health services and manpower and training concerns of Asian Americans. In U. S. President's Commission on Mental Health, *Report to the President from the President's Commission on Mental Health*. Washington, DC.

Yamamoto, J., James, Q. C., & Palley, N. (1968). Cultural problems in psychiatric therapy. *Archives of General Psychiatry, 19*, 45-49.

Yoshioka, R., Tashima, N., & Chew, M. (1981). *Mental health services for Pacific/Asian Americans*. San Francisco: Pacific Asian Mental Health Research Project.

Part III

MACRO INTERVENTION: Policy and Planning

DOUGLAS K. CHUNG

A fundamental problem for Asian Americans and their organizations as a whole is getting from where they are to where they want to be. The consideration of their current status, goals, and the means by which to get there results in a planned process for the whole—subgroups, organizations, families, and individuals—to achieve its goals. This planned process or strategy is referred to in two ancient Chinese classics: *I Ching* (*The Book of Changes*) by Confucius (c. 500/ 1989), which provides guidelines for individual or organizational changes; and *The Art of War* by Sun Tzu (c. 500/1963), which refers not only to military strategies but also to strategic consultation for multilevel planned changes. Confucianism, Hinduism, and many other Asian life philosophies provide strategic principles and perspectives for cyclical, patterned change for the well-being of the parts as well as the whole.

The term *strategy* among Asian Americans, then, means the assessment of the interdependency of individuals, institutions, situations, systems, and other components that make up the complex network of life in families, organizations, communities, societies, and the universe itself. Beyond this, strategy involves the design and implementation of subsequent actions that effect, manage, and evaluate change.

The Asian perspective for change is rooted in its culture and prescribes that each situation be thoroughly assessed from an interdependent worldview of all elements, including allied and counter forces, water, trees, values, oneness, and so on. The Asian concept of oneness is that conflict and consensus strategies are two sides of one coin. Oneness is perhaps best described by the Yin/Yang Theory, which assumes that the world (everything from quantum to solar systems) consists of two primary categories of existence, or Yin and Yang forces. These two forces are complementary interacting elements in any system. This inevitable coexistence of conflict and consensus has received strong support from the social science literature, according to Tropman and Erlich (1987). The tension between Yin and Yang is similar to that between task and process or quantitative and qualitative, and this tension leads to change or provides the opportunity for change. It is essential for helping professionals who work in the Asian American system to study the tension and interaction of counterforces influencing the system's structure and functioning.

In "The Confucian Model of Social Transformation," I present a holistic Confucian theoretical perspective on social transformation. The Confucian ideal welfare state is described and the Confucian social transformation technologies are introduced. Confucius prescribes seven steps, which integrate the micro and macro levels of social change into a single and comprehensive planned change. The ultimate goals of intrinsic and extrinsic harmonies are to be reached through the transformation of knowledge, attitude, behavior, and organizational performance among individuals, significant others, families, and social systems in an interdependent network. The keys to successful social transformation and various situational approaches are discussed and compared to contemporary social work practice.

The following two chapters present problematic cases illustrating the differential approaches used by Asian Americans to define and change their circumstances. In "The Economic Well-Being of Asian/Pacific Islander Female-Headed Households: Implications for Social Welfare Policy," Kathleen M. McInnis-Dittrich answers the questions: "Do the cultural qualities of self-discipline and industriousness attributed to Asians enable female heads to compensate for the disadvantages other female heads face in the American economy? How does membership in ethnic groups impact the well-being of disadvantaged women? How do Asian American women differ from non-Asian women in combining the income from family members for their economic support?" The Asian strategic concepts of interdependence and oneness are reflected in this chapter, and implications for welfare policies that meet their needs are discussed.

In "Policy Implications of Factors Associated With Economic Self-Sufficiency of Southeast Asian Refugees," Chi Kwong Law and Leonard Schneiderman indicate that in all likelihood it would probably take more than 5 years for Southeast Asian refugees to achieve economic self-sufficiency; therefore, the federal government's responsibility for providing cash assistance should be extended to 5 years.

English proficiency in particular, then vocational skills and access to labor markets markedly affect the economic self-sufficiency of refugees; hence, refugees should be exposed to English training first and vocational training second, which is contrary to most programs for refugees. While recommendations and implications are derived from the Southeast Asian refugee experience, they may be applicable to other non-English-speaking newcomers struggling for self-sufficiency.

REFERENCES

Confucius. (1989). *I-Ching* (T. Cleary, Trans.). Boston: Shambhala. (Original work published c. 500 B.C.). [Other versions by Fu Hsi (c. 3000 B.C.); King Wen (c. 1050 B.C.); and the Duke of Chou (son of King Wen).

Sun Tzu. (1963). *The art of war* (S. B. Griffith, Trans.). Oxford: Oxford University Press. (Original work published c. 500 B.C.)

Tropman, J. E., & Erlich, J. L. (1987). In F. M. Cox, J. L. Erlich, J. Rothman, & J. E. Tropman (Eds.), *Macro practice: Strategies of community organization*. Itasca, IL: Peacock.

Chapter 7

THE CONFUCIAN MODEL OF SOCIAL TRANSFORMATION

DOUGLAS K. CHUNG

In both micro and macro social work practice, a fundamental concept is social change or social transformation for the improvement of human well-being. While the literature describes several Western models for social change, it seldom presents models of social change used in Asian countries. Both Confucius and Gandhi espoused highly regarded models of social transformation. An Asian social transformation model for universal generalist social work practice is recommended. The holistic Confucian model of social transformation addresses Lauffer's claim (1987) of a "lack of comprehensiveness" in social planning.

This chapter describes the Confucian ideal welfare state as well as the Confucian social transformation model, and nine situational strategic approaches for incorporating the social transformation model to achieve harmony in society. Then the Confucian model and Gandhian approaches for social change are compared, and implications for social work practice are cited.

THE CONFUCIAN MODEL

Confucius (551-479 B.C.) is renowned as a philosopher and educator, but little attention is given to his roles as a researcher, statesman, change agent, social planner, social innovator, enabler, and advocate. Few Americans are aware that Confucius, a universal generalist, developed a general method to transform individuals, families, communities, and nations.

The Confucian Model of Social Transformation is a research-oriented, multidimensional, cross-cultural, multilevel, comprehensive approach applicable to both micro and macro systems. It is a life-style or an art of living to synchronize the systems of the universe to reach its potential. Webster defines *transform* as "to change markedly the form or appearance of; to change the nature, function, or condition of; to convert." The form means any perceived pattern, such as skin color, family structure, cultural values, and symbols. "Transformation" means to go beyond the present limited form experience and reach other forms, such as cross-cultural or the other side of non-form, which is the spiritual experience. It means to reach and experience that I, the system, am more than the form and taste, that I can feel various forms (different skins, cultures, and structures) in this endless life change process inherent to all systems. The Confucian Model of Social Transformation changes a system and helps it to reach its potential or excellence by examining the way the system interfaces in its interdependent network and planning for the change.

The Confucian Social Transformation Model consists of several characteristics: (a) determining and working with the truth when making changes; (b) integrating both individual and collective planned change; (c) basing the change plan on quantitative and qualitative research; and (d) integrating various intuitive, moral, rational, and spiritual approaches. The Confucian transformation model is useful for universal generalist social work practice because it is comprehensive and includes multilevel, multidimensional social change.

The values of Confucian social transformation are rooted in a belief in the capacity of individual transformation, and a recognition of the need for a democratic and caring society.

THE IDEAL WELFARE STATE

Today we are confronted with the problem of having no common agreement on what constitutes an ideal social welfare state. There is no clear long-term social welfare vision or policy statement for social work practice. There are a number of policy analysis models available (Flynn, 1987; Gil, 1981; Gilbert & Specht, 1986; Jansson, 1984; Karger & Stoesz, 1990; Pierce, 1984; Prigmore & Atherton, 1986) to evaluate the desirability of social conditions, and fragmented values are articulated in the 1958 and 1981 National Association of Social Workers Working Statements and in the 1979 NASW Code of Ethics; however, the type of ideal welfare society we are searching for is simply absent from our welfare literature.

Heus and Pincus (1986) explain this lack in the literature as due to the predominance of left-brain thinking in the American culture, where much focus is on science; hence, the United States has developed an extensive description of ethics because this task is essentially a rational or scientific clarification of values. On the other hand, Euro Americans have been unable to clarify values into a vision because this task requires intuitive or artistic effort.

The Asian culture, meanwhile, is relatively high-context, tends to be right-mind-dominated, and belongs to the intuitional school of thought. It is generally accepted that Western culture is more pragmatic and individualistic while Eastern culture is more idealistic and collective.

It is in the Asian culture, then, that we find a description of the ideal welfare state. Confucius prescribed an ideal society with the following values: equity, trust, respect, sharing, cooperative and nurturing community, democracy, adequacy in meeting human needs, efficient and effective use of resources, self- and societal actualization, and harmony. It is a complementary society and a part of the harmonious universe. Accomplishing of the ideal society depends upon successful individual self-discipline and the social care network.

Confucius (1967/500 B.C.) described the ideal welfare state in *Li Chi* (*Book of Rites*) as follows:

> When the Grand course was pursued, a public and common spirit ruled all under the sky; they chose men of talents, virtue, and ability; their words were sincere, and what they cultivated was harmony. Thus men did not love their parents only, nor treat as children only their own sons. A competent provision was secured for the aged till their death, employment for the able-bodied, and the means of growing up to the young. They showed kindness and compassion to widows, orphans, childless men, and those who were disabled by disease, so that they were all sufficiently maintained. Males had their proper work, and females had their homes. (They accumulated) articles (of value), disliking that they should be thrown away upon the ground, but not wishing to keep them for their own gratification. (They laboured) with their strength, disliking that it should not be exerted, but not exerting it (only) with a view to their own advantage. In this way (selfish) schemings were repressed and found no

development. Robbers, filchers, and rebellious traitors did not show themselves, and hence the outer doors remained open, and were not shut. This was (the period of) what we call the Grand Union. (pp. 365-366)

In such an ideal welfare state, it can be surmised, the residents individually and the state as a whole enjoyed equity and respect as they trusted and shared with each other. This state must have consisted of cooperative and nurturing communities where a democratic government efficiently used resources and provided for human needs. Self- and societal actualization or potential must have been achieved through excellent role performance, and all must have lived harmoniously in a state that was only part of an even larger harmonious universe. The above welfare state could only be achieved by living the goals of the social transformation model.

GOALS OF THE CONFUCIAN MODEL

The goals of social transformation prescribed by Confucius in *The Great Learning* (1971/500 B.C.) include: achieve illustrious virtue, renovate the people, and rest in the highest excellence. In other words, the overall goal is to cultivate the virtuous nature with which humanity is innately endowed and to renovate people daily for a tranquil and happy world. An expected outcome of the goals for individuals is self-started, self-controlled, and self-assumed responsibilities, with the dual aim of cultivating one's self and contributing to the attainment of an ideal welfare state.

The above goals indicate several characteristics important to understanding the social transformation model:

(a) all systems are committed to excellence and to these goals;

(b) these goals are primarily process-oriented;

(c) goals are simultaneously applicable to both micro and macro systems; and

(d) goals are based on education.

The goals and their characteristics indicate that the social transformation model was based on a clear understanding of people, their environment, and their interdependent relationship. This ecological-systems perspective of the ideal society is better understood with a review of the theoretical assumptions of the model.

THEORETICAL ASSUMPTIONS OF THE MODEL

Confucius's basic assumption was that lawlessness and social problems are due to unlearned individuals, a social structure without norms, and the inadequate relationship of these two systems. The author (1990) has identified the following Confucian social transformation assumptions based on worldviews found primarily in *I Ching* (Confucius, 1989), *The Great Learning* (Confucius, 1971/500 B.C.), *Confucian Analects* (Confucius, 1971/500 B.C.), and *The Doctrine of the Mean* (Confucius, 1971/500 B.C.):

(1) In the beginning, there is nothing (Wu-Chi).

(2) The Great Ultimate (*Tai Chi*) exists in the *I* (change). The Great Ultimate is the cause of change and generates the two forms, the Great Yang (a great energy) and the Great Yin, its opposing force.

(3) These two primary forms, Yang and Yin, are symbols of opposite and complementary forces, such as positive and negative, day and night, male and female, rational and intuitive.

(4) Yang and Yin interact and eventually produce everything.

(5) Everything or every system coexists in an interdependent network. Thus, one who knows the truth also cares.

(6) The dynamics, and therefore the tension between Yang and Yin forces in all systems, lead everything to an endless changing process; that is, production and reproduction and the transformation of energy. It is a natural order, an order in which basic moral values can be seen.

(7) The Great Ultimate (*Tao*) exists in everything and is the source or background of *I* (change). Human nature is inherently good. Human beings may go alone with the Great Ultimate (*Tao*) and engage in endless self-discipline to reveal the real self (nature of *Tao*) and enjoy the change.

(8) There are four principles of change:

(a) Change is easy.

(b) Change is a transforming process due to the dynamics of Yang and Yin. Any change in part of Yang or Yin leads to a change in the system and its related systems.

(c) Change is constant and changeless; change itself is unchanging.

(d) The best transformations promote the growth and development of the individual and the whole simultaneously, or reaching the excellence for all systems in the interdependent network.

(9) Any search for change should consider the following factors:

(a) The *status* of the object in the interdependent network; that is, who is the system and what is its role, position, rights, and duties?

(b) The *timing* in the interdependent network; that is, is this the right time to initiate change?

(c) The *mean position* or the most strategic position in dealing with the change in the interrelated network; *Tao* (Truth) exists in the mean (Chung).

(d) The *response* of Yin and Yang forces; that is, the willingness of opposing forces or parties to dialog, compromise, and so on.

(e) The *integration* between the parts and the whole; that is, the system in its economic, political, and cultural realms.

(10) There exists an interconnected individual network with the pattern of interdependent relationships in all levels of systems, from individual, through family and state, to the whole world. The whole is dependent upon the harmonious integration of all the parts, while the parts require the nurture from the whole. The ultimate unit perceived under this framework is the universe itself.

(11) Self is understood as a here-and-now link in a chain of existence from the past to the future, to be shaped by the way one performs his daily life roles. One's humanity is achieved only with and through others.

(12) The individual and social transformations are based on: self-cultivation, personal effort to search for the truth, and becoming a life-giving person. Searching for and finding the truth leads to: (a) an originality and creativeness of problem solution and development; and (b) a life-giving and sharing Jen characteristic or personality. Wisdom (truth), Jen (love), and courage are non-separable concepts in reality.

(13) Organizational effectiveness and efficiency are reached when systematically interconnected individuals or subsystems find and adhere to the truth. Existence is an issue of the interconnected whole. Methods that assume and take account of connections work better than those that focus on isolated elements. Organizational effectiveness improves through rearranging the relationships between the parts and the whole.

A balanced and harmonious development within the interdependent network is the most beneficial for all. Self-actualization and collective goals should be integrated, according to Confucianism.

There are many similarities between the Social Transformation Model and the ideas of Gordon's General Systems (1979) and Germain and Gitterman's Life Model (1980) as they define ecology. Confucius, guided by the above theoretical assumptions, prescribed the following social transformation method to reach the ideal caring society.

THE CONFUCIAN SOCIAL
TRANSFORMATION METHOD

In the Social Transformation Model, Confucius prescribed the following seven steps to achieve the ideal society:

(1) The *investigation of things or variables*; that is, find out the way things are and how they are related;

(2) The *completion of knowledge*; that is, find out why things are the way they are or why the dependent variable was related to other variables—the reality/truth, *Tao*. Since everything is in an interrelated network, the discovery of why the dependent variable was related to other variables will help transform one's attitude (step 3);

(3) The *sincerity of thoughts*; that is, one should be sincere in wanting to change or in setting goals, which is a commitment to excellence and the truth, *Tao*—a source of self-motivation, a root of self-actualization, and a cornerstone of adequate I-Thou and I-Thing relationships;

(4) The *rectifying of the heart*; that is, the motivation for change must be the right one, good for the self and the whole. It is a cultivation for consciousness (virtue), a moral self through intuitive integrity of Jen (humanity, benevolence, perfect virtue, compassion and love), *Yi* (righteousness), *Li* (politeness, respect), and wisdom (from steps 1, 2, and 3), which enables a real freedom from evil, moral courage, and the ability to be good;

(5) The *cultivation of the person*; that is, there must be lifelong integrity between the "knowledge self" (steps 1 and 2) and the moral self (steps 3 and 4) through self-discipline (education) and self-improvement. This is the key to helping the self and others;

(6) The *regulation of the family*; that is, one should use self-discipline within the family and honor parents, respect and care for siblings, and love children. One should understand the weaknesses of family members one likes and appreciate the strengths of those one dislikes to avoid disharmony in the family, and to prevent prejudice and favoritism in the society;

(7) The *governance of the state*; that is, the state must provide public education, set policies, care for the vulnerable people, appoint and elect capable and moral persons for public officials and employees, and apply the Mean management. This public administration should lead to the ideal welfare state (see Figure 7.1).

The Confucian Social Transformation Method can be used in universal generalist social work practice. It is self-cultivated practice that

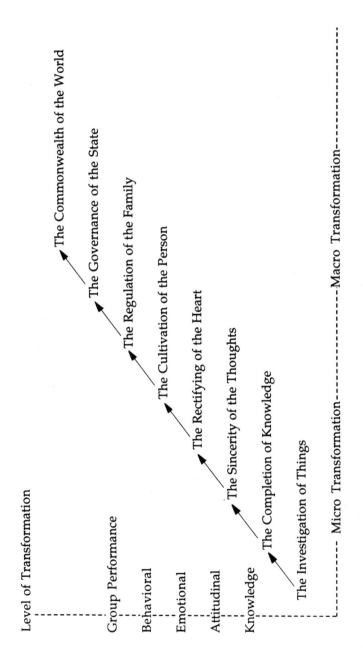

Figure 7.1. Confucian General Transformation Method

seeks the truth and is committed to the truth (*Tao*) as it brings about individual and social changes for an improved and more harmonious world.

NINE SITUATIONAL STRATEGIC APPROACHES

Nine major approaches are critical to incorporate the seven steps of the Confucian Social Transformation Method in changing individuals and society. These approaches constitute the skills of social transformation.

Comprehensive Education

Education is considered to be the most important approach in transforming the individuals, families, and nations to reach an ideal society.

The ancient Confucian school provided a comprehensive, integrated education for transforming individuals to be self-starters, self-controlled, and responsible for cultivating one's self and contributing to the attainment of a welfare state.

The school curriculum included *The Five Ching* and *The Four Shu*, considered to be the highest authority in the Chinese classics. *The Five Ching* are the five canonical works and include: *I Ching* (*The Book of Change*), *The Shu* (*The Book of History*), *The Shih* (*The Book of Poetry*), *The Li Chi* (*Record of Rites*), and *The Chun Chiu* (*Spring and Autumn*), a chronicle of events extending from 722 to 481 B.C. *The Four Books* (Confucius, 1971) include the *Lun Yu* (*Confucian Analects*), *Ta Hsio* (*The Great Learning*), *The Chung Yung* (*The Doctrine of the Mean*), and *The Works of Mencius*. In addition to studying these texts, the ancient Chinese education included music, horsemanship, archery, mathematics, politics, history, literature, law (rites), science, and physical education.

In *The Li Chi* the concept of *li* (politeness or respect) is discussed in an extensive ethical system that governed the conduct of all people in their interpersonal relations. Confucius used *li* and music as twin fundamental tactics for personal and social transformation. The function of *li* was to socialize human desire, while music was to transform human emotion.

Confucius established the liberal arts curriculum to develop integrated individuals who would be part of an ideal society. Confucius taught these doctrines to bring about social changes.

Cognitive Approach

Confucius was perhaps the earliest scholar to apply cognitive theory to social change. Confucianism advocates an expansion or modification of individual consciousness (virtue) through acquiring knowledge and truth in daily life until perception more nearly approximates reality or truth. It promotes a stilling and controlling of the mind as the way to reach unity of body, things, and spirit (Tao-Li and Chi) and to live within a state of higher consciousness. Confucianism focuses on the conscious thinking process. Confucius assumed the acquisition of knowledge (truth finding) would lead to an accurate perception of reality, which, in turn, would mold and shape attitudes, emotions, motives, and behaviors. *The Great Learning* (Confucius, 1971/500 B.C.), which includes the seven steps of the general method, provides an example of a cognitive approach for social planning to achieve social change. If, by such a process, the majority of the people in the society are transformed, the world would then become more tranquil and happy.

The Existential Stance

Self, in the Confucian view, is a here-and-now link in a chain of existence stretching from the past to the future, to be shaped by the way an individual performs his daily roles. Confucianism emphasizes the individual by looking at today and determining what one can do to improve one's self and the group's self. This positive existential viewpoint, as part of the cognitive approach, is clearly evident in the *Confucian Analects* when Confucius answered the question, what is filial piety, differently according to the varying backgrounds and needs of the person asking (Confucius, 1971/500 B.C.); hence, indicating the belief that current individual readiness is an important theme of the existential perspective, according to Van Kaam (1966).

Role Approach

Confucianism prescribes five basic role sets or social relationships, which form the basis of Chinese and other Asian social structures and relationships, a parts-whole relationship rearrangement that was discussed in Chapter 2. Role is one of the major approaches Confucius uses to transform individuals and the society through its moral-demanded content. It is widely believed that the economic prosperity of Japan, Taiwan, Hong Kong, Korea, and Singapore is due to the close association with and adherence to Confucianism, which emphasizes the importance of defined role concepts and ethics.

Jen Network and Dynamics

Jen network is critical for transforming individuals and society. Jen means benevolence, perfect virtue, compassion, and love. Jen network, highly favored by Confucius, means that helping professionals should establish social support networks that promote a caring, sharing, and loving society. To be fully human is to relate to others in a life-giving, sharing way.

Brandon's *Zen in the Art of Helping* (1976) (Zen is a school of Buddhism in Japanese) gives an example of the cognitive approach to truth-seeking and moral socialization aimed at reaching social transformation. Confucian social transformation is based on individual cultivation and the social role-network approach, integrated with Jen dynamics, which showed in the individual's virtuous action (Jen personality), the leader's Jen leadership, and Jen administration. In other words, Jen is the way to educate the truth-seeking individual, shape the community, and transform society toward the ideal welfare state.

The Leader's Example Is All in Administration

The leader's example in public administration is the most important example for social transformation to occur. Confucius emphasized the role, the Jen mind (personality), and the Jen leadership style of the leader.

Confucius believed that the best administration of government depended on getting the proper leaders. This assumption is derived from the fact that Jen (benevolence, perfect virtue, compassion, and love) can free people from selfishness and transform social mentality and norms. Being a leader or administrator depends on how much influence one can create in transforming the organization or society. Confucius assumed that the Jen mind and Jen leadership would attract and convince the public and eventually lead to social transformation.

The Mean Approach as Life Management and Public Administration

The Mean Approach is the way that leads to excellence and unification with *Tao*. In *The Doctrine of the Mean*, the Confucian comprehensive view of life and reality is again evident. *The Doctrine of the Mean*, or *Chung Yung*, promotes searching for the truth and adhering to it to attain excellence and perfection. It requires the system (from micro to macro) to define its mean position in the part-whole relationship. The harmonious cooperation of all systems arises from self-cultivation and self-consistency. It is a life and management philosophy committed to excellence.

I Ching as Programs
for Change Study and Consultation

The *I Ching* (*Book of Changes*) prescribes universal ontology, evolution processes, changing principles, and guidelines for change alternatives. The *I Ching*, considered to be the oldest of the Chinese classics, is a book of omen and advice that Confucius used as a text in dealing with personal and social transformation. It is a system of systems of changes. It is a symbolic system or tool used for evaluation, planning, implementation, and prediction among lay people, scholars, statesmen, and fortune-tellers for both micro and macro changes. There are different interpretations of *I Ching*, and the majors ones include: *I Ching the Tao of Organization*, by Cheng Yi (1988); *The Buddhist I Ching,* by Ou-i Chih-hsu (1987); *The Taoist I Ching,* by Liu I-ming (1986); and *I Ching Mandalas A Program of Study for the Book of Changes* (Cleary, 1989). The various versions of *I Ching* provide a good example of how Buddhism, Taoism, and traditional Confucianism were blended into neo-Confucianism, which profoundly affected the pre-modern Chinese, Korean, Japanese, and Vietnamese dynasties. Its worldview has been described in the section of theoretical assumptions. *I Ching* guides people to learn the truth-*Tao* for problem-solving and leads us to be harmonious with *Tao*-truth unification, which is the core of Confucianism. Use of *I Ching* provides an example of a spiritual approach for change consultation.

The Ecological-Systems Approach

Confucius perceived the person in the environment from an ecological-systems theory as he attempted to transform the person and the environment into an ideal society. The similarities between the ideas of Confucius, Gordon (1979), McMahon (1990), and those of Germain and Gitterman (1980), as they define ecology, may readily be seen in the following discussion. Confucius promoted both internalized self-cultivation and external role configuration (micro and macro systems) in a humanistic way to reach an ideal state; that is, individual lives are shaped and modified by the choices (self-cultivation) they make, given the situational opportunities present. By their choices and their efforts (seven steps in *The Great Learning*), they in turn shape the environment (transform family, state, and kingdom—various levels of organizational equilibrium). Confucius considered that both the person and the environment needed to be shaped (Jen personality, Jen administration, and Jen network) in order to achieve an ideal society. The family became the most immediate and decisive portion of the interdependent network.

Figure 7.2 describes the Confucian Social Transformation Model as an Ecological-Systems Perspective. It transforms the individual through knowledge, as well as through emotional, attitudinal, behavioral, and organizational performance changes. It integrates micro and macro transformation through education, role network, and Jen administration.

THE CONFUCIAN MODEL AND
THE GANDHIAN APPROACH

Both Confucius and Gandhi shared a close common ground in their social transformation method. Confucianism and Gandhian idealism developed from a worldview that emphasized the existence of truth in all phenomena, which human beings could not perceive because of personal limitations. They present a holistic worldview, looking into the basic unity of human diversity. The world is perceived as constantly moving toward its betterment, and human beings are advised to live in harmony with nature. Both emphasize the significance of change as a precondition to forming an ideal society. The crucial focus for both is a constant search for the goal of life, the unity with one's own self, and the belief that happiness comes from within.

The concept of ideal society according to Confucius and Gandhi depends on a deeper concern for humanity. All human beings are viewed as an extension of one's own self. A deeper human concern is based on self-actualization through living a simple life, devoid of materialistic glamour and individualistic megalomania. It is the group of people living a simple life dedicated to high thinking, not the material possessions, that will promote national growth. Both Confucius and Gandhi looked at the dignity of labor as central to building an equalitarian society. A self-contained person with a sense of dignity is perceived as being other-oriented and engaged in helping others.

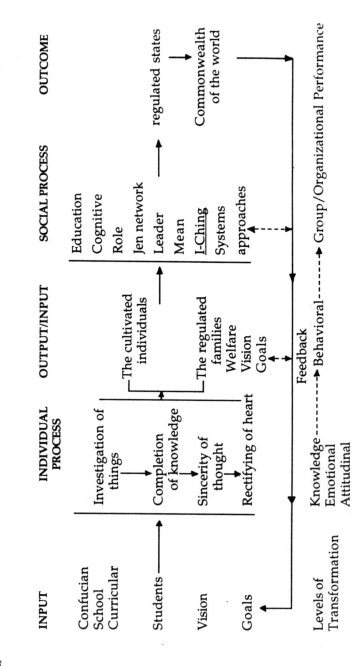

Figure 7.2. An Ecological-Systems Perspective of Social Transformation

The social order, according to Confucius and Gandhi, is based on self-discipline, mutual trust, and sharing. Such trust evolves out of the person's own sense of harmony, which Jen translated into caring, loving, and sharing. Gandhi tested the applicability of these concepts in his own theory and practice of nonviolence. His concepts of nonviolence incorporate a wide range of human feelings and behaviors non-injurious to self and others, and include even non-stealing and non-possession.

Following a path of self-discipline and self-realization, both Confucius and Gandhi aspired to create an ideal society with equality, justice, and love for all. Such an ideal society can only be formed through an absolute dedication to the truth—the central theme and goal of life. This desire to reach the truth became such an obsession for Gandhi that he inspired an entire nation to revolt against the British by burning British-made clothes, violating inhuman laws made by the British government, and marching to Dandi to make salt. This was Gandhi's unique way of translating the search for truth into macro-level social change.

The Gandhian strategy, upon close analysis, is quite compatible to the Confucian seven-step general transformation method. Truth-seeking as a life-style, a value system, and a way of problem solving have helped India gain independence and an economic position.

IMPLICATIONS FOR SOCIAL WORK PRACTICE AND CONCLUSIONS

The Confucian Transformation Model has many strengths. First, it provides a conceptual model that prescribes the nature of the relationship between the person and the environment on the individual, group, family, state, nation, and world levels. It defines the core of the social environment: We are the environment; the environment is us; we shape individuals; we shape the environment; the environment shapes us. The second strength of the Confucian Transformation Model is that it shapes the individual and the environment or the micro and the macro simultaneously through these comprehensive approaches: cognitive, existential, role, Jen network, leadership, mean, ecological-systems, and humanistic public administration under comprehensive private and public education systems.

Third, the Social Transformation Model assumes a positive human nature, which encourages the progressive forces in human nature and human growth at various levels of practice. It helps both the clients and practitioners to view human motivation in a positive way by identifying the progressive forces and removing obstacles in development processes; therefore, practitioners can be free from the fear of "creating dependency" in the helping process. Furthermore, the Confucian model views each person as a constituent rather than as a client, a perspective that Harrison (1989) also espouses. Fourth, it perceives that the cause of human dysfunction is due to individual and environmental causes; therefore, treatment must prescribe methods of individual internal change and adaptation; ways to change the environment; and transactions between individuals and their environments.

Fifth, the Confucian Transformation Model can serve as an approach for the universal generalist practice. It also has great potential to serve as an international social work model for world peace and human well-being due to its assumption of virtue, mean philosophy, systems interrelatedness, Jen leadership and administration, and its ultimate vision of human welfare throughout the world.

Confucius used the role approach because social disorder was the key social problem at the time, and defined social roles would help bring about social order. The implication is that the strategy or approach that a change agent selects should depend on the situation encountered. The change agent must study reality—the underlying contradictions or the Way Things Are—and then react. Absolute freedom to choose the strategy or approach does not exist. One has only a temporary and situational choice. This situational approach, which is the *I Ching's* approach, may be the appropriate leadership and management approach (mean management) for Asian American social work practice as well as for universal social work practice.

One of the weaknesses of the Confucian model is its lack of detail in operations to achieve planned change. Confucius's seven steps general method to reach the ideal society and mean philosophy, as described in *The Great Learning,* are too abstract for a plan of operation, making his technology more philosophical than scientific.

Chung (1990), based on the Confucian model, suggests a social transformation model for universal generalist social work practice to operationalize the Confucian Model. The model includes the following steps:

(1) Assess the situation by examining the underlying contractions and tension through quantitative and qualitative investigation of the way things are (truth) and why things are (knowledge completion).

(2) Design the change with commitment to excellence and consider goal determination for the entire interdependent network through choice of change strategies, tactics, and the change principles.

(3) Implement the change with commitment and situational approaches.

(4) Evaluate the parts and the whole interrelated network with quantitative and qualitative research, which will lead to an endless recycling and revitalizing process.

(5) Manage the change on knowledge, attitudinal, emotional, behavioral, and organizational performance levels to assure the integration of micro and macro transformation.

While Legge (Confucius, 1971) indicates that Confucius belongs to the intuitional school more than to the logical, it seems more accurate to say that the Confucian approach is both intuitional and logical. His seven steps transformation model is comprehensive and culturally sensitive to social work practice with Asian Americans as promoted by Chung (1989). It includes perception, cognition, emotion, attitude, personal behavior, and organizational performance changes. It has both the investigation of the way things are (left mind) and the way they might be (right mind). They are all of one piece, operating in situations creating the information that is being processed. Through the integration of knowing and valuing, the individual grows and transforms the self and the surrounding environment. The social work profession may honor Confucius as our professional mentor for his vision of the ideal society and for his comprehensive social transformation model for universal generalist social work practice. Further studies are needed to explore more conceptual guides and principles of Confucianism for social work practice.

REFERENCES

Brandon, D. (1976). *Zen in the art of helping*. Boston: Routledge & Kegan Paul.

Cheng Yi. (1988). *I Ching the tao of organization* (T. Cleary, Trans.). Boston: Shambhala. (Original work published 1050)

Chung, D. (1989). *Culturally competent social work practice for Asian Americans*. Paper presented at the 1989 NASW Annual Conference, San Francisco.

Chung, D. (1990, March). *Social transformation model for cross-cultural generalist social work practice*. Paper presented at the 1990 Council on Social Work Education 1990 Annual Program Meeting, Reno, Nevada.

Cleary, T. (Trans.). (1989). *I Ching mandalas a program of study for The Book of Changes*. Boston: Shambhala. (Original work published about 1,000 years ago)

Confucius. (1967). *Li chi* (J. Legge, Trans.). New York: University Books. (Original work published c. 500 B.C.)

Confucius (1971). *Confucian analects, the great learning and the doctrine of the mean* (J. Legge, Trans.). New York: Dover. (Original work published c. 500 B.C.)

Confucius. (1989). *I Ching* (T. Cleary, Trans. 1989). Boston: Shambhala. [Other versions by Fu Hsi (c. 3000 B.C.); King Wen (c. 1050 B.C.); and the Duke of Chou (son of King Wen)]. (Original work published c. 500 B.C.)

Flynn, J. P. (1987). *Social agency policy analysis and presentation for community practice.* Chicago: Nelson-Hall.

Germain, C. B., & Gitterman, A. (1980). *The life model of social work practice.* New York: Columbia University Press.

Gil, D. (1981). *Unravelling social policy.* Cambridge, MA: Schenkman.

Gilbert, N., & Specht, H. (1986). *Dimensions of social welfare policy.* Englewood Cliffs, NJ: Prentice-Hall.

Gordon, H. (1979). General systems theory and social work. In F. J. Turner (Ed.), *Social work treatment: Interlocking theoretical approaches* (2nd ed.). New York: Free Press.

Harrison, W. D. (1989). Social work and the search for postindustrial community. *Social Work, 34*(1), 73-75.

Heus, M., & Pincus, A. (1986). *The creative generalist: A guide to social work practice.* Barneveld, WI: Micamar.

Jansson, B. S. (1984). *Theory and practice of social welfare policy.* Belmont, CA: Wadsworth.

Karger, H. J., & Stoesz, D. (1990). *American social welfare policy.* New York: Longman.

Lauffer, A. (1987). Social planners and social planning in the United States. In F. M. Cox, J. L. Erlich, J. Rothman, & J. E. Tropman (Eds.), *Strategies of community organization* (pp. 311-326). Itasca, IL: Peacock.

Liu, I-ming. (1986). *The Taoist I Ching* (T. Cleary, Trans.). Boston: Shambhala. (Original work published 1796)

McMahon, M. O. (1990). *The general method of social work practice.* Englewood Cliffs, NJ: Prentice-Hall.

National Association of Social Workers. (1958). Working definition of social work practice. *Social Work, 3*(2),18-25.

National Association of Social Workers. (1979). *Code of ethics.* New York: NASW.

National Association of Social Workers. (1981). Working statement on the purpose of social work. *Social Work, 26*(1), 6.

Ou-i, Chih-hsu. (1987). *The Buddhist I Ching* (T. Cleary, Trans.). Boston: Shambhala. (Original work published 1599-1655)

Pierce, D. (1984). *Policy for the social work practitioner.* New York: Longman.

Prigmore, C. S., & Atherton, C. R. (1986). *Social welfare policy analysis and formulation.* Lexington, MA: Heath.

Van Kaam, A. (1966). *The art of existential counseling.* Wilkes-Barre, PA: Dimension.

Chapter 8

THE ECONOMIC WELL-BEING OF ASIAN/PACIFIC ISLANDER FEMALE-HEADED HOUSEHOLDS: *Implications for Social Welfare Policy*

KATHLEEN M. McINNIS-DITTRICH

Often seen as the "model minority," Asians enjoy one of the highest mean incomes in the United States. However, with a national aggregate poverty rate of 13.1% (U.S. Census, 1983), average income may be a deceptive measure of socioeconomic well-being. High mean income and high poverty rates suggest both that Asians are concentrated in the lowest and highest income brackets and that there is substantial variation between specific ethnic groups within the general category of Asians.

Female-headed households are the most economically disadvantaged in the United States. Little research addresses Asian female-headed households. Do the cultural qualities of self-discipline and industriousness attributed to Asians enable female heads to compensate for the disadvantages other female-headed households face in the American economy? What influence, if any, does nativity (native versus foreign birth) as well as membership in particular ethnic groups have on the well-being of these women? How do Asian women differ from other women and among themselves in combining income from a number of sources to provide for their families?

The focus of this research is threefold. First, the socioeconomic characteristics of Asian female-headed households will be examined on an aggregate and ethnic group level. Asian female heads will be compared to the general population of female-headed households by personal and familial characteristics and sources of income.

Recent research shows female heads rarely rely on a single source of income such as earnings or public assistance (McInnis, 1987; Oberheu, 1982; Rein & Rainwater, 1978). Women draw on a number of sources, including their own earnings and the earnings of other household workers, along with asset income, Social Security, child support, alimony, and public assistance. This combination of income sources comprises their "income package." The second focus of this research is an analysis of the income packaging strategies of Asian women compared to the general population of female-headed households.

Third, the implications of these findings for social welfare policy based on a model of "economic choices" for women will be examined.

REVIEW OF THE LITERATURE

Female Heads of Household

Although two-thirds of all female heads show some income from employment, one-half remain below the poverty line (McInnis, 1987). Fewer years of education is only one factor that limits the wage that women overall are able to command in the labor market (Duncan, 1984; Featherman, 1971; Schiller, 1989; Wallace, Datcher, & Malveaux, 1980). In addition, women are more likely to show a disrupted labor force experience, being forced to withdraw at least temporarily due to child bearing and rearing responsibilities. As mothers, they may return to only part-time employment, further restricting their earning power (Bumpass & Sweet, 1981; Ferber, 1982; McEaddy, 1976; Polacheck, 1981; Smith, 1980; Wiseman, 1977).

Minority female heads of household suffer a dual disability. Racial or ethnic group membership is second only to education as a predictor of socioeconomic success among female heads of household (Duncan, 1984) due to the influence of the combination of gender and racial discrimination (Schiller, 1989).

Asians

Asian cultural values contribute to self-reliance and a fierce sense of inter-dependence within Asian families. The traditional Asian family is a cohesive extended network, with strong ties of obligation and respect for parents and siblings. These attributes combined with the "self-selection" of better educated immigrants suggest Asians of either gender are less likely to be dependent on public assistance than their non-Asian counterparts (McInnis, 1987; Moulton, 1978; Owan, 1980). Strong devotion to family further suggests that multiple workers may be expected to contribute to the well-being of a family unit in times of economic need.

Asian women have done better than other minority women. Higher education levels, disproportionate representation in professional and technical fields, and small families lead to higher incomes (Owan, 1980; Wong & Hirschman, 1983; Woo, 1985). They possess a less volatile position in the labor market due to their small numbers, a larger proportion of highly skilled immigrants, and geographical concentration in the more prosperous Western states (Leiberson, 1980; Wong & Hirschman, 1983). This optimistic picture, however, neglects several important factors that influence the overall economic well-being of Asian female-headed households.

First, although Asians are concentrated in five prosperous states (California, Illinois, New York, Washington, and Hawaii), these states have the highest costs of living in the country. When controlling for regional variation in the cost of living, Woo (1985) found that Asian women were frequently less well-off than their Euro American counterparts.

Second, Woo (1985) found that Asian women do not earn incomes commensurate with their educational levels when compared to Euro American men and women, even in professional or technical fields with full-time employment. This finding suggests past and present racial discrimination.

Third, any attempt to describe the economic well-being of Asian women that does not desegregate the population into the ethnic groups overlooks critical differences that may help policymakers identify groups that are particularly high risk for poverty. Native versus foreign birth, circumstances surrounding immigration, and unique adaptations to the U.S. economy all influence the economic well-being of Asian female heads of household.

Japanese women, half of whom are native born (McInnis, 1987), are among the most acculturated of Asian women. Interracial marriage rates, the empirical indicator of the permeability of ethnic group boundaries, are the highest for Japanese women, compared to all other Asian groups. The financial support required to emigrate to the United States from Japan further suggests that female heads of household represent a better educated middle-class population.

Chinese, Korean, Filipino, and Asian Indian women have smaller proportions of native born, but faced similar circumstances surrounding immigration. Pre-1965 Asian immigrants were given permission to enter the United States only as needed professional and technical workers or to join family members. Even with the revision of immigration laws in 1965, only Asians with substantial financial resources and marketable labor skills could realistically come to the United States.

Chinese, Japanese, and Asian Indian women preserve a reverential attitude about work and education for all family members, two strong predictors of economic success. A strong commitment to employment combined with the cultural values of helping family members in times of need suggest that these three groups will do well economically on their own strengths, and also suggest that they can be expected to seek the financial support of other family members in lieu of receiving public assistance.

Southeast Asian (Vietnamese, Lao, Cambodian, Khmer, Hmong, and Mao), Hawaiian, and other Asian women are expected to be less successful economically. Although these women may share a cultural commitment to hard work and family, lower levels of human capital may present significant barriers in the labor market.

EMPIRICAL ANALYSIS

The Data Set

The empirical analysis that follows used a subsample of the 5% A-sample of the Public Use Microdata Sample files of the 1980 United States Census of the Population and Housing. Households identified as Japanese, Chinese, Filipino, Korean, Asian Indian, Southeast Asian, Hawaiian, and Other Asian (Pacific Islanders) were included in the subsample. The total sample size was 2,382. Female-headed families classified in the census as subfamilies (those in which a different individual is considered the primary household head) were eliminated because these mothers are primarily young, never married women residing with their parents, 70% of which are above the poverty line (McInnis, 1987).

General descriptive statistics for all Asian female heads and by ethnic category appear in Table 8.1. The category "U.S. Female Heads" refers to the aggregate population of female-headed households in the United States, inclusive of all Euro Americans and non-Euro Americans. These figures are based on previous work by the author from the 1980 U.S. Census and are included for purposes of discussion (McInnis, 1987).

Summary of Descriptive Statistics

Asian women are more frequently "married but separated" than the general population of female heads, 17.1% versus 3.7%, respectively. They become female heads of household more frequently as a result of widowhood rather than divorce or out-of-wedlock pregnancy. In fact, the population of single/never married mothers is very small compared to all female heads (8% versus 17%). Hawaiians are an exception to this observation, with 22% of the sample being single/never married mothers. These figures indicate that Asian women have greater marital stability, a significant factor in reducing the likelihood of poverty (Bane & Ellwood, 1983).

Asian female heads show higher levels of education and higher employment rates than the general population of female heads of household and thus are found more frequently in professional or managerial positions, the highest paying occupations, than female heads in general (16.3% versus 11.6%, respectively). Asian women work more weeks per year and more hours per week.

Despite this strong attachment to the labor force, the poverty rates for Asian versus all female heads is almost identical (44.4% versus 44.9%). The descriptive statistics suggest there is a bipolar distribution of economic well-being within the population of Asian female heads of household. Japanese, Chinese, Asian Indian, Korean, and Filipino women (Group 1) appear to be the most economically stable of the ethnic groups. Southeast Asians, Hawaiians, and Other Asians have a much less stable economic position (Group 2).

Group 1 Asian female heads of household show a smaller number of persons per household, fewer and older children than either the general population of female heads or those in Group 2.

As expected, Group 1 is disproportionately represented in professional-managerial and technical positions. Among Chinese and Korean female heads, however, approximately one-fifth of all female heads are operator-laborers, the lowest paying occupations. This is a larger percentage than even the numbers of women in these occupations in Group 2, the

text continued on page 151

Table 8.1

Asian and Pacific Islander Female Heads of Households

General Descriptive Statistics

Characteristic	All Female Heads	All Asian Female Heads	Group 1						Group 2	
			Japanese	*Chinese*	*Filipino*	*Korean*	*Asian Indian*	*SE/East Asian*	*Hawaiian*	*Other*
Marital Status:										
Married/separated	3.7%	17.1%	8.3%	22.9%	24.4%	20.4%	15.6%	18.1%	6.4%	14.7%
Widowed	11.8	19.1	19.2	23.2	15.2	22.2	18.3	27.4	10.8	18.1
Divorced	45.0	40.0	52.4	37.5	36.8	36.2	49.5	26.4	46.2	32.7
Separated	22.5	15.8	15.4	11.1	15.4	18.6	11.0	20.7	14.5	23.3
Never married	17.0	8.0	4.7	5.3	8.2	2.6	5.6	7.7	22.1	11.2
Total	100.0	100.0	100.0	100.0	100.0	100.0	100.0	100.0	100.0	100.0
Persons in Household:	3.54	3.61	3.00	3.43	3.69	3.24	3.35	4.31	4.04	4.53
Education (yrs):	11.0	11.7	12.7	11.3	13.1	11.0	12.6	8.8	11.7	11.0
8th grade or less	18.1%	15.8%	4.7%	23.2%	11.1%	19.5%	17.4%	38.8%	6.4%	15.5%
Some high school	23.2	12.4	9.6	7.0	9.5	14.0	14.7	15.4	23.3	18.1
High school grad	34.6	33.8	44.8	26.1	24.9	40.2	22.9	22.1	53.8	42.2
Some college	17.3	19.2	25.9	20.2	21.0	12.7	14.7	16.7	12.1	18.2
College grad	6.8	18.8	15.0	23.5	33.5	13.6	30.3	7.0	4.4	6.0
Total	100.0	100.0	100.0	100.0	100.0	100.0	100.0	100.0	100.0	100.0
Number of Children in Household:	2.1	1.96	1.6	1.8	1.9	1.7	1.8	2.4	2.4	2.7
Ages of Children: All under 6 yrs.	18.6%	18.5%	12.6%	14.1%	23.0%	21.3%	15.6%	17.1%	23.3%	24.2%

All 6-18 yrs.	63.9	67.0	77.8	78.0	60.4	70.1	72.5	60.9	54.2	56.0
Both age groups	17.5	14.5	9.6	7.9	16.6	8.6	11.9	22.0	22.5	19.8
Total	100.0	100.0	100.0	100.0	100.0	100.0	100.0	100.0	100.0	100.0
Labor Market Characteristics:										
At work	55.5%	62.9%	69.2%	67.7%	70.9%	71.9%	63.3%	48.5%	47.4%	41.4%
Job/not working	1.8	1.9	1.9	2.4	1.9	1.8	2.7	1.3	2.4	.9
Unemployed	6.3	4.7	4.5	5.6	2.4	5.5	9.2	4.2	5.6	6.0
Not in labor force	36.2	30.5	24.4	24.3	24.8	20.8	24.8	45.8	44.6	51.7
Total	100.0	100.0	100.0	100.0	100.0	100.0	100.0	100.0	100.0	100.0
Mean number of weeks worked in 1979	27.5	30.4	32.9	33.4	34.5	33.8	32.1	21.3	23.8	20.4
Mean number of hours worked in 1979	24.4	27.4	27.6	30.7	31.2	31.3	28.9	20.5	21.6	19.4
Mean number of weeks unemployed in 1979	2.8	2.6	2.2	3.9	2.1	2.9	2.5	3.1	2.9	1.6
Class of worker:										
Never worked	22.9%	17.6%	16.9%	13.5%	10.7%	10.9%	12.8%	30.8%	23.7%	37.1%
Private sector	58.6	61.9	63.0	66.6	67.4	68.3	54.1	54.5	55.4	44.8
Public sector	16.5	16.3	15.4	13.1	18.7	15.4	29.4	11.4	18.8	15.5
Self-employed	.3	2.9	4.5	5.9	2.7	5.4	3.7	2.7	2.1	2.6
Unpaid family worker	1.7	1.3	.2	.9	.5	.0	.0	.6	.0	.0
Total	100.0	100.0	100.0	100.0	100.0	100.0	100.0	100.0	100.0	100.0
Occupation:										
Managerial-Prof.	11.6%	16.3%	18.2%	20.8%	20.6%	13.1%	27.5%	6.0%	10.8%	8.6%
Tech-Sales-Admin.	30.1	27.9	27.1	29.6	37.7	19.9	33.9	13.0	28.9	25.0
Service	16.7	19.4	22.0	11.1	17.6	27.1	9.2	21.4	27.3	14.7
Farm, Forest, Fish	2.4	.7	.4	.3	.7	.5	.9	1.0	2.0	0.0
Production-Craft	2.3	3.0	2.8	4.4	2.6	6.3	1.8	7.0	.4	2.6

continued

Table 8.1
Continued

General Descriptive Statistics

Characteristic	All Female Heads	All Asian Female Heads	Group 1						Group 2	
			Japanese	Chinese	Filipino	Korean	Asian Indian	SE/East Asian	Hawaiian	Other
Operator-Laborer	13.8	14.1	12.4	20.3	9.6	21.3	12.8	30.4	6.9	12.1
No occupation	23.1	18.6	17.1	13.5	11.2	11.8	13.9	31.2	23.7	37.0
Total	100.0	100.0	100.0	100.0	100.0	100.0	100.0	100.0	100.0	100.0
Poverty Status:										
At or below poverty line	44.9%	44.4%	27.7%	29.6%	28.7%	37.1%	31.2%	54.5%	49.4%	51.7%
Immigrant cohort										
Native born		36.2%	48.2%	31.3%	28.2%	5.9%	40.4%	2.3%	98.8%	50.9%
1975-1980		22.8	3.8	24.3	17.4	33.9	14.7	76.3	.4	17.2
1970-1974		17.2	8.8	18.2	22.4	38.5	26.6	16.4	.4	10.3
1965-1969		9.7	10.0	11.1	14.0	12.7	12.8	4.3	.0	9.5
1960-1964		7.2	17.6	5.6	9.0	3.1	2.7	.0	.0	6.9
Total		100.0	100.0	100.0	100.0	100.0	100.0	100.0	100.0	100.0
Number of Cases		2,332	468	341	579	221	109	299	249	116

disadvantaged group. This suggests another bipolar socioeconomic picture within the Korean and Chinese population of female heads of household. The importance of the occupation of the head of household is further supported when poverty rates are compared. Overall, Asians have a poverty rate similar to the general population of female heads. This aggregate rate is due primarily to high poverty rates among the ethnic groups in Group 2. Poverty rates are almost 10% higher for Koreans than Japanese, Chinese, and Filipino heads. The distribution in occupational and educational classifications explains much of this variation.

Group 2 shows the highest percentage in the "no occupation stated" category. This category includes women who have never worked or have not worked long enough in a particular position to establish an occupational identity. Rein and Rainwater (1978) found the ability to state an occupation inversely related to the probability of being in poverty.

More than 70% of all Asian household heads have a high school diploma or better. Group 1 Asian women show the highest educational attainment of all Asian groups, with the largest number of women with college and graduate degrees. Despite an unstable economic picture, 70% of Hawaiians have a high school diploma or better. Hawaii has nearly the highest cost of living and the highest percentage of working women with children. These women often work for low wages in a tourist-agricultural economy and have relatively low welfare payments if not working.

Group 1 women show higher labor force participation, less unemployment, and greater numbers of hours worked per week and weeks worked per year than Group 2 women and the population of all female heads.

Sources of Income

Sources of income for all female heads, all Asian female heads, and specific Asian ethnic groups appear in Table 8.2. Asian women show a greater dollar amount in earnings by head of household than the general population of female heads ($7,011.81 versus $5,509.00) but not a large difference in the percentage of total household income derived from earnings (54.9% and 54.2%, respectively).

The difference in the percentage of total household income derived from public assistance received by the head of household is noteworthy.

Female heads of household in general receive almost 10% of their total income from public assistance, while this figure is only 5.5% for Asian/Pacific Islander female heads of household.

Earnings from other household members are slightly higher for Asians, as opposed to the general population (25.3% versus 22.1%), suggesting a more substantial work effort by others in Asian household units. The percentage of total household income represented by Social Security and other categories is similar between Asian and all female heads.

As was noted in Table 8.1, disaggregation of income sources by ethnic group presents a much more dramatic display of differences (see Table 8.2). Group 1 (Japanese, Chinese, Filipino, Korean, and Asian Indian) women average 15% to 20% more of their total household income derived from earnings than their Group 2 counterparts (Southeast Asians, Hawaiians, and Other Asians). Likewise, Group 2 women average from three to six times the percentage of total household income from public assistance as Group 1 women. Larger families, more out-of-wedlock pregnancy, and low-paying occupations contribute to the need to supplement meager incomes with welfare among Group 2 women. Group 2 women also appear to rely more heavily on the earnings of others in the household than their Group 1 counterparts.

Hawaiian female heads receive almost one-fifth of their total income from public assistance, twice the percentage of female heads in general. Despite their relatively high level of education, educational attainment does not translate into economic stability.

Overall, every Asian group, with the exception of Southeast Asians, has a higher mean total household income than the general population of female heads, indicating that even the most economically disadvantaged of Asian women do better than the aggregate population of female heads of household. For Group 1 Asians, higher earnings by the head of household account for most of the difference. For Group 2 women, earnings may be lower but they appear to supplement earnings with larger amounts of income from public assistance and the earnings of other household members.

INCOME PACKAGING STRATEGIES

The figures reported in the tables that follow are percentages of households showing income from selected sources. The computation of

Table 8.2
Percentage and Amount of Income From Specific Sources by Ethnicity

Source of Income	All Female Heads	All Asian Female Heads	Japanese	Chinese	Group 1 Filipino	Korean	Asian Indian	SE/East Asian	Group 2 Hawaiian	Other	ETA-SQ
From Head of Household:											
Earnings/Assets	$5,509.00	$7,011.81	$7,620.10	$8,245.06	$8,173.49	$7,398.85	$8,656.33	$4,013.77	$4,702.03	$4,334.91	.0479
	(54.2%)	(54.9%)	(59.2%)	(62.4%)	(56.9%)	(66.5%)	(58.9%)	(40.5%)	(44.5%)	(42.6%)	
Social Security	241.20	235.69	327.51	251.03	216.69	153.71	261.38	72.17	172.21	183.32	.0071
	(2.4%)	(1.9%)	(2.5%)	(1.9%)	(1.4%)	(1.4%)	(1.8%)	(.7%)	(1.6%)	(1.8%)	
Public Assistance	1,006.04	706.89	497.29	386.36	617.28	337.74	489.82	1,246.15	1,896.35	1,296.08	.0734
	(9.9%)	(5.5%)	(3.9%)	(2.9%)	(4.3%)	(3.0%)	(3.3%)	(12.7%)	(18.1%)	(12.7%)	
Other	889.76	1,298.38	1,674.70	909.96	766.84	964.48	865.87	437.73	514.96	721.17	.0175
	(8.7%)	(10.2%)	(13.0%)	(6.9%)	(5.3%)	(8.7%)	(5.9%)	(4.4%)	(4.9%)	(7.1%)	
From Other Household Members:											
Earnings/Assets	2,247.76	3,237.12	2,445.75	3,180.26	4,348.46	2,107.01	4,091.79	3,699.18	1,766.20	3,410.78	.0107
	(22.1%)	(25.3%)	(19.0%)	(24.1%)	(30.3%)	(18.9%)	(27.8%)	(37.4%)	(26.4%)	(35.5%)	
Social Security	161.01	153.48	220.35	172.21	96.58	87.22	208.81	144.25	199.18	88.84	.0048
	(1.6%)	(1.2%)	(1.7%)	(1.3%)	(.7%)	(.8%)	(1.4%)	(1.5%)	(1.9%)	(.9%)	
Public Assistance	116.35	126.81	98.72	72.00	154.86	83.89	121.51	280.57	228.45	149.96	.0090
	(1.1%)	(1.0%)	(.7%)	(.5%)	(1.1%)	(.8%)	(.8%)	(2.8%)	(2.2%)	(1.5%)	
Total Household Income	1,0171.12	1,2770.18	1,2879.33	1,3216.88	1,4374.20	1,1132.90	1,4695.51	9,903.82	1,0479.38	1,0185.06	.0236
	(100.0%)	(100.0%)	(100.0%)	(100.0%)	(100.0%)	(100.0%)	(100.0%)	(100.0%)	(100.0%)	(100.0%)	
Number of cases	—	2382	468	341	579	221	109	299	249	116	

percentages identifies the prevalence of each of these income packaging strategies, in addition to the dollar amounts reported in Table 8.2.

Income packaging strategies are divided into three general categories. The first category is referred to as households using employment-intensive strategies. These strategies are those in which:

(1) Only the head of household works.
(2) The head of household works and a nonworking adult is present in the household to serve as a potential child-care giver, although it cannot be determined whether the nonworking adult actually provides child care.
(3) The head of household and other members of the household work.

The second category is defined by households using welfare-intensive strategies. Welfare is defined as any means-tested cash transfer program. Welfare-intensive strategies include:

(1) A nonworking head of household who receives welfare and may be receiving non-employment income (this may include the earnings of other household members.)
(2) The head of household combines work and welfare.
(3) Welfare is the sole source of income.

The third income packaging strategy is identified as non-employment/non-welfare packaging. Income in these households is derived from social insurance payments, alimony, child support and/or unemployment benefits. These categories are not intended to be mutually exclusive.

Employment-Intensive Strategies

Column 1 of Table 8.3 shows the percentage of households showing income from an employed head of household. Japanese, Korean, Chinese, Filipino, and Asian Indian women have a greater percentage of households with employed heads than the general population of female heads. Substantially fewer female heads are employed among Southeast Asian, Hawaiian, and Other Asian women, not surprising in view of the low employment incomes noted in Table 8.2.

Overall, there is no clear pattern indicating that either native-born or foreign-born heads consistently show greater work effort when results are examined on the basis of nativity. The Cramers V indicates that the disaggregation of the population on the basis of ethnic groups is a more

Table 8.3

Percentage of Households Showing Employment-Intensive Strategies by Ethnic Group and Nativity

	(1) Percentage of Households With a Working Head			(2) Percentage of Households With a Working Head With Nonworking Adult in Home			(3) Percentage of Households With a Working Head With Multiple Household Workers		
	Native	Foreign	C.	Native	Foreign	C.	Native	Foreign	C.
All Female Heads	67.1%	69.5%	.01006	59.1%	70.1%	.05404	74.8%	76.4%	.00800
All Asian Heads	73.1	79.2	.07068	74.1	79.9	.16949	79.7	84.4	.06036
Japanese	83.6	76.1	.09183	70.4	70.6	.00237	91.7	82.4	.13676
Chinese	90.6	78.3	.14656	83.3	75.9	.06710	90.9	88.4	.03487
Filipino	71.2	83.7	.14078	85.0	87.8	.03213	74.2	84.9	.12500
Korean	100.0	81.7	.11319	100.0	92.9	.04222	100.0	87.5	.10758
Asian Indian	75.0	81.5	.07838	70.0	83.3	.15842	63.6	85.7	.24604
Southeast Asian	42.9	55.5	.03838	33.3	48.3	.05362	0.0	62.9	.11959
Hawaiian	61.4	100.0	.08674	54.3	—	—	73.6	100.0	.08743
Other	49.2	50.9	.01724	25.0	38.9	.14430	57.9	60.9	.03017
Cramers V:									
By Ethnic Group—All			.24326			.3952			.2394
By Ethnic Group—Native-Born			.28762			.3688			.2886
By Ethnic Group—Foreign-Born			.25870			.4027			.2526

powerful explanatory factor than nativity. In other words, differences between Japanese and Koreans are the product of membership in these ethnic groups rather than the result of native versus foreign birth.

Column 2 of Table 8.3 shows the percentage of households in which the household head works and a nonworking adult is present. It is expected that the presence of a nonworking adult as a potential caregiver would increase the frequency of working heads among Asian heads of household.

The figures for the general population of female heads indicates that 60% of native-born and 70% of foreign-born extended households have a working head, but these figures do not suggest that the presence of a nonworking adult in the household increases the frequency of a working head. Differences between ethnic groups account for almost 40% of the variation observed in this income packaging strategy.

Column 3 of Table 8.3 examines an additional income packaging strategy—the presence of a working head and multiple household workers. Among female heads in general, three-quarters of households with a working head also show income from other workers. This suggests that if a woman works, it is likely that there will be other workers in the household. More than 90% of Japanese and Chinese households with a working head also show income from the earnings of other workers. An employed head of household may, by her example, encourage work by others in the household.

In a previous work by this author, working foreign-born heads of households consistently showed a greater prevalence of multiple household workers (McInnis, 1987). This pattern does not hold true of Asian women. Native-born Japanese, Chinese, and Koreans show greater use of multiple household workers than their foreign-born counterparts. Among the remaining groups, foreign-born heads use multiple workers more frequently than native-born heads, suggesting that foreign-born heads may expect more in terms of work effort when faced with economic need. Ethnic group disaggregation accounts for almost one-quarter of the variation observed (Cramers V = .24326) and is more powerful in explaining the variation for native-born (Cramers V = .28762) than for foreign-born (Cramers V = .25870) heads.

Welfare-Intensive Strategies

Column 1 in Table 8.4 displays the percentage of households in which public assistance payments are received by the head of household.

Table 8.4

Percentages of Households Using Welfare-Intensive Strategies by Ethnic Group and Nativity

	(1) Percentage of Households Receiving Welfare			(2) Percentage of Households Combining Work and Welfare			(3) Percentage of Households With Welfare as Sole Income		
	Native	Foreign	C.	Native	Foreign	C.	Native	Foreign	C.
All U.S. Female Heads	38.2%	25.1	.11485	11.3%	8.2%	.2020	3.1%	5.1%	.02365
All Asian Heads	28.0	13.2	.18155	12.1	6.3	.10207	14.3	10.4	.04161
Japanese	14.2	14.8	.0084	6.2	7.0	.01554	1.8	5.8	.10295
Chinese	12.3	12.3	.0010	6.6	4.7	.02977	2.8	8.9	.11049
Filipino	35.0	11.1	.27071	14.7	6.5	.12955	2.5	5.3	.06144
Korean	23.1	12.0	.07798	23.1	8.2	.12133	0.0	6.7	.06488
Asian Indian	29.5	7.7	.028876	13.6	1.5	.23533	2.3	6.2	.09065
Southeast Asian	0.0	39.0	.12065	0.0	13.0	.05898	0.0	9.6	.16281
Hawaiian	45.5	0.0	.09935	17.5	0.0	.05039	3.3	0.0	.02012
Other	42.5	35.1	.07453	11.9	7.0	.08242	6.8	12.3	.09346

Cramers V:

By Ethnic Group—All	.28414	.12115	.10034
By Ethnic Group—Native-Born	.30624	.15296	.21855
By Ethnic Group—Foreign-Born	.29282	.11325	.07734

Almost 40% of native-born heads receive welfare compared to only 25.1% of all foreign-born heads in the U. S. population of female heads. This pattern is consistent among Asians as well, with the exception of Southeast Asians, Hawaiians, and Other Asians. Although for Chinese and Japanese the difference is minimal, native-born Filipino women show three times the amount of public assistance utilization as their foreign-born sisters. Native-born Asian Indians use four times more public assistance than their foreign-born counterparts. Direct comparisons are difficult for Southeast Asians and Hawaiians, in part due to their small numbers. The Cramers V for both general racial disaggregation and within immigration cohorts indicates that ethnic category explains almost one-third of the variance observed in the utilization of public assistance.

Ethnic group is less powerful, however, in explaining the differences observed in the work and welfare combination income package (See Column 2, Table 8.4). Japanese and Chinese women show a smaller percentage of households with work and welfare combination incomes, the effect of the small numbers of households that receive welfare at all. If a Japanese, Chinese, or Filipino household receives any welfare, almost one-half of those households combine welfare with employment, a much greater percentage than other groups. Among native-born Koreans, all heads combine welfare and work, if they receive welfare at all.

The small numbers of native-born Southeast Asians and foreign-born Hawaiians make comparisons based on nativity difficult for these groups. However, approximately one-third of foreign-born Southeast Asians and native-born Hawaiians supplement welfare with earnings, similar to the pattern of female heads in general.

The extent to which "welfare only" income packaging strategies are used is somewhat surprising (See Column 3, Table 8.4). Among all foreign-born Asians, if the head receives welfare, it is more frequently the sole source of income than for native-born Asians and female heads in general. This indicates that although public assistance utilization is low among this population, those who do receive public assistance are those least successful in combining assistance with other sources to improve their economic well-being.

Non-Welfare/Non-Employment Strategies

Table 8.5 shows the percentage of households who receive income from non-welfare/non-employment sources. These sources include child

Table 8.5

Percentage of Households Showing Income From Non-Earnings,
Non-Welfare Sources by Ethnic Group and Nativity

Ethnic Group	Native	Foreign	C.
All Female Heads	28.3%	27.8%	.01823
Asians:			
All Heads	31.1	28.7	.02571
Japanese	35.6	35.0	.00602
Chinese	37.7	20.9	.17519
Filipinos	18.4	21.6	.03581
Koreans	15.4	18.3	.01763
Asian Indians	20.5	23.1	.03104
Southeast Asians	0.0	17.1	.06921
Hawaiians	17.5	0.0	.05039
Other Asians	18.6	10.5	.11400
Cramers V:			
By Ethnic Group—All	.16148		
By Ethnic Group—Native Born	.21137		
By Ethnic Group—Foreign-Born	.15212		

support, social insurance, alimony, and unemployment benefits. Unfortunately, the census does not distinguish the sources of income included in this category. Japanese and Chinese native-born female heads appear to be more successful in procuring income from these sources than any other ethnic or nativity group. All other Asians receive less than female heads in general.

This analysis is included primarily because of the research interest in the receipt of child support payments by female heads of household. Although this category includes sources of income other than child support payments from an absent father, the figures in Table 8.5 do indicate that "other sources" provide income for only one-fifth to one-third of Asian female heads of household. Even if child support were the only source included in this figure, it would indicate that not only does the "other income" category constitute a small portion of total household income but also that few households derive income from this source. This suggests that, with the exception of Japanese and Chinese households, child support is not a major source of income and is not obtained in proportion to the numbers of divorced and separated female heads of household.

In general, Japanese, Chinese, Korean, Filipino, and Asian Indian women are the most economically stable of Asian women. This is due to higher levels of education, more work effort, and smaller families. Southeast Asians, Hawaiians, and Other Asians are among the most severely disadvantaged groups of all female heads, regardless of nativity. This is apparently due to poor human capital, concentration in low-paying occupations, and limited labor force participation. Although these groups represent a relatively small percentage of female heads in general, they represent a population very similar to other disadvantaged minorities, such as Hispanics and African Americans. Therefore, any recommendations for policy must address issues that affect all low-income female heads, including Asian heads of household, regardless of racial or ethnic group or nativity.

ECONOMIC CHOICES FOR
FEMALE HEADS OF HOUSEHOLD

Based on these findings, the economic choices for female heads of household are summarized in Table 8.6. In Columns 1 and 2, the economic choices available to female heads of household have been identified. Column 3 identifies those elements of public policy intervention that are necessary to support and maximize these economic choices.[1]

A woman becomes a female head of household through divorce, widowhood, or an out-of-wedlock pregnancy. If she has sufficient independent resources (i.e., investment income, Social Security, child support or other non-employment income), seeking employment is a true choice, not a necessity (See Table 8.6). For a majority of female heads of household, the choices are not as clear-cut. If a woman has sufficient human capital to command a wage high enough to support her children, full-time employment is a viable strategy.

These two economic choices (Choices 1 and 2 in Table 8.6) are those most frequently made by Japanese, Chinese, Korean, Asian Indian, and Filipino women. This choice is made possible primarily because of the high levels of education attained by these women.

Combination incomes, represented by Choices 3 and 4, are used less frequently by these women but do represent an alternate that maximizes employment effort and minimizes welfare use. Southeast Asian, Hawaiian, and Other Asian women appear to be less able to contribute substantial

Table 8.6

Economic Choices and Policy Consideration for Female Heads of Households

Woman's Situation	Economic Choices	Policy Consideration
1. Has sufficient non-employment income to support self and children.	Employment optional but not required.	Continued child support enforcement.
2. Has high level of human capital and strong labor force attachment.	Full-time employment (with child care). Supplement income with child support.	Affordable, quality child care. Continued child support enforcement.
3. Has low to moderate human capital due to little education or experience.	Seek and retain employment.	Adult education.
	Supplement work with child support.	Continued child support enforcement.
		Affordable, quality child care.
	Supplement earnings with welfare.	Restore work incentive to AFDC.
4. Has low to moderate human capital but lives in extended family.	Seek and retain employment.	Adult education.
	Supplement work with child support and earnings of family.	Continued child support enforcement.
		Affordable, quality child care.
	Supplement work with welfare.	Restore work incentive to AFDC.
5. Cannot work due to size of family or disability.	Welfare. Child Support.	Continued child support enforcement.

amounts of income from their own employment, and they therefore rely more heavily on public assistance and the earnings of others (if living in extended households).

It is apparent from Table 8.6 that none of these income packaging strategies can be successful without the existence of affordable and quality child care and/or enforcement of child support obligations from the absent parent. Even the provision of adult training programs will be minimally effective if no child care is available or if welfare benefits are taxed at 100% with employment.

If a woman cannot work at all due to the size of her family or a disability, her choices are limited. She can rely on child support if it has been awarded and can be collected. Or, she can rely on public assistance, which guarantees that she and her children will live below the poverty line.

Employment-intensive strategies obviously lead to economic success, while welfare-intensive strategies lead to a reduced level of economic well-being.

IMPLICATIONS FOR SOCIAL WELFARE POLICY

Social welfare policymakers must set goals that will help all ethnic minority women achieve some level of economic well-being. This research has shown the common perception—that Asian women, like their male counterparts, are economically successful—to be true for only a small portion of the Asian population. Asian female heads of household face formidable obstacles in their struggle to support families on limited income. The suggestions for social policy discussed below pertain to all ethnic minority women.

In the economic choices model, women with high levels of human capital are the only ones who can hope to support their children at a level above the poverty line. Therefore, the first policy goal is to enhance the human capital of female heads of household. This must focus not only on obtaining employment for female heads of household but also on improving the kinds of employment they obtain. More than two-thirds of female heads work, yet one-half remain below the poverty line (Bane & Ellwood, 1983). The problem therefore is not a resistance to work, but the inability to work sufficient hours or command a wage high enough to move out of poverty. For Asian women, this situation is further complicated by the effect of racism and discrimination in the employment market. Southeast Asian, Hawaiian, and Other Asian, along with Hispanic and African American women, need to become target groups for human capital enhancement programs designed and executed in close cooperation with business and industry in the geographical area in which target women live. Jobs must be developed and maintained in the private sector to insure long-term viability. Nontraditional secondary education programs are necessary for teenage mothers who may have dropped out of high school to have and care for children. Unless these young women return to school and at least earn a high school diploma, their economic choices in the future will be limited to public assistance.

A second goal of public policy must focus on child care. Even if mothers are able to secure employment, without convenient and affordable child care, it is unrealistic to expect that they will work even part-time. Child care options include both the direct provision of subsidized child care and tax incentives that make child care more cost-effective for middle and working-class mothers. Subsidized child care is most crucial for moderate and low wage earners, who will never earn enough to stay above poverty and pay for the child care they need.

A third goal of social welfare policy pertains to the reinstatement of the work incentives that were eliminated under the Omnibus Reconciliation Act of 1981 (OBRA). The 1980 U. S. census data used in this analysis were collected prior to OBRA. Therefore, it is assumed that the number of female heads of household in the data set who indicated work and welfare combination incomes may be higher in this analysis than currently exists. Other research that has followed up on the well-being of AFDC mothers affected by the elimination of work incentives has found that many recipients did not stop work immediately to retain their benefits (Hutchens, 1984; Moffitt, 1984). However, their economic well-being declined significantly. With the reinstatement of a work incentive for AFDC recipients, an ongoing attachment to the labor force by female heads would be encouraged.

Retention of medical assistance benefits would protect the welfare of the children of part-time employed heads, those usually not eligible for employer-provided health care. The Family Support Act of 1988 has made a one-year extension of medical assistance possible for recipients who leave the program for employment. It is unlikely that one year of employment in a low-wage job will make women eligible for employer-sponsored health insurance. Government-subsidized health insurance must be made available for longer than one year or female heads will return to AFDC for medical insurance benefits. Such behavior would defeat the intent of extending medical assistance benefits.

The fourth and final policy focus is on a rigorous and comprehensive support of court-mandated child support payments. Less than one-half of all women awarded child support in divorce settlements actually receive support from the non-custodial parent (Garfinkel, 1982, 1983). Given that only one-half of these women receive the full amount, consistent enforcement is indicated.

Child support payments will not eliminate the need for AFDC, but will certainly reduce the proportion of public welfare funds currently being spent on dependent children whose non-custodial parents can provide financial support. The Family Support Act of 1988 requires that states make concerted efforts to collect delinquent child support payments for women receiving AFDC. This is a valuable first step but needs to be extended to benefit women who do not receive AFDC, yet are entitled to child support payments.

CONCLUSIONS

Asian female heads of household are excellent examples of the ability of female heads to survive economically if adequately prepared for the labor force. The direct connection between marketable human capital, greater labor force participation, and less welfare is graphically illustrated. Although ethnic minority status may create a dual disability for some female heads, human capital can partially compensate for the disadvantages of ethnic minority status. Until the issue of enhancing human capital is addressed by social welfare policy, disadvantaged groups, such as Southeast Asians, Hawaiians, and Other Asians, will continue to remain poor.

Adequate and publicly subsidized child care, adult training programs tied to local industry, and the reinstatement of the work incentive are offered as additional recommendations to both enhance human capital and encourage labor force participation. Enforcing child support obligations of the non-custodial parent would relieve some of the financial pressures placed on female heads of household. It would also reaffirm the legal obligation of both parents to provide financial support for their children.

Asian women have been more successful than most female heads of household in attaining financial well-being. Clearly, their ability to compete successfully in the labor market as well as tap a wide variety of income sources to comprise their income package accounts in part for this success.

NOTE

1. Use of the term *choices* does not imply that these options are necessarily voluntary, but rather suggests a number of variations in economic behavior for female heads of household.

REFERENCES

Bane, M. J., & Ellwood, D. (1983). *The dynamics of dependence: The routes to self sufficiency* (Mimeograph). Cambridge, MA: Urban Systems Research & Engineering, Inc.

Bumpass, L., & Sweet, J. A. (1981). *A demographic perspective on the poverty population* (Discussion paper 669-681). Madison: Institute for Research on Poverty, University of Wisconsin-Madison.

Duncan, G. J. (Ed.) (1984). *Years of poverty, years of plenty.* Ann Arbor: University of Michigan, Institute for Social Research.

Featherman, D. L. (1971). The socioeconomic achievement of white religio-ethnic subgroups: Social and psychological explanations. *American Sociological Review, 36*, 207-222.

Ferber, M. A. (1982) Women and work: Issues of the 1980's. *Signs: Journal of Women in Culture and Society, 8*(2), 273-295.

Garfinkel, I. (1982). *The role of child support in antipoverty policy* (Discussion Paper 713-782). Madison: Institute for Research on Poverty, University of Wisconsin-Madison.

Garfinkel, I. (1983). *Evaluation design for child support demonstration* (Discussion Paper 714-782). Madison: Institute for Research on Poverty, University of Wisconsin-Madison.

Hutchens, R. (1984). *The effects of the Omnibus Budget Reconciliation Act of 1981 on AFDC recipients: A review of studies* (Discussion Paper 764-784). Madison: Institute for Research on Poverty, University of Wisconsin-Madison.

Leiberson, S. (1980). *A piece of the pie.* Berkeley: University of California Press.

McEaddy, B. J. (1976). Women who head families: A socioeconomic analysis. *Monthly Labor Review, 99*(6), 3-9.

McInnis, K. M. (1987). *Income packaging strategies among native and foreign born female heads of household.* Unpublished doctoral dissertation, University of Wisconsin-Madison.

Moffitt, R. (1984). *Assessing the effects of the 1981 federal AFDC legislation on the work effort of women heading households* (Discussion Paper 724A-84). Madison: Institute for Research on Poverty, University of Wisconsin-Madison.

Moulton, D. (1978). The socioeconomic status of Asian families in five major SMSA's. In *Summary and recommendations: Conference on Pacific and Asian American families.* Washington, DC: Government Printing Office.

Oberheu, H. (1982). *1979 AFDC recipients characteristics study.* Washington, DC: U. S. Social Security Administration.

Owan, T. (1980). *Asian Americans: A case of benighted neglect* (Occasional Paper Number 1). Chicago: Asian American Mental Health Research Center.

Polacheck, S. W. (1981). Occupational self-selection: A human capital approach to sex differences in occupational structure. *Review of Economics and Statistics, 63*(1), 60-69.

Rein, M., & Rainwater, L. (1978). Patterns of welfare use. *Social Service Review, 52*(4), 511-534.

Schiller, B. (1989). *The economics of poverty and discrimination.* Englewood Cliffs, NJ: Prentice-Hall.

Smith, J. P. (Ed.). (1980). *Female labor supply.* Princeton, NJ: Princeton University Press.

U. S. Bureau of the Census (1983). *The 1980 U. S. census: General economic characteristics, part 1* (U.S. Summary PC-80-1-Cl.) Washington, DC: Government Printing Office.

Wallace, P., Datcher, L., & Malveaux, J. (1980). *Black women in the labor force.* Cambridge: MIT Press.

Wiseman, M. (1977). *Change and turnover in a welfare population.* Berkeley: University of California Press.

Wong, M. G., & Hirschman, C. (1983). Labor force participation and socioeconomic attainment of Asian-American women. *Sociological Perspectives, 26*(4), 423-446.

Woo, D. (1985). The socioeconomic status of Asian American women in the labor force. *Sociological Perspectives, 23*(3), 307-338.

Chapter 9

POLICY IMPLICATIONS OF FACTORS ASSOCIATED WITH ECONOMIC SELF-SUFFICIENCY OF SOUTHEAST ASIAN REFUGEES

CHI KWONG LAW
LEONARD SCHNEIDERMAN

The term *refugee* is defined in the 1980 Refugee Act as someone outside his country of nationality who is unwilling or unable to return to that country "because of persecution or a well-founded fear of persecution on account of race, religion, nationality, membership in a particular social group, or political opinion" and who is not firmly resettled in any foreign country. The Act limits admission to those refugees "of special humanitarian concern" to the United States.

Southeast Asian refugees form the largest group of Asian immigrants to the United States in recent years. More than 700,000 Southeast Asian refugees were admitted to the United States between 1975 and 1985. They bring into American society new cultural elements, and their experience of assimilation provides new insight into how recently arrived immigrants integrate into the host society. In this chapter, we shall examine one particular aspect of assimilation—economic assimilation. This chapter reports findings from the literature and data taken from a study of the Aid for Families with Dependent Children (AFDC) population in Los Angeles County.

In this chapter, the term *refugees* indicates refugees in general. The term *Southeast Asian refugees* is used whenever this refugee group is referred to specifically. This is not to imply either that all refugees are Southeast Asian refugees or that Southeast Asian refugees form one homogeneous group. It should be noted that there are many different nationality and ethnic groups of Southeast Asian refugees, including Lao, Cambodians, Vietnamese, ethnic Chinese, Hmong, and others. The experience of each national and ethnic group in the United States deserves more attention than what can be provided in this chapter.

THE REFUGEE RESETTLEMENT PROGRAM

The stated goal of the Refugee Resettlement Program is to promote *economic self-sufficiency*, within the *shortest possible time* after a refugee enters a state, through the planned and coordinated use of support services, with cash and medical assistance as transitional aid where necessary. This chapter examines conceptual and policy issues related to the two major aspects of this goal, namely, *economic self-sufficiency* and *shortest possible time*.

Under the existing policy, the federal government assumes the full cost of cash assistance to refugees eligible for AFDC, SSI (Supplemental Security Income), and General Assistance for the first 31 months under a 100% reimbursement arrangement with the state and local government. Refugees not eligible for this program are entitled to Refugee Cash Assistance during the first 18 months after their arrival. Apparently, the federal government intends to assist refugees over the period required to reduce welfare dependency ratios to those of non-refugees. Can refugees, and Southeast Asian refugees in particular, reduce welfare dependency ratios to those of non-refugees within 31 months? This chapter provides some answers to this question.

To understand how to promote economic self-sufficiency within the shortest possible time, we need to look at the factors that account for variation in economic self-sufficiency of the refugees and to identify which of these factors are amenable to programmatic solutions. Furthermore, there has been continuous debate on the appropriateness of providing cash assistance to the refugees through the existing AFDC structure. Data drawn from the Los Angeles County AFDC population will shed some light on this issue.

Table 9.1
Welfare Dependency and Poverty Level in Summer 1982
for Southeast Asian Refugees (Entered United States after October 1978)

	Dependency on welfare		
	Totally dependent	*Partially dependent*	*Not dependent*
Number of samples	482	354	271
Sufficiency			
below poverty	64%	28%	12%
above poverty	36%	72%	88%
Total	100%	100%	100%

ECONOMIC SELF-SUFFICIENCY

Haines (1983) considered that economic self-sufficiency denotes the ability of people to meet their own financial needs through their own efforts. In the California State Plan for Refugees in 1987, economic self-sufficiency is defined as gainful employment in a non-subsidized job and receipt of a wage adequate for the basic economic needs of the person and family without reliance on public assistance.

There are two related concepts within economic self-sufficiency, namely, *dependency* and *sufficiency*. In terms of dependency, a refugee may have (a) no income and rely on welfare benefits, or (b) some earned income but still rely partly on welfare benefits, or (c) earned income and be off welfare. In other words, dependency on public assistance can be total, partial, or nil.

Defining sufficiency in terms of meeting one's own financial needs or being adequate for the basic economic needs of the person and family is still quite vague. Operationally, sufficiency can be defined as having an income above poverty level as defined by the federal government.

Bringing the two operational definitions together, we have six categories that can be illustrated using the data collected by the Institute for Social Research in the summer of 1982 (Caplan, Whitemore, & Bui, 1985). In a survey of Southeast Asian refugees arriving after October 1978, the Institute for Social Research obtained the figures presented in Table 9.1.

We note that among those totally dependent on welfare, 64% were living below the poverty level. On the other hand, among those who did not depend on welfare at all, 88% were living above the poverty level. Yet, this group constitutes only 22% of the total sample. Thus, the ultimate goal of promoting economic self-sufficiency is for all refugees to move out from *total dependency on welfare and living below the poverty level* to *not depending on welfare and living above the poverty level*.

THE SHORTEST POSSIBLE TIME

Within the context of the Refugee Resettlement Program, shortest possible time simply means the shortest time that is possible for the refugees to achieve economic self-sufficiency. However, it depends on how long the accounting period is to assess whether a refugee is self-sufficient.

Placing refugees into the labor market as soon as they can find a job would reduce dependency, but may or may not bring about sufficiency, depending on the wage they receive. The wage may be so low that it does not help to lift the refugee family above the poverty line. There may be little chance for advancement, and the refugee may live in poverty for an extended period of time. Moreover, due to job insecurity, the refugee may return for welfare assistance periodically. If a program can place refugees in employment at a high rate, such as 80% in the first year, and yet most of those placed in jobs return for welfare assistance within a month or so, it cannot be claimed that the program is truly successful.

Thus, the shortest possible time should not be defined with respect to measurements such as how fast a refugee can be placed on a job, or how soon a refugee leaves the welfare roll. On the other hand, it may not be possible for all refugees to become self-sufficient all of the time. Shortest possible time can be measured by the time required for an "average refugee" to achieve what an "average American" can achieve. In other words, it is the time required by the refugees as a group to achieve the same proportion of their population living above poverty as that of the general population in the United States.

DURATION REQUIRED TO ACHIEVE ECONOMIC SELF-SUFFICIENCY

There are research studies that attempt to answer the question of how long it takes a refugee to achieve economic self-sufficiency. Most studies, including those quoted below, do not single out the effects of the existing support services and welfare benefits when attempting to estimate duration. In other words, if a research study finds that it takes a refugee 5 years to become self-sufficient, this fact of "5 years" is confounded with the effects of existing support services and welfare benefits that are available to refugees in general. Without these services, the refugees might take much longer to become economically self-sufficient. In spite of this limitation, we will examine the existing evidence on how long it takes a refugee to become economically self-sufficient, taking into account the current levels of support services and welfare benefits.

Bach and Bach (1980) analyzed the Immigration and Naturalization Service data and observed that 58% of the 1975 arrivals reported having a job, and the rate was virtually the same as the employment rate found among the general U.S. population in the same month. They concluded that employment increases significantly with time in the United States, and perhaps it would take only 3 years for most refugees to reduce any dependency on public assistance. It is noted that the *3 years* period suggested by Bach refers to leaving dependency but not necessarily achieving sufficiency, let alone that *obtaining employment* means *leaving welfare dependency totally*.

Based on data collected by various U.S. government departments, Baker and North (1984) concluded that the 1975 Southeast Asian refugees would reach the employment-population ratio (approximately 60%) of other Americans in 5 years. Yet, *5 years* is still an optimistic estimate. In general, subsequent waves of Southeast Asian refugees have fewer years of education completed and a lower level of English proficiency than earlier Southeast Asian refugees (ORR annual reports); therefore, the time required by these waves of Southeast Asian refugees to reach the employment-population ratios of other Americans would conceivably be much longer. This point can be illustrated by the contrast between the time required by different cohorts to achieve labor participation rates comparable to that of the U.S. general population.

Table 9.2

Percentage Below Poverty by Period in United States

Number of Years in United States	Percent Below Poverty Level
1	67
2	57
3	43
4	30
5	18 (projected)
6	6 (projected)
U. S. population	15

The Office of Refugee Resettlement (ORR) Report to the Congress in 1982 indicated that the labor participation rates of those Southeast Asian refugees arriving in the United States in or before 1978 surpassed that of the U.S. general population in about 4 years. But the labor participation rates of the 1980 and 1981 cohorts at their 5th year in the United States were still 10% and 20% below those of the U. S. general population in 1985 and 1986, respectively (ORR, 1986, 1987).

The empirical evidence collected in the studies mentioned above focuses primarily on the employment ratios instead of occupational status or earned income. However, refugees, like other types of immigrants, suffer downward occupation movement in their beginning years in the new country, and they usually earn less than native-born Americans with a comparable level of education and years of working experience. Following this logic, one would expect that the percentage of Southeast Asian refugees falling below the poverty line would still be larger than that of other Americans, even when they have reached the employment-population ratios of other Americans. This point can be illustrated in Table 9.2, using the results obtained in the Institute for Social Research study (Caplan et al., 1985) mentioned earlier.

Unfortunately, the Institute for Social Research study collected information only on those who entered the United States within a 4-year period. However, if we extrapolate the numbers, we would expect that the percentage of Southeast Asian refugee households living below poverty would be approximately equal to that of the U. S. population at around the 6th year.

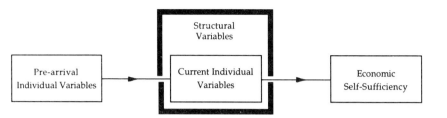

Figure 9.1. Factors Affecting Economic Self-Sufficiency

Another source of information is research literature on the analysis of the income of immigrants. Chiswick (1978), in one of his most frequently quoted studies on the earnings of foreign-born adult white men, found that the age-earnings profile of immigrants crosses the age-earnings profile of native-born Americans about 10 to 15 years after immigration. One would expect that the time required by Asian refugees would be even longer due to language and cultural barriers.

In light of the evidence gathered so far, the estimation of the average time for a Southeast Asian refugee to become economically self-sufficient is far from being accurately known. The 31-month arrangement in the cash assistance program is probably too short. It may take 5 years or even 10 to 15 years for Southeast Asian refugees to become economically self-sufficient at the same level as the general population. By using the celeration line approach (Bloom & Fisher, 1982), we can expect that the average time required for Southeast Asian refugees to become economically self-sufficient is 6 years (Table 9.2).

FACTORS AFFECTING ECONOMIC
SELF-SUFFICIENCY

A review of the research literature suggests a large number of factors related to the economic assimilation of refugees in the United States (Law, 1988). These factors can be broadly classified into structural and individual factors, as presented in Figure 9.1; and the list of relevant variables for structural and individual factors is provided in Table 9.3.

Pre-arrival characteristics of refugees, such as their cultural background, are important but not amenable. The provision of English and

Table 9.3

Factors Affecting Economic Self-Sufficiency

Structural Variables Characteristics	Individual Variables	
	Pre-Arrival Characteristics	Current
Site of resettlement	Previous education	Household composition
Welfare benefits levels	Previous occupation	Age
& eligibility standard	Previous work experience	Sex
Availability of services	Arrival English	English proficiency
child care	Urban/rural background	Enrollment in ESL
public transportation	Trauma of war & escape	Vocational training
social support services		Employment
Ethnic community services		Migration
Race relations within U.S.		Car ownership
		Health status
		Motivation to acculturate
		Family member
		left behind

vocational training in the asylum camp and participation in camp activities are important to the adjustment of refugees in the host country (Boesen, 1985; Clark, 1986). These factors are primarily relevant to the planning of overseas refugee programs. Variables such as age, education received in their country of origin, and sex of the refugees cannot be altered by any programmatic means.

The length of time the refugee has spent in the United States is consistently found to be one of the most significant variables accounting for the variation in economic self-sufficiency. However, the variable of time in the United States includes the effects of various events that occur as time passes, such as acquiring English proficiency, familiarizing oneself with the employment structure of the community, establishing social networks that help to find employment, and even having young children grow older and enter school, thereby freeing an adult to enter the labor market. For policy and service considerations, we would be more concerned with what happens or does not happen in the adjustment process of the refugees.

Within the limited scope of this chapter, we shall focus on factors the domestic Refugee Resettlement Program aims to influence: English proficiency, vocational skills, access to the labor market, and welfare benefits.

English Proficiency

English proficiency at the time the refugee enters the U. S. (Caplan et al., 1985; Downing, Hendricks, Mason, & Olney, 1984) and the current level of English proficiency (Aames, Aames, Jung, & Karabenick, 1977; ORR, 1982-1987) account for a significant portion of variation in different measures of economic self-sufficiency. According to the ORR annual reports, while 32% of the 1975 Southeast Asian refugees spoke English well or fluently at the time of arrival, the percentage dropped below 10% for subsequent waves.

In a study conducted by the authors on a sample of 108 refugees out of a total of 1,046 AFDC recipients as of the end of June 1986, in Los Angeles County, 62% of the refugees did not speak any English, as compared to only 5% of the other AFDC recipients (Schneiderman, Furman, & Law, 1988). Moreover, of those who had looked for jobs in the past year, 61% of the refugees reported language as the major problem encountered in their job hunt, compared to only 4% of the other AFDC recipients reporting. Nearly all of those who did not speak English—both refugee and non-refugee AFDC recipients—found language to be the major problem in securing a job.

ORR (1987) also reported that Southeast Asian refugees who spoke no English had a labor force participation rate of only 8.6% and an unemployment rate of 28.6%, while those who could speak English fluently had a labor participation rate of 61% and an unemployment rate of only 15%.

There are two different approaches to improving English proficiency for refugees. One approach is characterized by front-loading, or providing English training at the beginning of the resettlement process of the refugees. The other approach is to help the refugee find a job as soon as possible, with the assumption that the refugee will gradually pick up language proficiency at the workplace. However, as shall be discussed in later sections, the kinds of vocational skills provided to refugees and the types of work that the refugees look for are very much related to their level of English proficiency. Consequently, refugees with low English proficiency are frequently hired for jobs that require little communication with other workers. The refugee would not be expected to acquire English proficiency readily in such a workplace.

In a study conducted by the Northwest Regional Educational Laboratory (NREL, 1985), it was found that among people of similar backgrounds, those who received language training were able to acquire more English than those who did not. Language training was found to be a more significant predictor of English gain than was employment because, at the end of a 6-month period, the gains in English as demonstrated by those in full-time language training were significantly greater than the gains in English demonstrated by those in employment. Although those in employment generally started at a higher level of English proficiency, the language training group surpassed the language ability of the employed group at the end of the 6-month period.

McManus (1985) analyzed the labor market costs of language disparity and estimated that the present lifetime cost of not being fluent in English ranges from $19,000 for the most nearly fluent to $36,000 for the least fluent. In other words, if the cost of English training is less than $19,000 or $36,000, depending on the current English proficiency, then there is a potential net gain for obtaining such training. The above cost-benefit analysis addresses mainly individual gains instead of public benefits. A complete analysis should at least include estimates of gains from increase in tax received by the government and reduction in welfare benefit payments.

Vocational Skills

Downward occupation mobility among Southeast Asian refugees upon migration has been reported frequently (Kelly, 1977; ORR, 1982-1987; Stein, 1979). The three major reasons for downward mobility of refugees are lack of language proficiency, non-recognition of qualification, and lack of local experience (Samuel, 1984).

The first wave of Southeast Asian refugees in 1975, who came from mainly professional backgrounds, may nevertheless have had difficulties in adapting to the United States. Subsequent waves of Southeast Asian refugees, who came from rural or small business backgrounds, found it harder to adapt to the local labor market. In the authors' Los Angeles sample of refugees receiving AFDC, 49% of the male respondents reported never having been employed for wages before. Unfamiliarity with the labor market and the lack of capital to establish small businesses in the United States became major handicaps for these refugees.

About 28% of our sample were currently enrolled in trade, technical, or vocational training at the time of the study. Nearly 85% of the training received prepared them primarily for blue-collar jobs such as construction, machine shop trades or crafts, automotive repair, electronics, and assembly work. It should be noted that these jobs usually do not require much communication skill in English. By contrast, the other recipients in the AFDC program received training primarily in typing or clerical work, medical or dental aids, or computer skills. Although part of this difference may be due to individual educational level, one cannot ignore the English communication skills factor.

Hitherto, there have been few empirical studies demonstrating how well Southeast Asian refugees are prepared for employment after receiving vocational training. The major empirical evidence is provided by Caplan et al. (1985), who found that those who had received vocational training were *more* likely to have earned income than those who had not (47.1% versus 36.5%); and those who had received vocational training were *less* likely to be on cash assistance than those who had not (58.3% versus 66.9%). However, due to the fact that the more capable ones tend to be able to enroll in training programs, the results turned out to be not significant after controlling other variables in the multivariate analysis.

Nevertheless, the cost-benefit analyses of vocational training programs for the disadvantaged are generally positive. For example Bassi (1983), having reviewed various empirical studies, concluded that the benefits of classroom training and on-the-job training to economically disadvantaged workers had probably exceeded the costs to taxpayers. Such findings were particularly applicable to women and participants with lower pre-program earnings. We would expect that these observations would also apply to the Southeast Asian refugees as a disadvantaged group.

Access to the Labor Market

Whether one can find a job depends on the type of services that one can offer and one's degree of access to major information channels in the labor market. In the authors' sample of refugees in Los Angeles, the kinds of work being sought were slightly more diversified and yet very much similar to the kind of vocational training they were receiving. The common types of work refugees sought were miscellaneous craft or trade, electronics, auto repair or mechanics, services, and operative work such as sewing, pressing, factory, and so on; whereas the most common types of work that the non-refugee AFDC recipients sought were clerical or secretarial, operative, cashiers, sales, and technical.

The types of work refugees sought depended not only on personal desire, but also on the kinds of jobs offered them. Downward occupational mobility experienced by refugees during early resettlement was due partly to their low level of English proficiency, which, in turn, provided them with the rationalization for this downward mobility.

Job placement, job development, and job counseling programs have been successful. For example, in the Chicago project, the Refugee Policy Group (1983) reported that 74% of the 246 employable refugees held jobs at the end of the project. However, as noted earlier, caution has to be taken in reading figures on placement rates. Success in obtaining a job is the beginning. It is yet uncertain whether one can maintain the job and earn enough money to raise one's family above the poverty level. As noted by Downing et al. (1984), the jobs Hmong refugees secured often paid below the level of public assistance and included no health benefits.

Furthermore, overall placement rates of employment services do not necessarily tell us how successful an employment service is. Refugees may be able to find jobs even without the help of employment services. A comparison of the employment rate of those receiving employment service with the employment rate of those not receiving employment service would be more useful. In this regard, it should be noted that 55% of the refugees in the authors' Los Angeles sample who had been looking for a job depended primarily on friends and relatives.

Though the effectiveness of employment service in promoting economic self-sufficiency is unclear, employment service accounted for the largest share (29%) of the budget in 1981 and 1982 contracts for support services under the Refugee Resettlement Program (ORR, 1982, 1983), followed by English as a Second Language (22%), and vocational training (13%). Research in the cost-effectiveness of employment service is needed to assess whether the largest share of money is well spent.

Welfare Benefits

High welfare benefits are usually associated with high welfare dependency. Theoretically, with higher welfare benefits, a welfare recipient will prefer to wait for a better paying job before taking an offer, and the duration on welfare assistance may be lengthened. On the other hand, those who manage to find a better paying job may stay on the job longer; thus, the chance of returning to the welfare rolls is reduced.

Empirical studies on the relationship between welfare benefits and welfare dependency based on the general population provide mixed results. Masters and Garfinkel (1977) found no consistent AFDC program effect on labor supply. In Danziger, Haveman, and Plotnick's (1981) estimates, AFDC reduces only 0.6% of the total work hours of all workers.

The evidence that higher welfare benefits will cause higher welfare dependency among the Southeast Asian refugees is primarily indirect in nature. In the analyses performed by Baker and North (1984), Caplan et al. (1985), and Bach and Carroll-Seguin (1986), the variable site or place of residence was significantly related to welfare dependency, labor participation, and having income above the poverty level. Invariably, being in California adversely affects all three dependent variables. As California has higher welfare benefits than the other "sites" under study, the authors then associate high welfare benefits with the adverse rates in welfare dependency, labor participation, and poverty rate.

California's high level of welfare benefits is also blamed for attracting Southeast Asian refugees into the state. Strand and Jones (1985) noted that Oregon, which has no General Assistance program, reported about 15% of its total refugee population moving, mostly to California, in anticipation of the changes in federal funding.

On the other hand Law (1988), using the 1980 5% Census Public Use Microdata Samples, found that Southeast Asian refugees who migrated from one state to another tended to move away from states with small population size, low per capita income, and high unemployment rate. After these factors were controlled, the level of welfare benefits was not related to the decision to move. There are definitely other factors that attract Southeast Asian refugees to California, such as its warm climate and a large Southeast Asian community that is already there.

PROVIDING CASH ASSISTANCE THROUGH EXISTING STRUCTURES

The current welfare system has the advantage of providing assistance to refugees at benefit levels consistent with those provided to other American residents. An administrative advantage of using the current system is the existence of mechanisms, such as an extensive network of offices, experienced workers, and accounting systems. With the spasmodic and unpredictable influx of the refugee population, a separate independent administrative system would be deemed expensive. Kogan, Jenny, Vencill, and Greenwood (1982) found good provisions for financial accountability and generally satisfactory completion of the refinements in the cash assistance system that was necessary for refugees at the state level of government.

The major criticism of the current public welfare system is that it encourages the use of assistance and fosters dependency. Second, the current system is not oriented to the transitional nature of the refugees' adaptation to the new country. Another criticism is that all refugees are similar in terms of their transitional adjustment process and yet receive different levels of assistance depending on where they reside, due to variation in benefit levels and eligibility requirements of the states. For instance, some refugees may receive AFDC for the unemployed in one state but not in another.

From the Los Angeles County data, the authors (Schneiderman et al., 1988) found that refugees differed substantially from other AFDC recipients in aspects such as demographic characteristics, household composition, educational attainment, English proficiency, vocational skills, and employment history. For instance, the average age of children in the refugee households was higher than those in the other AFDC households (7.3 years versus 4.7 years), and refugees tended to be living with an intact family. It is not certain that a single program can be responsive to these differences.

POLICY IMPLICATIONS AND CONCLUSIONS

The time that the Southeast Asian refugee population takes to achieve a level of economic self-sufficiency comparable to that of the U. S. population in general is not accurately known. In all likelihood, it would probably take more than 5 years for Southeast Asian refugees to achieve self-sufficiency. Admission of refugees is primarily a decision of the federal government, and refugees have the right to choose the state they live in. On the other hand, if the duration of federal responsibility in providing cash assistance is shorter than the duration required by the refugee population to become economically self-sufficient, then the financial burden will be shifted from the federal government to the individual states. *Thus, the current period of 100% federal responsibility for providing cash assistance should be extended to 60 months to reduce interruption of refugee transition due to the possibility of shifting the financial burden from the federal government to individual states or local governments.*

Economic self-sufficiency is influenced by many factors. Factors amenable to programmatic solutions include English proficiency, vocational skills, and access to labor markets. However, the effectiveness of the respective services in bringing about economic self-sufficiency among refugees is yet to be assessed.

Evidence indicates that English proficiency is one of the most important variables affecting economic self-sufficiency. Furthermore, English proficiency is apparently related to the kind of vocational training and subsequent employment obtained. Since the gains in English proficiency due to full-time language training were significantly greater than the gains due to employment, the authors recommend the front-loading approach of *providing English training first and vocational training second.*

Furthermore, the authors expect that after improving their English proficiency, refugees will automatically increase their chance of gaining employment and obtaining a better paying job. Therefore, if there is a choice between providing employment service or English training, one should always provide the latter.

Moreover, Strand (Strand & Jones, 1985) also found that Southeast Asian refugees attending English training were less likely to be employed. This suggests that English training classes should also be provided in the evening or on weekends for those who are currently working or actively looking for jobs.

As noted earlier, downward occupational mobility among Southeast Asian refugees was consistently observed. Service programs, which aim at providing supplementary professional training required for local accreditation standards, should be made available to Southeast Asian refugees whose professional qualification are not recognized in the United States.

Data from the Los Angeles study suggest that the demographic characteristics and service needs of refugees and other recipients of AFDC differ in significant ways. It is not certain that a single program can offer services that are responsive to these differences. Given the obvious importance of using an established, nationally available program to accommodate the largely unanticipated arrival of large numbers of refugees, there is need for further analysis of service needs and service outcomes to determine whether the AFDC program offers the best programmatic structure within which to administer future cash assistance services to refugees.

The present state of knowledge does not warrant a definitive answer to the above questions. However, there are ongoing experimental efforts, such as the Refugee Demonstration Project in California, which aim at increasing refugee employment and self-sufficiency by removing those refugees applying for or receiving federally assisted AFDC from the program and placing them in an alternative state-supervised, county-administered program. Evaluation of these experiments will be very useful for future plans.

REFERENCES

Aames, J. S., Aames, R. L., Jung, J., & Karabenick, E. (1977, September). *Indochinese refugee self-sufficiency in California: A survey and analysis of the Vietnamese, Cambodians and Lao and the agencies that serve them.* Report submitted to the State Department of Health, State of California.

Bach, R. L., & Bach, J. B. (1980, October). Employment patterns of Southeast Asian refugees. *Monthly Labor Review,* 31-38.

Bach, R. L., & Carroll-Seguin, R. (1986). Labor force participation, household composition and sponsorship among Southeast Asian refugees. *International Migration Review, 20*(2), 381-404.

Baker, R. P., & North, D. S. (1984). *The 1975 refugees: Their first five years in America.* Washington, DC: New TransCentury Foundation.

Bassi, L. J. (1983, September). CETA—Did it work? *Policy Studies Journal, 12*(1), 106-118.

Bloom, M., & Fischer, J. (1982). *Evaluating practice: Guidelines for the accountable professional.* Englewood Cliffs, NJ: Prentice-Hall.

Boesen, I. W. (1985). From autonomy to dependency: Aspects of the dependency syndrome among Afghanistan refugees. *Migration Today, 18*(5), 7-21.

Caplan, N., Whitemore, J. K., & Bui, Q. L. (1985, January). *Southeast Asian refugee self-sufficiency study.* Institute for Social Research.

Chiswick, B. R. (1978). The effects of Americanization on the earnings of foreign-born men. *Journal of Political Economy, 86*(5), 897-921.

Clark, L. (1986, May). Views quoted in "Dependency syndrome: Another look" by Refugee Policy Group. *Refugee, 29,* 35-37.

Danziger, S., Haveman, R., & Plotnick, R. (1981, September) How income transfer programs affect work, savings, and the income distribution: A critical review. *Journal of Economic Literature, 19*(3), 975-1028.

Downing, B. T., Hendricks, G., Mason, S., & Olney, D. (1984, May). Hmong resettlement. *Cura Reporter, 14*(3), 1-8.

Haines, D. W. (1983). Southeast Asian refugees in the United States: An overview. *Migration Today, 11*(2/3), 9-13.

Kelly, G. P. (1977). *From Vietnam to America.* Boulder, CO: Westview.

Kogan, D., Jenny, P., Vencill, M., & Greenwood, L. (1982, September). *Study of the state administration of the refugee resettlement program: Final report.* Berkeley, CA: Berkeley Planning Associates.

Law, C. K. (1988). *Economic assimilation of refugees: Human capital, job information and ethnic enclave*. Unpublished doctoral dissertation, University of California at Los Angeles.

Masters, S. H., & Garfinkel, I. (1977). *Estimating the labor supply effects of income maintenance alternatives*. New York: Academic Press.

McManus, W. (1985, September). Labor market costs of language disparity: An interpretation of Hispanic earnings differences. *American Economic Review, 75*(4), 818-827.

Northwest Regional Educational Laboratory (NREL). (1985). *A study of English language training for refugees in the United States* (Vol. I-III). Portland, OR: NREL.

Office of Refugee Resettlement (ORR). (1982, May). *Refugee resettlement program: Employment services, a report on model practices in employment for refugees*. Washington, DC: Department of Health and Human Services.

Office of Refugee Resettlement (ORR). (1982-1987). *Report to the Congress: Refugee resettlement program*. Washington, DC: Department of Health and Human Services.

Office of Refugee Resettlement (ORR). (1983, January). *Special report to Congress: Alternative methods for the provision of cash assistance, medical assistance, and case management for refugees*. Washington, DC: Department of Health and Human Services.

Refugee Policy Group. (1983). *The Chicago project: An alternative resettlement*. Washington, DC: U. S. Catholic Conference.

Samuel, T. J. (1984). Economic adaptation of refugees in Canada: Experience of a quarter century. *International Migration* (Geneva), *22*(1), 45-55.

Schneiderman, L., Furman, W. M., & Law, C. K. (1988) *Recipients of AFDC in Los Angeles County: Refugees and non-refugees*. Los Angeles: UCLA Center for Child and Family Policy Study.

Stein, B. N. (1979). Occupational adjustment of refugees: The Vietnamese in the United States. *International Migration Review, 13*(1), 25-45.

Strand, P. J., & Jones, W., Jr. (1985). *Indochinese refugees in America: Problems of adaptation and assimilation*. Durham, NC: Duke University Press.

Part IV

LIFE CYCLE: Vulnerable Groups

FARIYAL ROSS-SHERIFF

Asian Americans today live in a nation that is different from the one that isolated and rejected the earlier immigrants. Supported by ethnic community, religious organizations, and an array of kin, the family remains a source of socialization and refuge in times of cultural discontinuity. This last part includes four chapters to help readers understand three vulnerable groups among Asian Americans at different stages in the family life cycle. The three critical groups highlighted are adolescents, women, and the elderly, all of whom experience high levels of stress and related mental health problems (Ross-Sheriff, 1990).

Adolescents are of vital concern to Asian Americans because they represent the future. The stereotype of high-achieving Asian youths has its roots in the efforts of the Asian adult immigrants who work hard, sacrifice comforts, and skimp on necessities so that their children may attend college. Asian parents strongly believe that education provides access to economic and social opportunities. However, serious conflicts arise for adolescents and their families, both recent arrivals and even those who were born in the United States, when the normal stresses of identity development during adolescence are confounded by their minority status as people of color, by their ethnic differences from the Euro Americans, and by the disadvantages of their immigrant status (Takaki, 1989). The problem is further compounded emotionally for those immigrant youths whose parents, grandparents, or other relatives are unsuccessful according to the economic and social standards of either the Asian or the American culture. The resolution ranges from becoming achievement-oriented students to becoming members of ethnic gangs in Los Angeles and Chicago, cities with large Asian populations. The chapter by Brij Mohan, "Trans-Ethnic Adolescence, Confluence, and Conflict: An Asian Indian Paradox," addresses the identity issues for Asian Indians.

Asian women generally bring substantial strengths to the family through defined role responsibilities for nurturance and cultural preservation to ensure the socialization of family members and cultural continuity. Yet, Asian American women encounter especially difficult obstacles, one of which is combining employment with their traditional roles as wives, mothers, homemakers, and caregivers for elderly family members. The combination of these roles creates severe stresses especially for those women in households wherein the resident men feel it is socially or culturally inappropriate for them to help with child-rearing and household tasks. Access to support networks becomes important. The chapter by Pauline Meemeduma, "Support Networks of Sri Lankan Women Living in the United States," presents results of an ethnographic research study on support networks of a select group of Asian women.

Tensions within families result from conflicting demands for change versus demands for constancy in cultural practices, and from conflicting expectations and attitudes of women and their husbands about the wife's role as a wage earner—a role often seen as a necessary, but culturally undesirable, feature of life in the United States. The levels of physical abuse of Korean women and the relationships between abuse, cultural attitudes, and immigrant status, are described in Young I. Song-Kim's chapter, "Battered Korean Women in Urban United States."

A large proportion of elderly Asian Americans, whether early or recent immigrants, experience severe stresses as a result of their increased physiological vulnerability and dependency on others. These stresses are exacerbated by the psychological distresses in their adjustment to the United States. They had the most to lose in leaving their home countries and the least to gain in their new lives. For many, their loss of self-worth is compounded by their increased isolation in the United States. Paul K. Kim and Jung-Sup Kim describe the problems confronting elderly Korean Americans and present social work practice and policy implications in "Korean Elderly: Policy, Program, and Practice Implications."

The focus in these chapters on specific Asian groups does not necessarily imply that the strengths or stresses described are characteristic of only these particular groups. For example, the discussion of high achievement among Asian Indians does not necessarily indicate that the high-achievement syndrome is more characteristic of this group of Asian Americans than of any other group. Similarly, the description of abuse suffered by Korean American women neither implies that abuse is prevalent among all groups of Asian Americans, nor does it imply that among Asian Americans only Korean women experience abuse. Rather, these chapters identify vulnerable groups and present examples of problems that require the prevention and supportive services of social workers.

REFERENCES

Ross-Sheriff, F. (1990). Displaced populations. *Encyclopedia of Social Work* (18th ed.) (Supp.). Silver Spring, MD: National Association of Social Work.

Takaki, R. (1989). *Strangers from a different shore: A history of Asian Americans.* New York: Little, Brown.

Chapter 10

TRANS-ETHNIC ADOLESCENCE, CONFLUENCE, AND CONFLICT: *An Asian Indian Paradox*

BRIJ MOHAN

The romantic myth of a stable Asian Indian family is in question. Cultural transplantation of Asian Indian youths poses difficult and challenging dilemmas for them and their families. Although the problem is not endemic, contextual considerations suggest an analytical approach to unravel the complexity of trans-ethnic adolescence. Trans-ethnic adolescence is a new phenomenon of old experiences, as past generations of immigrants and their children must have gone through this adaptation. These adolescents represent a new generation of primary immigrants from the Indian subcontinent who settled in the United States. Because Asian Indian ethnicity is an emerging phenomenon, the study of Asian Indian youths is a challenging area of inquiry.

METHODOLOGY

This chapter uses direct observations and case studies conducted by the author and descriptive information from existing literature. The methodology involved both longitudinal and cross-sectional observations analyzed in an analytic-descriptive design. In addition, case studies illustrate the validity of particular situations. Three aspects of trans-ethnic behavior are described in this chapter: (a) characteristic variables; (b) identity, confluence, and conflict; and (c) implications for social work education, practice, and research.

CHARACTERISTIC VARIABLES

Demographic data on Asian Indian youths in the United States are unavailable. Statistics pertaining to age, income, gender, family occupations, and place of origin have not been collected systematically yet. Only sketchy details are extracted from the Bureau of Census and other sources that provide limited data on demographics of specific populations. However, Dutt (1989) reports that the percentage of foreign-born Indian youths in the United States has decreased, and he analyzes the ramifications:

> From 22 percent of foreign-born Indians above 14 years of age in 1979, such young people formed only 13 percent of the total in 1988. . . . More Indian children are now born in the United States, a natural evolution of the immigration process. The majority of such youths, however, may be average performers and have so called average ambitions. But they have nevertheless borne the pressure of trying to prove their high calibre. . . . Statistics on immigration show a rise in the number of incoming relatives of citizens, which has meant a lowering of the educational levels of newer Indians as they must depend to a lesser degree on their professional qualifications to make it in America. (p. 16)

Conceptually, using achievement and performance as measurable criteria, Asian Indian youths fall into three categories: (a) overachievers, (b) average performers (Dutt, 1989), and (c) underachievers. However, adaptive and maladaptive behaviors cut across these categories. Adolescent growth of trans-ethnic youths represents both confluence and the conflicts of the parents. In addition, the youths' mode of adaptation is markedly different from that of the first generation. These premises highlight two aspects of trans-ethnicity: (a) adolescent development in a pluralist society and (b) intergenerational strife.

Overachievers

Overachievers constitute a group of high performers who are strongly motivated by success and achievement. These individuals are propelled by family and individual pride; they are proud strivers for the "American Dream." Usually their family background is sound socially and materially. Acquisition of knowledge, education, and wealth is their passion. A supportive family milieu and free access to the opportunities in American society generally yield amazing results. For example, in nearly all branches of science, technology, medicine, and the arts, Asian Indian youths are thriving as "God's blessed children" (Sikri, 1989b, p. 16).

Are these second-generation Asian Indian overachievers, who either moved to the United States as toddlers or were born in this country, as happy and content as they appear? If material achievement were the sole criterion of happiness, then the answer is yes. The following case studies illustrate different outcomes for these overachievers. (Pseudonyms are used to maintain confidentiality.)

> Roshan, 16, graduated from high school with exceptional scholastic grades and scores and was almost selected the valedictorian. He was offered a prized scholarship by one of the top universities in the United States. This summer he is graduating from college in record time with enviable offers from some of the best professional schools for higher education. Roshan is a model of academic achievement; however, he is not very sociable and his friends call him an ideal "nerd."

> Sohan, 19, attended a medical college. Both of his parents are professionals. After a year or so in medical school, he dropped out from the college and ran away "to find peace." His peers call him "weird."

People generally talk about the success stories of Roshans in the Asian Indian community, but not about the Sohans. Even though "climbing" behavior of overachievers seems to be a pattern, definitive profiles in subjective experiences are unavailable. For example, two young brothers, John and Tom, recently dropped out of college after their parents separated. They are extremely sensitive, creative, and gifted children, but their achievement scale is clouded by familial conflicts. Their parents are highly respected by others but have irreconcilable differences. Both John and Tom still aspire to be top ranking artists in their fields, but they are extremely discontent. Passive protest defines their life-style, and this results in mental health problems. Casualties of the tangle of pathology arising from similar situations within Asian Indians generally remain uncovered under the secretive mist of family pride and prestige.

Average Performers

Average performers are healthy, well-adjusted youths usually involved in average middle-class jobs and occupations. They do not attend Harvard or Yale, nor do they aspire to win a Nobel prize. Their sense of reality helps them adjust to the new environment, and they are admired for their social achievement. Many of them are married to Euro Americans. Both primary and secondary Asian Indian immigrant families have average performers. Their level of achievement is attributed to both motivational and sociological factors. Individual differences aside, it seems that familial and environmental conditions determine their behavior and performance, as the following case studies suggest:

> Chand preferred not to attend college after high school. He is assisting his father with plans to expand and diversify the family business. He is modest, hard-working, conscientious, and responsible. Unlike other youths in business, Chand does not like to brag about his material assets.

> Suraj already has a college degree and is in business. He is married to a Euro American and is involved in numerous community activities. He believes in Asian Indian integration and is proud to be an Indian. His father wanted him to pursue further education, but Suraj did what he wanted to do. He feels he has settled down and is content with his family life and work.

Chand and Suraj represent the life pattern of work, family, and a modest sense of fulfillment. However, maladaptive behaviors are not necessarily alien to this pattern. These youths often are vulnerable to the dysfunctional attractions and stresses of life.

Underachievers

Underachievers manifest low self-esteem, a high sense of deprivation, and an ambivalent attitude toward life. They lack either opportunities or self-awareness to realistically relate to their life circumstances. They often encounter a saddening withdrawal, dissipation, and regression. Family pathology, unemployment, discrimination, poverty, and mental and physical illness are some of the conditions that characterize the background of underachievers. The following case studies typify underachievers' life situations:

> Roy and Ben are brothers. They were neglected as children due to parental disharmony. Father's professional problems and mother's mental health

condition deprived both of security and love in the family. Their education was disrupted several times until they dropped out of school completely. Ben is happily married, pragmatic, and compromising; however, he suffers from a severe sense of educational deficit. Roy married a Euro American who divorced him a year later. Roy has remarried, but is dependent on others for financial support. He is frustrated and tired of dead-end, low-paying jobs. Roy is reflective and fatalistic.

Dolly, 18, married an Indian rather than pursue a career or education, which were not encouraged due to family circumstances. A relatively early marriage provided a sense of security that did not last long. However, a concerted devotion to familial obligations resulted in stability and relative prosperity for the family. The young couple, however, want to go back to India.

Underachievers sometimes explode the myth that Asian Indian youth always go to Ivy League colleges. They also shatter the romantic image of achieving youth whose success stories are the highlights of social gatherings and party gossip.

What has happened to the "American Dream" for the children of these new and diverse citizens? Sikri (1989a, 1989b) reveals the answer through descriptions, ranging from intergenerational conflicts to widespread discrimination. The "American Dream" for these youths is filled with mixed voices of excitement and rage, fulfillment and denial, and joy and frustration. Wilke and Mohan (1984) suggest that the "Asian American experience in the U. S. is an indictment as well as a testimony to the nation's pluralism" (p. 29). In general, Asian Indian youths are strangers from a different shore (Takaki, 1989b). Takaki (1989a) succinctly observes, "My family has been here more than 100 years, yet people still ask me what country I'm from. . . . Our universities are not educating us about our diversity" (p. A3).

The prosperity and plight of Asian Indians is increasingly becoming a subject in the literature. For example, Mahapatra (1988) profiles the Asian Indian community as an affluent group. Mukherjee (1988), on the other hand, portrays the strife and woes of a people who are existing in the twilight of the American dilemma. New Asian Indian immigrants come from socially reputed strata of the Indian society. Despite their being discriminated against, Asian Indians' identification with oppressed ethnic groups is incomplete. In the American society, Asian Indians are unofficially treated as "elites."

The oppressed elites present a most intriguing paradox. For example, the mother of a young graduate says, "My daughter can't get into a medical school because Asian Indians are proportionately over-represented [in the school]. Had she been black, she would have received a scholarship from Harvard! We have all the disadvantages of being a minority without any safeguards."

CRISIS OF IDENTITY: CONFLUENCE, CONFLICT, AND CONTEXT

Asian Indian youths have a veritable problem of identity. Although their parents, mostly first-generation immigrants, lead a very active life in a self-imposed exile, young boys and girls are striving hard to find a meaningful sense of identity. Some of them, maybe most of them, do not think about it systematically, but their goals, commitments, lifestyles, and aspirations reflect a mix of nostalgia and abhorrence about certain fundamental aspects of life. The new culture of capitalism and pluralism has sharpened their consciousness to the extent that a conflict with native endowment and adopted new culture seems unavoidable. Two issues constitute the crux of the problem: (a) identity and (b) freedom of choice in career and profession and in socialization.

Identity

Asian Indian youths, even those who are born, raised, and educated in the United States or Canada, are at best confused or puzzled about identity-related issues. The extremely active life-style of their parents—Indian party followed by a Bombay movie on Saturday night, *pooja* (worship) or its variant practice on Sunday morning, and American work ethic from Monday through Friday—is simply unacceptable to these maturing young adults. They, as educated Asian Indians, want the best of two cultures without paying a significant price. The societal context that breeds alienation further complicates this process of self-exploration. Jindal (1989), who studied at Brown University, wrote about his search for identity in a highly introspective manner:

> I remember the first time I took a standardized test at school. When I came to the inevitable question concerning "ethnic origin" I filled in "American Indian" without hesitation. In the first grade, I had always told my friends that I was half Indian and half American. I had even decided that my right side was Indian and left side was American. When I came home I learned

the difference between John Wayne's Indians and Gandhi's Indians. I was "Oriental" or "Asian" or "Other," but was definitely not "American Indian." I still hesitate when people ask me where I am from. They are not satisfied with Louisiana and are annoyed until I state that my parents are from India. I wonder what my kids will say. Having parents born and raised here, they will have to reach back to their grandparents to explain their complexion. When do my descendants gain the same right as European immigrants to call themselves Americans? (p. 5)

Likewise, Naipaul, the world's leading English writer, recently returned to his "mother country" to discover his roots. "I was born in Trinidad, but the fact of my Indian origin remained the cornerstone of my identity" (Naipaul, 1990, p. 7). I am a naturalized American but certain contacts I have known for about 15 years still address me as a "Hindu," "Man from the East," and "Indian." The striving for identity persists.

The search for identity is the essence of trans-ethnic behavior. It involves special significance in the lives of youths who encounter confusion, lack of clarity, and preponderance of blurred boundaries of role expectations. Erikson (1979) observes that:

> Each generation of descendants of immigrants from all the world's nations and creeds had a chance to become a new and (this is immensely important for the viability of any new world views) a type of [person] that could include and absorb many origins and types; and whose aspirations could be predictably fulfilled if [he or she] only persisted in renewing [himself or herself] by remaining open to chances and ready for change. (p. 24)

Ramanujam (Erikson, 1979) concludes that adolescence assumes an identity of adjustment rather than of choice because

> [T]he social structure does not permit the emergence of a cogent adult role as perceived in adult societies. Subordinating one's individual needs to the interests of the group, be it a family, a kinship group, a clan or a class, is upheld as a virtue. . . . Thus, self-assertion becomes selfishness, independent decision making is perceived as disobedience. . . . Under such circumstances it is easier to play safe . . . by passive aggressive behavior or regression into total passivity. (p. 25)

Asian Indian youths seek to transcend the structural-normative elements of their parental endowments. The problem of "identity reconstruction in a pluralist society" (Mohan, 1989, p. 199) assumes a distinct character in the confluence and conflict of what is felt by youths as repressive quality of parenting with a continuation of permissive adaptation. Adolescent trans-ethnicity is inherently troubled by the pangs of freedom. The individual striving for identity, self-exploration, and self-awareness in the context of Asian Indian culture partakes a special significance for scientific research and inquiry.

Career and Socialization Choice

Freedom of choice for career and socialization are two other difficult aspects with which Asian Indian adolescents must cope. Most parents understandably want their children to succeed and prosper in their chosen fields, and they support their children in these endeavors. However, the material dimension and parentally induced incentives outweigh individual aptitudes and values. For example, a 17-year-old radio disc jockey and director of a jazz program contends, "One thing I am sure of, I am not going to be a doctor." Another youth, on the contrary, says, "I am programmed to be a doctor. What choice do I have?" Both of these boys are gifted, and other youths perhaps share in these dilemmas. Sanjay, 17, the newly elected youth governor of Louisiana, asserts, "If Connie Chung can become an anchor woman, why can't I become an anchor man?"

However, self-direction and determination are not universal attributes for youth. Those lacking either these traits or proper guidance sometimes fail despite their potential. Karan, a recognized genius, gave up his career and joined a cult. Problems of socialization in the permissive society are serious. Many parents are traumatized when their children forge interracial relationships beyond the trappings of caste and religion. For example, the following case study epitomizes trans-ethnic confluence and conflict.

> Bela, a young student from a Brahmin family in Bombay, became a single parent of a child whose father, a married African American, refused to assume any parental obligation. Communications with family, severely deteriorated relationships, and the notice of deportation served by the Immigration and Naturalization Service deepened the crisis.

In addition, Sikri (1989a) quotes others as they describe a frightening cultural gap in dating among Asian Indian youths:

(1) "It is a schizophrenic attitude," said Ritu Sinha. "On one hand parents want their daughters to have careers. . . . But they also want children never to open their mouths in front of elders or to go out on a date."

(2) Sapna Patel, a 10th grade student, said, "My parents feel the American culture is dumb. They don't let us eat meat. They don't let us go on dates. I resent it very much. My friends think it's weird."

(3) "I feel like running away from home," said one high school student.

(4) Akbar Matadar, a physician in Pittsburgh, said, "The issue is screaming out for attention. There have been suicides."

(5) "The schizophrenia is on the part of the children. They develop two identities, one for the home and one for the world out there," said a school counselor. (p. 17)

Most Asian Indians in the United States are strongly wedded to their cultural ancestry regardless of their ethnic variations. Adherence to one's caste, class, and religion is a common phenomenon. The construction of this ethclass of Asian Indians is a new wrinkle in American pluralism. It is, however, fraught with unsettling consequences for the first and second generations. One cannot escape an alarming conclusion: There is an Indian equivalent of the American Dilemma. Implications of this human condition for policymakers, practitioners, community leaders, and Asian Indians are both intriguing and far-reaching from academic and practical considerations.

IMPLICATIONS FOR SOCIAL WORK EDUCATION, PRACTICE, AND RESEARCH

By definition, trans-ethnicity involves a kind of transcendence that can be viewed from different angles. How people look at this phenomenon reflects individual and societal values and ideologies. A value-neutral approach is neither scientific nor humane. A critical assessment, therefore, offers a rational-humane perspective. In this section, the transcendental context of Asian Indian adolescence is related to social work education, practice, and research.

How are the youth reacting to the dual culture transplantation?

Are there maladaptive consequences of this new experience? What, if any, professional help is available? What is the content and modality of professional assistance? A typical profile of Asian Indian youth is difficult to formulate. Generally they are acquisitive, productive, and successful, although a significant number end up as losers. Three characteristics of Asian Indian youths appear in the literature: (a) a sense of insecurity is outweighed by acquisitive and self-assertive drives; (b) loss of identity is not loss of humanity because trans-ethnicity, an aspect of new ethnicity, seeks to survive and sustain despite the challenges of regressive forces; and (c) Asian Indian ethnicity is likely to become a victim of its own success if preventive measures are not taken soon. The confluence and conflict of ethnic transformation may permanently damage the Indian psyche if authentic self-awareness is not pursued.

A professional response to these issues calls for a trans-ethnic model of social work education, practice, and research that involves:

- awareness, recognition, and acceptance of human diversities
- a network of social arrangements that promotes human relatedness at the expense of alienation, arrogance, and authoritarianism
- pluralism, equality, and justice as guiding principles of a civil order.

Devore and Schlesinger (1987) formulated the following four assumptions of ethnic-sensitive practice: (a) individual and collective history have a bearing on the generation and solution of problems; (b) the present is most important; (c) nonconscious phenomena affect individual functioning; and (d) ethnicity is a source of cohesion, identity, and strength as well as a source of strain, discordance, and strife (p. 514). Moreover, they state that suggested practice principles involve coercive and voluntary routes to the social worker; simultaneous attention to individual and systemic concerns; cognitive, affective, and behavioral skills; and ethnic competence in the human services (pp. 515-516). Trans-ethnic practice will benefit from these formulations in direct and indirect services in the processes of assimilation, accommodation, and conflict.

It is premised that the Council on Social Work Education and the National Association of Social Workers espouse, promote, and advocate these elements toward a just and egalitarian system that is conducive to the development of diverse human groups. Nevertheless, oppression and racism remain pervasive challenges to human progress. For example, anti-Asian activity in the form of violence, vandalism, harassment, and intimidation continue to occur across the United States, skinheads are on the march (Leo, 1988), and racial discrimination incidents occur on college campuses (Tifft, 1989). Children who are victims of such discrimination cannot remain untouched by the cruelties of the system that degrades their heritage. A sense of inescapable demoralization creeps into their psyche. Although some ethnic minorities express their resentment and frustrations, others endure a self-torturous ordeal.

Social work education, practice, and research must strengthen curricula designs and dynamic modalities of practice that promote individual identity, group morale, and social responsibility. The American creed is gentle and lofty; however, its practice is less than ideal. Social work education, practice, and research must seek to humanize the system that produces alienation, oppression, inequality, and injustice.

Trans-ethnic youths' vulnerability to these developmental barriers ought not be underestimated. Regardless of their performance level and sociocultural background, youth crisis is a monumental human encounter. Trans-ethnic practice is equipped to deal with the diversity of adolescence; it is a professional response to the postmodern complexity of adolescent transcendence—an urge to achieve one's potential. Trials and tribulations of this delicate phase represent, in Sartre's words, "the tragedy of freedom as contrasted with the tragedy of fate" (1943, p. 187). Asian Indian youths represent a postmodern phenomenon, defying modernists' ideology of assimilationism. Their sense of responsibility and commitment to what they hold authentic appears to unlock the mystery of the crisis of identity.

However, traditional methods of American social work practice cannot adequately encompass the problems of trans-ethnic adolescence. Existing modes of intervention simply are not designed to deal with the vicissitudes of this phenomenon. Often, Asian Indians may resist or ignore professional help. Likewise, professionals may show ineptitude and may lack trans-cultural sensitivity. Client-worker incompatibility becomes a barrier even before a plan is formulated. Suggestions of clinical intervention alienate many Asian Indians who need help but do not want to be labeled. The following case example illustrates the difficulties of providing professional help to Asian Indians:

Shalini, 15, reported a case of possible child molestation with incestuous overtones involving a 10-year-old girl whom Shalini was babysitting. Shalini's parents were both shocked and worried. Her father was concerned because his own daughter had been exposed to a vicious environment.

He likened professional help, in that situation, to a cultural trap without any exit. Although there is a general growth of awareness among the youth, their families remain skeptical about the purpose and nature of social work practice.

Social workers who have knowledge and understanding of Asian Indian culture and experiences, or those who are of Asian Indian ethnic background and can work with both parents and adolescents, usually are unavailable in most communities. Those few Asian Indian social workers who are in practice seldom get Asian Indian clients. Moreover, their inherent immunity ill-equips them to intervene in situations in which they are neither welcome nor sought out. The Asian Indian component of ethnic-sensitive practice is still in an embryonic stage. Ethnocentrism of American social work practice further compounds the development of new tools and methods.

Professional help, as a dynamic element of social work education, practice, and research, must reorient its epistemology for developing better strategies for human and social transformation (Mohan, 1988). Explorations in clinical philosophy, a field that needs to be developed, will strengthen trans-ethnic knowledge, practice, and research (S. Z. Hasan, personal communication, March 5, 1990). Specific trans-ethnic "adolescence" can be incorporated into the main repertoire of social work education, practice, and research through research and analysis that undergird a conceptually valid relationship between facts and values. Cartesian dualism and materialistic frameworks do not adequately encompass a cosmic worldview that would unravel trans-ethnic adolescence in a humane and holistic manner. An incessant search for creative paradigms sustains the pulse of a continuing thrust for knowledge and freedom.

CONCLUSIONS

Analysis and case examples presented in this chapter briefly signify the complexity of a new ethnic diversity. Asian Indians represent a group of new Americans, sometimes labeled as "elitist," who are living a self-created paradox of ethnic duality. Zachariah, speaking about the source of intergenerational conflicts, said that tensions play an important role in the personality formation of young South Asians (Jain, 1990). As parents, "We are dismayed that unlike us, our children are 'brown' on the outside but 'white' inside—like a coconut," Zachariah noted, asserting that parents consider this a betrayal (Jain, 1990, p. 33). This human situation presents an area of study where cultural and structural aspects of pluralism present challenging issues with particular reference to (a) identity formation and (b) ethnic conflict. This exploratory essay proffers a few suggestive leads that practitioners, policymakers, and researchers may find useful to link their efforts in social planning and intervention strategies. It is by no means an exhaustive and/or final account of the present situation. Conclusions drawn here reflect this author's observations, experiences, and understanding of the new ethnicity phenomenon as applied to Asian Indians in the United States. Implications suggested by the author are premised on the assumption that social work education, practice, and research constitute a dynamic whole responsive to the emerging aspirations and needs of a multicultural society.

REFERENCES

Devore, W., & Schlesinger, E. G. (1987). Ethnic-sensitive practice. In A. Minahan et al. (Eds.), *Encyclopedia of social work. Vol. 18* (pp. 512-516). Silver Spring, MD: National Association of Social Workers.

Dutt, E. (1989). Becoming a 2nd generation. *India Abroad, 22*(2), 16.

Erikson, E. H. (1979). Report to Vikram: Further perspective on the life cycle. In S. Kakar (Ed.), *Identity and adulthood* (pp. 13-34). Delhi: Oxford University Press.

Jain, A. (1990). 'Brown' outside and 'white' inside. *India Abroad, 20*(28), 33.

Jindal, P. (1989). Asian American or American Indian. *Sanskrati, 1*, 3, 5.

Leo, J. (1988, January 25). A chilling wave of racism. *Time*, p. 57.

Mahapatra, M. K. (1988). *A study of affluent Indians in the United States*. Hong Kong: Asian Research Services.

Mohan, B. (1988). *The logic of social welfare: Conjectures and formulations*. New York: St. Martin's Press.

Mohan, B. (1989). Ethnicity, power, and discontent: The problem of identity reconstruction in a pluralist society. *Indian Journal of Social Work, 50*(2), 199-212.

Mukherjee, B. (1988). *The middleman and other stories*. New York: Grove.

Naipaul, V. S. (1990). Naipaul seeking his roots. *India Abroad, 20*(4), 7.

Sartre, J. P. (1943). *Les mouches*. Paris: Gallimard.

Sikri, A. (1989a). Dating: A scary cultural gap. *India Abroad, 20*(2), 17.

Sikri, A. (1989b). Inside America's possible dream. *India Abroad, 20*(2), 16.

Takaki, R. (1989a). Portrait. *The Chronicles of Higher Education, 11*, A3.

Takaki, R. (1989b). *Strangers from a different shore: A history of Asian Americans*. New York: Little, Brown.

Tifft, S. (1989, January 23). Bigots in the ivory tower. *Time*, p. 56.

Wilke, A. S., & Mohan, R. P. (1984). The politics of Asian Americans: An assessment. *International Journal of Contemporary Sociology, 21*, 3-4, 29-71.

Chapter 11

SUPPORT NETWORKS OF SRI LANKAN WOMEN LIVING IN THE UNITED STATES

PAULINE MEEMEDUMA

Immigration to a new country, no matter how desired the move, involves serious disruption to the support relationships of the individual. The newcomer must deal with the loss of individual supportive relationships in the home country as well as the need to establish new supportive relationships in the host country. The importance of support networks in facilitating the psychosocial well-being of individuals is now a commonly accepted practice tenet within the social work profession (Collins & Pancoast, 1976; Hoppa, 1986). Access to a support network potentially provides the individual with: (a) instrumental support or material and informational resources such as finance, accommodations, goods, and employment; (b) social support or an opportunity for meeting others and learning about social and recreational activities; and (c) personal support or an avenue to share self and establish self-worth and identity. The existence of support networks provides both a sense of belonging and a means of providing a set of resources to enable individuals to manage crises, stress, and life transitions (Belsky & Rovine, 1984; Collins & Pancoast, 1976; Stack, 1974).

Despite such evidence, little is known about the nature of immigrants' support networks in the host country and the factors that shape these networks. In the study reported in this chapter, these questions are addressed in relation to the support networks of a group of Sri Lankan women living in a large metropolitan area in the United States. The support networks of the Sri Lankan women are described with regard to whom they turned to for support, and why, and the type of support provided by support network members.

The study questions are particularly important in relation to the support network experiences of immigrant women. Women traditionally are pivotal to the maintenance of supportive relationships, as they contribute to and invest more in supportive relationships than men. Such relationships are more integral to the well-being of women (Bell, 1981). Immigration, therefore, as a process of dislocation to the supportive networks of the home country, has an implicitly greater cost in terms of loss for women.

Regardless of how desired the move was, the dislocation from the world one understands, is accepted in, and has a known place in, has significant impact on self-cohesion and identity. In reestablishing support networks in the United States, the immigrant woman faces the need to reintegrate the often unclear, conflictual, and contrary American norms and values within the normative context of her home country (Rack, 1977; Shuval, 1982). This process of reintegration must be done in a way that enables the woman to achieve a cohesive and consistent psychosocial functioning. Although the process of reintegration is carried out as part of daily life over a long period, it clearly has significant consequences for determining the nature of immigrant women's settlement and adaptation experiences in the United States.

Researchers acknowledge the importance of the cultural setting of the individual in shaping the structure, process, and function of the support network (Bott, 1957; Vaux, 1985). Cultural norms act to shape the support need cues that will be expressed and in what manner they will be expressed, as well as who will respond and in what manner they will respond. Cultural norms also act to shape the meaning and value of the support relationship to both the individual and the collective group. Hence, support networks are a crucial component of how the individual understands himself or herself as a cultural being and how the individual understands and responds to his or her external world.

This research study on the support networks of Sri Lankan women living in the United States arose from the author's experience while living in Sri Lanka from 1982 to 1984. As a Westerner married to a Sri Lankan, the author was able to observe the support networks of Sri Lankans. These networks were shaped by the individual's membership in an extensive network of family/kin relationships. Family/kin membership was characterized by concern with responsibilities and rights toward the family/kin group; the importance of the family/kin group over the individual; an emphasis upon cooperation, harmony, and loyalty between family/kin members; and a concern for the maintenance of family/kin respectability and status. This emphasis on the family/kin group was expressed in the norms and rules surrounding the conduct of social relationships and, hence, significantly shaped the character and functions of support networks. In Sri Lanka, the support networks available to the individual predominantly consisted of family/kin members who provided extensive instrumental, social, and personal support, which was long-term and unconditional, devoid of expectations of equitable reciprocity between receiver and giver.

Although the family/kin-based support networks in Sri Lanka were clearly important to both males and females, it appeared that Sri Lankan women depended more on the family/kin support network for instrumental, social, and personal support. What happens to these women, and to many others from family/kin-based cultures, when they emigrate to such countries as the United States? Generally, these women face a host country that has minimal or nonexistent family/kin supports; where the initiation and conduct of social relationships and, hence, support networks is based significantly on different cultural prescription, and where they face the normal stress of immigration dislocation, settlement, and adaptation. To answer the above question, several further questions were posited, three of which are discussed in this chapter: What was the world of support the women had left in Sri Lanka and how did it act to shape their support network experiences in the United States? What were the support experiences of the women during their first 6 months of settlement in the United States? What were the women's support network experiences after the initial period of settlement?

METHODOLOGY

The study consisted of 45 Sri Lankan women who lived within a large metropolitan area in the United States. All of the women had immigrated to the United States as adults of 18 years or older. All had been residents in the United States for a minimum of 6 months.

The research design used was ethno-methodological. The study was concerned with enabling the Sri Lankan women to "tell their own story," limiting the influence of the researcher's own cultural perspective

(Becerra & Zambrana, 1985). Paton's (1980) general interview guide was used to formulate general questions. The women were interviewed from May to August 1987, and their stories were tape-recorded and transcribed.

The Sri Lankan women interviewed for the study were predominantly married with children. Because of the professional occupations of their partners, the women may generally be characterized as middle class, although a significant majority had markedly lower educational qualifications and occupational statuses than their partners. The ethnic distribution of the sample was primarily Sinhalese (58%, $n = 26$), Tamil (24%, $n = 11$), and the remainder, Burghers of part European descent and Malay (18%, $n = 8$). The religious distribution of the women was Christian (44%, $n = 20$), Buddhist (42%, $n = 19$), Hindu (11%, $n = 5$), and Moslem (2%, $n = 1$). The mean age of the women at the time of arrival in the United States was 34 years, with a range from 18 years to 65 years. The mean age of the women at the time of the study was 42 years, with a range from 19 years to 73 years. The relative recency of immigration of these Sri Lankan women to the United States is reflected in both the figures for the length of stay and for the family/kin group members available in the United States. The median length of stay was 5.2 years. At the time of migration, only 40% ($n = 18$) of the women and 20% ($n = 9$) of the women's partners had a family/kin member living in the United States.

RESULTS

The support networks left behind in Sri Lanka described by the women were dominated by family/kin members. It was a world within which day-to-day responsibilities were shared, in which the support provided was unconditional, and in which family/kin rights and responsibilities were valued and functional. As a consequence, the women described feeling part of a social and psychological whole:

> In Sri Lanka, there is some relationship connection to everybody and you are related to so many people. In Sri Lanka, it is impossible to be lonely the way you are here [in the United States]. Where we lived was a central spot so people were always dropping in. I didn't feel lonely at all. (33-year-old woman in the United States for 6 months)

Many women throughout the interviews utilized the remembered support world of Sri Lanka to contrast their support experience in the

United States. The comparison overwhelmingly reflected a negative perception of their support world in the United States. Many women contrasted the absolute certainty of the provision of support in Sri Lanka with the uncertainty of such support in the United States. One woman said, "I know they (family/kin) would help. They have always helped me. That is so hard about here, you are not sure who would help."

The Sri Lankan women in the study clearly were aware that they could not expect the environment and support in the United States to be the same as in Sri Lanka. They could articulate the impediments in the United States to having a Sri Lankan support network, yet it was evident during the interviews that they continued to realize a Sri Lankan model of support networks to understand and shape their support networks experiences in the United States. It was as if normative expectations of support networks were integral to their understanding of themselves as Sri Lankans. Hence, their persistence in referring to the culturally prescribed support network, despite contextual incongruence, resulted in dysfunctional consequences for some of the women.

SUPPORT DURING THE FIRST 6 MONTHS IN THE UNITED STATES

During the interviews, the Sri Lankan women described the support they had received during their first 6 months in the United States. Their support was divided into three categories: (a) instrumental, (b) social, and (c) personal. Characteristics of support network members were divided into four categories: (a) family/kin, (b) co-national, (c) American, and (d) other. Given the immediate needs of settlement, the women predominantly expressed receiving instrumental and social support during the first 6 months in the United States (Table 11.1).

The first 6 months in the United States remained vivid in the memories of the Sri Lankan women in this study. The women spoke of loneliness, homesickness, fears, problems, misunderstandings, and successes. They constantly referred to dislocation from their family/kin group in Sri Lanka: "I have always been homesick. I did not have anyone. I am not used to staying away from family this long. I couldn't believe it when I came here, how could people live like this without family around?" (25-year-old woman in the United States for 3 years).

It was clear in interviews with the Sri Lankan women that they had a hierarchical preference for particular types of support network members

Table 11.1

Type and Source of Support Networks

| | Source of Support (Percentage) | | | |
Type of Support	Family	Co-National	American	Other
Instrumental	43	60	57	0
Social	42	61	47	0

and that this preference was associated with the type of support provided. Without exception, if family/kin members were available, they were the support networks members used for instrumental and social support during the first 6 months in the United States. If family/kin were unavailable, then co-nationals were the next utilized support network members for instrumental and social support. In contrast, the Sri Lankan women in the study did not indicate that they expected to receive support from Euro Americans.

Family/kin members who were available in the United States at the time of settlement were reported as having provided extensive instrumental and social support. "The only people who helped me were his [spouse's] sister and brother-in-law. We stayed with them for one year. They paid our fare here, paid our medical insurance and food" (42-year-old woman in the United States for 3 years).

The extended nature of Sri Lankan kinship meant that support could also be obtained from more distant relatives, even though, in several cases, the woman had no previous contact with the individual relative. The family/kin relationship was sufficient in itself to define the support expectations and obligations: "The people who first helped me were Mr. and Mrs. C., distant relatives, my cousin's wife's people" (30-year-old woman in the United States for 3 years).

Family/kin members, when available, also constituted the social support network of the women: "My sister-in-law's people were there so it was like a little Sri Lanka. I didn't meet anyone except family people then" (19 year-old woman in the United States for 6 months).

Reliance on family/kin members for instrumental and social support, although mitigating the more stressful aspects of immigration settlement, acted to truncate the support network available to the Sri Lankan women in the study who had family/kin in the United States. The tendency and expectation that the forced support needs of the immigrants would be met within the family/kin support network precluded the development of adaptive resources and skills, as well as rendering the women highly dependent on the resource and skill capacity of their family/kin networks. When the resources and skills available to the family/kin support network were inadequate to respond to the settlement needs of the Sri Lankan woman, there were no alternate support networks available: "My sister-in-law and her people did everything. We were staying with my sister-in-law so we didn't meet anyone else" (35-year-old woman in the United States for 2 years).

When family/kin members were unavailable, the Sri Lankan woman preferred to turn to other Sri Lankans for instrumental and social support: "Somehow as a Sri Lankan we feel closer to other Sri Lankans than to foreigners" (52-year-old woman in the United States for 14 years).

However, access to co-nationals depended greatly on an informal network of social contacts originating in Sri Lanka. These informal contacts became a co-national support network in the United States. The contacts enabled the giver and receiver to be "known" to each other. This "knowing" process is a group process of interaction, primarily at the family/kin level of interaction, and has less to do with prior individual contact.

Although co-national instrumental and social support for the women studied was not extensive or as prolonged as family/kin support, the women reported impressive levels of support:

> They [other Sri Lankans] came to my house and asked what to do. They tell me what to do, what not to do. They came and talk with us, they take us places, helped me clean, they take us shopping, they told me about schools for the children. (44-year-old woman in the United States for 13 years)

Co-nationals also played an important social support function during the first 6 months in the United States. Sri Lankans frequently hosted social dinners, lunches, and picnics, which, in most cases, were exclusively for Sri Lankans, and thus provided access to other Sri Lankans. These social contacts also were the means by which previous contacts in Sri Lanka (that is, "knowing") could be established and, hence, co-national support network development could be facilitated.

It became readily apparent in the conversations with the Sri Lankan women that the culturally prescribed expectations in terms of the support role were similar for co-nationals and family/kin. In addition, the women described that being a family/kin member and co-national meant to support and to be supported by Sri Lankans.

Americans were outside the complex cultural norms that guided support relationships with family/kin members and co-nationals. Overall, the women in the study did not expect any support role from non-Sri Lankans, although they reported being appreciative when support was received.

A majority (57%, $n = 24$) of the women indicated receiving instrumental support from Americans during their first 6 months of settlement. Slightly fewer than half (47%, $n = 19$) indicated receiving some form of social support. Much of this instrumental and social support, however, was unlike family/kin or co-national support, as it involved contact limited to the provision of advice or an invitation to lunch or dinner. "There was an old couple, Mr. and Mrs. V., Americans, who lived in the next apartment. They used to give me advice or call me a taxi if I needed one" (53-year-old woman in the United States for 3 years).

Access to Americans, in such a way that support could be made available, depended significantly on introductory and welcoming programs offered by church groups, educational organizations, or business establishments. Without these programs, a significant number of women had no social contact with Americans and, hence, no opportunity to develop support network relationships during the first 6 months of settlement.

DEVELOPING PERSONAL SUPPORT NETWORKS

After the Sri Lankan woman has been in the United States for some time, do the culturally prescribed support norms continue to act to shape her support experiences? To address this question, information was sought on the member composition of the women's personal support network at the time of the study (Table 11.2).

Again, when available in the United States, family/kin members were the utilized support network: "In the United States, I cannot discuss any private things with friends. I am not so close to them and I would feel embarrassed if they knew. I would be more comfortable going to my sister-in-law" (42-year-old woman in the United States for 2 years).

Table 11.2

Sources of Personal Support

| Support Received | Family/Kin | Source (Percentage) | | Other |
		Co-National	American	
Yes	42	36	40	16
No	58	64	60	84

NOTE: A "yes" was recorded where the respondent indicated at least one person in the particular category

In contrast, utilization of co-nationals as their personal support network was significantly lower than utilization of co-nationals for instrumental and social support. Interestingly, a number of Sri Lankan women reported at least one American as a part of their personal support network.

The findings seem to suggest two issues in relation to the personal support networks of the Sri Lankan women studied: First, the preference for family/kin members remains persistent over time, and second, there is a differential use of the support roles of co-nationals and Americans.

The preferred utilization of Americans over co-nationals as personal support network members seemed to assume that something other than cultural similarity was important in personal support networks. The Sri Lankan women explained that trust and gossip in the development and maintenance of their personal support networks was more important than cultural similarity. It was assumed, unless proven otherwise, that family/kin would not gossip, non-family/kin co-nationals would, and Americans would not.

There appeared a basic contradiction in that Sri Lankans knew each other too well to be trusted to be part of the personal support network. Co-nationals, however, could be used extensively as instrumental and social support network members because the culturally prescribed concept of trust did not apply. Equally, this culturally prescribed concept of trust could perhaps explain the appeal of Americans as personal support network members. Americans by definition could neither "know" a Sri Lankan in a collective family/kin sense nor have access to the means (other Sri Lankan family/kin groups) to gossip about family/kin matters. Although Americans were generally seen as friendly, this friendliness was seen as superficial, symbolic of a "hi and goodbye" process.

CONCLUSIONS

The study of the support networks of Sri Lankans living in the United States has several implications for social work practice, not only with Sri Lankan women, but also with other Asian women with similar cultural backgrounds. Social workers cannot begin to facilitate the development of appropriate support networks for Asian women without a clear understanding of the cultural factors that impinge on these networks (Murase, 1987). It is important for the social worker to be aware of the cultural norms that dictate who can provide support and what type of support can be given, the roles of the receiver and giver, the appropriate support need cues, and so on. To gain an understanding of the cultural context of women's support network, the social worker should encourage clients to describe their cultural world.

In addition, the social worker should seek information about those members their clients would turn to for support, those who would not be used for support, the type of support that would be given, and the support experiences of their clients in the home country.

The findings of the study question the practice of imposing intragroup homogeneity on ethnic minority communities. This approach assumes that common national or ethnic status overrides all intragroup differences. As the study results show in relation to support network development, there are clear intragroup interactive differences operating, based on a trust in individuals to maintain family/kin status and respectability. These differences operate to shape the differential support use of certain categories of individuals. Thus, the social worker must be aware of the appropriate support need and specific network. For example, co-nationals may be appropriately utilized for instrumental and social support needs and yet may be inappropriately used for personal support needs.

The study results also indicate that individual Sri Lankan women do not differentiate themselves from the collective family/kin group. There is a need for social workers to be aware of the role and importance of the family/kin group in shaping individuals' understanding of themselves and their social world (Kavolis, 1984).

Issues surrounding the preparation of social workers for culturally sensitive practice are also raised by the study. Culturally sensitive practice is clearly more than being aware of ostensible cultural differences. Rather, it requires a social work educational process that enables the student to move into the world of the other—to see the world as a

Sri Lankan does. Finally, the study raises questions about the complex issues of the compatibility between the cultural normative base of professional social work practice and the family/kin normative base evidenced in the Sri Lankan community. To be "trusted" generally requires an individual to be a family/kin member or a subsumed family/kin member. Once a non-family/kin member is subsumed within the kin group, that member is expected to adhere to the norms, rights, and obligations of the group. Norms such as not talking or gossiping outside the family/kin group about family/kin matters, and the provision of extensive and unconditional support, for example, seem to sit uneasily with the social work professional norms of case conference discussion and professional detachment.

Clearly, the dynamics of culture have an important role in shaping the support network experiences of ethnic minority women in the United States. Further research in this area is an exciting challenge to the social work profession in the 1990s.

REFERENCES

Becerra, R., & Zambrana, R. (1985). Methodological approaches to research on Hispanics. *Social Work Research and Abstracts, 21*(2), 42-49.

Bell, R. (1981). *The worlds of friendship*. Beverly Hills, CA: Sage.

Belsky, R., & Rovine, M. (1984). Social network contact, family support and the transition to parenthood. *Journal of Marriage and the Family, 46*, 455-482.

Bott, E. (1957). *Family and social networks: Roles, norms and external relationships in ordinary urban families*. New York: Free Press.

Collins, A., & Pancoast, D. (1976). *Natural helping networks*. Silver Spring, MD: National Association of Social Workers.

Hoppa, S. (1986). The catch in social support. *Social Work, 31*, 419-420.

Kavolis, J. (Ed.). (1984). *Designs of selfhood*. London: Associated University Press.

Murase, K. (1987, June). *Help seeking behavior of Southeast Asian refugees*. Paper presented at the 1987 Minority Issues Conference of the National Association of Social Workers, Washington, D. C.

Paton, M. (1980). *Qualitative evaluation methods*. Beverly Hills, CA: Sage.

Rack, P. (1977). *Race, culture and mental disorders*. London: Tavistock.

Shuval, J. (1982). Migration and stress. In L. Goldberger & S. Breznitz (Eds.), *Handbook of stress: Theoretical and clinical aspects* (pp. 677-691). New York: Free Press.

Stack, C. (1974). *All our kin: Strategies of survival in a black community*. New York: Harper & Row.

Vaux, A. (1985). Variations in social support associated with gender, ethnicity and age. *Journal of Social Issues, 41*, 89-110.

Chapter 12

BATTERED KOREAN WOMEN IN URBAN UNITED STATES

YOUNG I. SONG-KIM

The lives of battered Korean women in the United States are an extension of thousands of years of subjugation, with the additional conflicts
resulting from adjustment to a new culture. To fully understand the
problem of battered women in Korean immigrant families, it is necessary to consider this phenomenon in light of its historical precedent as
well as the current social and economic conditions arising from resettlement experiences in a different culture.

Throughout history Korean women have been the victims of physical
and psychological abuse. Specifically, the battering of women has been
justified by the conventions of Korean culture, which is deeply rooted in
the philosophy of male domination. The language reflects the stratification
and segregation of the sexes and their interpersonal relations in Korean
thought. For example, a wife speaks of her husband as *uri chip ju in* (the
master of our house). She also may refer to him as the *pa-kaat yang-ban*
(outside gentleman). In sharp contrast, the wife is the husband's *chip saram*
(house person) or his *an saram* (inside person) (Crane, 1967).

Korean society has taught men not only to expect services from and
to have authority over women, but also to discipline their wives by any
means, including violent punishment. Meanwhile, that same society has
taught women to accept their subordinate position, to obey their husbands, and to blame themselves for any family problems, including the
occurrence of domestic violence. Added to these factors are the pressures on Korean immigrant families to adapt to a new socioeconomic

environment—an adjustment for which few are prepared. As is often the case in many immigrant families, the husband is unable to fulfill his traditional role as sole provider because of unemployment or underemployment, and this results in his sensing a weakened status. In the words of Yu (1980), "Absolute male dominant sex roles in the traditional Korean family cannot be maintained intact in the United States" (p. 127).

Battered women has been broadly researched. It is experienced as the perception of absolute dominance and need for control by male partners (Adler, 1966; Bandura, 1977; Baum & Singer, 1980; Langer, 1983; Perlmuter & Monty, 1979; Seligman, 1975). Male sex-role socialization, which establishes the male as the ultimate authority and power, increases the likelihood of experiences of anger and resultant violence when his position of dominance is threatened (Dutton & Browning, 1988; Gondolf, 1985; Pleck, 1981). Considerable evidence indicates that situational stresses, many of which relate to the traditional male role of the provider, result in domestic violence. Unemployment, job dissatisfaction, and financial difficulties, for example, frequently are associated with episodes of battering women (Gelles, 1972; Prescott & Letko, 1977; Roy 1977), and these stresses have been linked to abuse in Korean immigrant families (Yim, 1978).

Given these considerations, the primary objectives of the current study were to describe the level and frequency of conjugal violence in Korean immigrant families and to examine the relationships between cultural conflicts arising during the adjustment to life in a foreign country and conjugal violence. Three hypotheses were tested in the study:

(a) Korean women who have more traditional attitudes experience more abuse than women who have less traditional attitudes,

(b) Korean women who live by more rigidly defined traditional sex-role tasks experience more abuse than women who share sex-role tasks with their spouses, and

(c) Korean women in households with higher levels of stress arising from their immigrant status experience more abuse than women in households with lower levels of stress.

METHODOLOGY

The data for the study were collected by interviewing 150 Korean women residing in Chicago. Participants in the study consisted of women, ages 18 years and older, who had resided in the United States for not more than 10 years. Participants were selected by two methods: (a) from the directories of several Korean associations and lists of subscribers of Korean newspapers and (b) from a list of names elicited from interviewees, thus partially using a snowball sampling method. Data were collected by means of structured interviews using a standardized questionnaire format. The standardized interview schedule elicited this demographic information: age, level of education, employment status, religious affiliation, and length of residence in the United States; performance on specific household tasks by wife, husband, or both; attitudes about Korean tradition regarding sex roles; and type, severity, and frequency of abusive behaviors experienced by the respondents. After the initial telephone contact, participants selected from directories and subscribers' lists were contacted by telephone and interviewed at their homes. Interviews also were conducted at various locations, including churches, temples, Korean restaurants, grocery stores, shops, and nursery schools.

The combination of this particular sampling strategy, with the concentration of the sample group in one major city, raises questions about generalizing the findings to a broader Korean population. However, careful data collection procedures were followed to reduce biases and provide critical information related to the target population.

RESULTS AND DISCUSSION

Background Information

The Korean immigrant women in the sample consisted primarily of married participants (82%, $n = 123$) whose average length of residence in the United States was 5 years. Only 1% ($n = 2$) of the women in the sample were never married. The participants on the average were 36 years of age, and 27% ($n = 41$) were college graduates. Of the respondents, 46% ($n = 69$) had a monthly family income of less than $2,000, and 30% ($n = 47$) were unemployed. The largest group of respondents, 80% ($n = 120$) were Christians.

Levels of Abuse

Findings showed that a significant proportion of Korean immigrant women suffer from conjugal violence. Of the 150 respondents, 60%

(n = 90) reported being battered, and the remaining 40% (n = 60) reported not being battered. An analysis of the type of abusive act, the frequency and severity of abuse for the 90 respondents reporting physical abuse, and the type of resultant injury is presented in Table 12.1. The frequency and intensity of abusive behaviors varied widely.

In two extreme cases, the batterers attempted to kill their wives. Seventy percent (n = 63) of the battered women had experienced bruises, 10% (n = 9) had damaged teeth, and 17% (n = 15) suffered from concussions. Moreover, 9% (n = 8) of the victims had miscarriages, and 7% (n = 6) had been hospitalized as a result of domestic violence. In terms of frequency, 24% (n = 22) of the battered women suffered from violence at least once a week, and an additional 37% (n = 33) had been subjected to violence at least once a month.

The highest level of abuse in Korean immigrant families, 75% (n = 68), occurred within 3 to 5 years of establishing residence in the United States. Thus, the findings of this study indicate high levels and frequency of experiences of abuse among urban Korean immigrant women. This estimate of the level of physical abuse in Korean women only is significantly higher than the figures for reported abuse among American women for physical, verbal, and psychological abuse (Walker, 1979).

FACTORS CURRENTLY CONTRIBUTING TO THE INCIDENCE OF BATTERED WOMEN IN KOREAN IMMIGRANT FAMILIES

Cultural Factors

Information on cultural factors was obtained in two areas: (a) performance of household tasks by gender and (b) attitude toward traditional cultural sex-role tasks. A list of categories of sex-role tasks was developed in consultation with Korean sociologists and psychologists.

Sex-Role Task Performance and Traditional Attitudes

The results of this study showed that a significant proportion of Korean immigrant wives, regardless of their employment status, continued to live by rigidly defined traditional sex roles. In Korea, there is a clear-cut distinction of certain roles that wives and husbands, respectively, assume.

Table 12.1

Levels of Abuse

Degree: Description of Abusive Acts	n	%
Low		
My husband/partner yelled at me	125	—
My husband/partner swore at me	71	78.9
My husband/partner destroyed my property	39	43.3
My husband/partner threw an object at me	46	51.1
Moderate		
My husband/partner threatened to hit me with an object	31	34.4
My husband/partner threatened to hit me with his fist	51	56.7
My husband/partner hit me with a closed fist	51	56.7
Somewhat Severe		
My husband/partner slapped me	38	42.2
My husband/partner hit me with an object	19	21.1
My husband/partner threatened me with a knife	14	15.6
My husband/partner threatened to kill me	20	22.2
Moderately Severe		
My husband/partner threatened to kill himself	13	14.4
My husband/partner threatened me with a gun	4	4.4
My husband/partner forced me to have sex with him	33	36.7
Severe		
My husband/partner squeezed or pinched me	23	25.6
My husband/partner choked me	22	24.4
My husband/partner burned me	4	4.4
My husband/partner broke my bone	7	7.8
My husband/partner stabbed me	3	3.3
Very Severe		
My husband/partner attempted to kill me	2	2.2
Resulting in		
Low		
Bruises	63	70.0
Moderately severe		
Black eye	34	37.8
Minor cuts or burns	27	30.0
Cuts, burns, or bruises requiring medical attention	13	14.4
Very severe		
Concussion	15	16.7
Damage to teeth	9	10.0
Broken bones	8	8.9
Joint injury	3	3.3
Spinal injury	1	1.1

(continued)

Table 12.1

Continued

Degree: Description of Abusive Acts	n	%
Injury to internal organs	2	2.2
Miscarriage	8	8.9
Emotional/mental distress requiring medial care	26	28.9
Physical injury requiring hospitalization	6	6.7
Frequency of abuse		
At least once a day	3	3.3
At least once a week	22	24.4
At least once a month	33	37.0
At least once a year	32	35.6

NOTE: $n = 125$ here is larger than the $n = 90$ who reported abuse, because the term *battered* did not include verbal or psychological abuse. Even though such abuse is undeniably damaging and painful, the overall consensus among the Korean women studied was that verbal abuse is not an actual occurrence of abuse.

The roles of driver, cook, baby-sitter, and shopper are rarely performed by the husband in Korea.

Even the design of living space in Korea exemplifies these divisions. For instance, the kitchen, which in Korea is off-limits to men under normal circumstances, intrudes conspicuously in the United States into the living room, which must be shared by all family members. The living arrangement is apparently more distressful to immigrant Korean men than women, because (a) men have had less experience than women in intense domestic environments and (b) these changes occur when the men already feel extremely vulnerable because of stresses arising from the transition from the Korean to the American Korean culture.

This study measured the patterns of the respondents' sex-role performance by how each couple divided and shared household chores. The majority of recent Korean immigrant women performed traditional tasks—cooking (83%, $n = 125$), washing dishes (73%, $n = 109$), laundry (67%, $n = 101$), child care (59%, $n = 88$), making the bed (63%, $n = 94$), and cleaning the house (61%, $n = 91$). However, certain tasks that required outside activities were shared by many men, such as: deciding to buy something (60%, $n = 90$), deciding to buy a house (59%, $n = 88$), shopping for groceries (57%, $n = 85$), and driving the car (80%, $n = 120$). Household tasks carried out exclusively by a large percentage of husbands included driving the car (37%, $n = 56$), paying bills (35%, $n = 52$), and making the

Table 12.2

Distribution of Respondent's Sex-Role Performance in the Household Tasks

Task	Battered (n = 90)				Nonbattered (n = 60)				Grand Total (n = 150)			
	Wife	Husband	Both	Total	Wife	Husband	Both	Total	Wife	Husband	Both	Total
Cooking	77 / 85.5%	0 / 0%	13 / 14.4%	90 / 100%	48 / 80%	0 / 0%	12 / 20%	60 / 100%	125 / 83%	0 / 0%	25 / 17%	150 / 100%
Washing dishes	69 / 76.6%	2 / 2.2%	19 / 21.1%	90 / 100%	40 / 66.7%	2 / 3.3%	18 / 30%	60 / 100%	109 / 73%	4 / 3%	37 / 28%	150 / 100%
Laundry	66 / 73.3%	4 / 4.4%	20 / 22.2%	90 / 100%	35 / 58.3%	4 / 6.6%	21 / 35%	60 / 100%	101 / 67%	8 / 5%	42 / 28%	150 / 100%
Driving the car	13 / 14.4%	42 / 46.7%	34 / 37.8%	90 / 100%	5 / 8.3%	14 / 23.3%	42 / 68.3%	60 / 100%	18 / 12%	56 / 37%	76 / 51%	150 / 100%
Shopping for groceries	43 / 47.7%	2 / 2.2%	45 / 50%	90 / 100%	20 / 33.3%	0 / 0%	40 / 66.6%	60 / 100%	63 / 42%	2 / 1%	85 / 57%	150 / 100%
Buying clothes	55 / 61.1%	2 / 2.2%	33 / 36.7%	90 / 100%	30 / 50%	5 / 5%	27 / 45%	60 / 100%	85 / 57%	5 / 3%	60 / 40%	150 / 100%
Paying bills	39 / 43.3%	32 / 35.5%	19 / 21.1%	90 / 100%	16 / 26.7%	20 / 33.3%	24 / 40%	60 / 100%	55 / 37%	52 / 35%	43 / 29%	150 / 100%
Taking care of children	61 / 67.8%	1 / 1.1%	28 / 31.1%	90 / 100%	27 / 45%	0 / 0%	33 / 55%	60 / 100%	88 / 59%	1 / 1%	61 / 41%	150 / 100%
Talking to teachers	56 / 62.2%	13 / 14.4%	21 / 23.3%	90 / 100%	12 / 20%	5 / 8.5%	43 / 71.6%	60 / 100%	68 / 45%	18 / 12%	64 / 43%	150 / 100%
Making bed	67 / 74.4%	1 / 1.1%	22 / 24.4%	90 / 100%	27 / 45%	4 / 6.7%	29 / 48.3%	60 / 100%	94 / 63%	5 / 3%	51 / 34%	150 / 100%
Cleaning house	68 / 75.5%	1 / 1.1%	21 / 23.3%	90 / 100%	23 / 38.3%	4 / 6.7%	33 / 55%	60 / 100%	91 / 61%	5 / 3%	54 / 36%	150 / 100%
Deciding to buy something	18 / 20%	30 / 33.3%	42 / 46.7%	90 / 100%	7 / 11.7%	5 / 8.3%	48 / 80%	60 / 100%	25 / 17%	35 / 23%	90 / 60%	150 / 100%
Deciding to buy house	10 / 11.1%	43 / 41.1%	37 / 41.1%	90 / 100%	5 / 8.3%	4 / 6.7%	51 / 85%	60 / 100%	15 / 31%	47 / 31%	88 / 59%	150 / 100%

decision to buy a house (31%, $n = 47$). Therefore, the data indicate that very few Korean men take primary responsibility for household tasks.

A chi-square comparison was made to test the relationship between sex-role performance and battered status. The results indicated a statistically significant relationship between sex-role performance and battered status ($\chi^2 = 25.14$; $df = 2$, $p<.05$). Couples who adhered to rigid sex-role performance standards were more violent than those who did not. Eighty-four percent of the couples with high congruency, as opposed to 45% of those with low congruency, experienced violent situations. More than 58% of the battering occurred in families with high conformity to rigid sex roles, whereas only 17% of nonviolent families conformed to the rigid Korean patterns of sex-role performance.

A chi-square comparison was made to test the relationship between traditional attitudes and battered status. The results indicated a statistically significant relationship between traditional attitudes and battered status ($\chi^2 = 6.17$; $df = 1$; $p<.01$). Korean women with more traditional attitudes in terms of appropriate husband-wife relationships experienced more abuse than those with less traditional attitudes. More than half of the battered women (52%, $n = 47$) as opposed to fewer than one-third of the nonbattered women (32%, $n = 19$) scored "high" on the scale of traditionalism. Alternatively interpreted, nearly three-quarters (71%, or 47 of 66) of the respondents with a more traditional attitude were victims of domestic violence compared to half (51%, or 43 of 86) of the women with a less traditional attitude.

Explanations for these findings are that the Korean immigrant wife may accept the traditional attitudes with which she was raised in her country of origin in terms of self-role task; her attempts to maintain these traditional roles in an environment with multiple stressors creates the potential for abusive situations; and Korean wives, in the process of observing and internalizing the values of the host U. S. culture, may question and challenge traditional Korean values, which would result in marital conflict and, hence, violence. For those women who are in situations in which their spouses have internalized the values of the host culture and thus have started sharing sex-role tasks, the potential for conflict and violence would be less.

Stress-Evoking Factors

The sources of stress and frustrations among Korean immigrant families, especially those who recently arrived, seem to be a combination of many factors, including unsatisfactory employment status, lack of social contacts, and language problems. Although language difficulties and a lack of social contacts may isolate the immigrants, they are not expected to result in the severe level of stress of unsatisfactory employment status. Upon arrival in the United States, a majority of immigrants face the harsh reality of the unfavorable labor market. For example, many Korean college graduates hold blue-collar jobs, and many professionals are either unemployed, underemployed, or have turned to nonprofessional jobs.

Language barriers, discrimination in hiring, and the lack of job information force most newcomers to begin their occupational career at the bottom of the ladder, as low-skilled and low-paid blue-collar or service workers. These stress-evoking factors may be a source of, and provide an understanding of, the causes and strategies of domestic violence in Korean immigrant families.

A chi-square comparison was calculated to test the relationship between employment status and battered status. The results indicate a statistically significant relationship between the incidence of battering and inconsistency in the pre-immigration and post-immigration employment status of husbands (χ^2 = 25.2; df = 1; $p<.05$). Fifty-eight percent (n = 52) of the batterers, as opposed to 17% (n = 10) of nonviolent husbands, held lower employment status upon immigrating to the United States. Interpreted from another perspective, more than four-fifths (84%, n = 76) of the men who held lower employment status were found to be wife batterers, whereas fewer than half (43%, n = 39) of those who assumed the same or higher employment status instigated violence.

Social contacts of the respondents were measured in terms of frequency of contact with friends, physical mobility, or participation in organizations. A cross-tabulation of social contacts and battered status was done to describe the relationship between these two factors. Lack of social contact was found to be significantly higher among battered women than nonbattered women. Only 7% (n = 6) of battered women went out frequently, whereas 20% (n = 12) of the nonbattered group went out daily. Similarly, nearly half (n = 43) of the battered women spoke to friends and relatives less than once a week or hardly at all, and 36% (n = 22) of the nonbattered women talked to friends or relatives at least once a week. Additionally, 89% (n = 53) of the nonbattered women participated in Korean or other social or professional activities.

Language problems were associated, to some extent, with episodes of battering. About one-fourth ($n = 24$) of the battered women evaluated their English skills as "poor" or "not at all," while none of the non-battered women reported being unable to speak English.

Thus, the current study clearly indicates a relationship between wife-battering and stress-evoking factors, such as unsatisfactory employment status, language problems, and a lack of social contacts. The findings of the study on factors associated with the occurrence of violence against immigrant Korean women can be illustrated by the following case presentation.

> The husband had a very successful career as an engineer in Korea, but couldn't practice his profession in the United States because of problems in obtaining a license. After soliciting suitable employment for 2 months, out of desperation he took a job as a janitor in an office building. Although he continued to apply for better employment at other places, he was continually turned down because of his poor English language skills. The wife, who had never been employed, took a job at a local garment factory, working 12-hour days and 10 hours on Saturdays. She subsequently brought in more money than her husband. Despite her long working hours and economic contributions to the home, the husband consistently complained that since they moved to America, the wife had become too "Americanized." She left dirty dishes in the sink and occasionally did not have meals ready on time, using the excuse that she had to "rush to go to work." The husband wanted his wife to be a good Korean wife. He insisted that, even though she was in America, she should still fulfill the Korean wife's role. The husband obviously felt frustrated in what he perceived as his wife's abandonment of the female role, and she reported feeling an acute sense of inequality and being overburdened with the absolute demands of the traditional Korean wife's role in addition to the long hours employed in a small and dusty workroom.

Dealing with the stress of immigration, as well as adapting to the demands of a new culture and one in which a woman's status is so different, invariably results in a strain on established family roles. The frustrations resulting from these stresses appear to accumulate over time and reach a breaking point at which inhibitions against violence are dropped. This study shows the breaking point to happen somewhere between 3 and 5 years after establishing residence in a new country.

Korean traditionalism apparently is strongly linked to battered women. Women who adhere to rigid sex roles experience more violence than women who are in households in which tasks traditionally carried out by females are shared with their male partners. In fact, the victims of battering may exemplify the society's old image of ideal womanhood: submissive, religious, nonassertive, self-blaming, and accepting of whatever the husband's life brings (Davidson, 1978). This bears out Pagelow's hypothesis (1984), which states that the more intense the wife's traditional ideology, the more likely she is to remain in an abusive situation. Additionally, couples who conceptually agree with traditional sex roles produce more violent situations. Where abuse is believed to be justified, it is much more likely to occur.

Researchers have suggested that battered women remain in a violent relationship because of many social and economic obstacles (MacLeod, 1980; Strube & Barbour, 1983, 1984), including fear of increased violence, lack of support and resources, and fear of loneliness. Korean women are no exception to this generalization. The majority of women studied rarely speak with anyone regarding their abuse. There also is evidence that social isolation of battered women constitutes part of both the cause and the consequence of abuse. According to Walker (1979) and Martin (1983), the batterer tends to systematically isolate the woman from others. She, in turn, also withdraws to protect herself from further harassment.

The traditional Korean culture views the wife as causing the abuse. Abuse is seen as a reaction to an unhappy home life. The assumption is that if a man is unhappy enough to hit his wife, she deserves it. Hence, blame and shame are yet other impediments to articulating the problem.

IMPLICATIONS FOR SOCIAL WORKERS AND CONCLUSIONS

The implications of these findings for the mental health profession are manifold. Those who have helping roles with this population should endeavor to acknowledge the problems Korean immigrants face in their attempts to obtain employment equivalent to that which they held in their native country, and should try to help them gain required job and language skills. Although Korean families oftentimes do not welcome institutional assistance because of cultural bias against it, informational materials and services should be made available to both Korean men and Korean women. Such educational efforts will help them accept and understand the changes in cultural norms that are inconsistent with contemporary American values and are not economically viable to their family unit.

Most respondents in the study had little knowledge of what resources were available to them. Hence, information written in the Korean language about existing programs should be disseminated before initiating new public services programs. Further research of the problem may indicate a need for new services, for both battered women and their spouses.

Despite the emotions and anxieties aroused by the interviewing process, many women in the study said that being able to talk about the abuse had been helpful. They felt they gained insight and a better understanding of their situations. Even though there was no actual counseling, the discussion of wife-abuse in an accepting, nonjudgmental setting appeared to be quite therapeutic. As one battered women reported, "I didn't want to admit that I was a battered woman, that this ugly thing was really happening in my home. I thought I had done something terrible wrong, but when I confessed it . . . I found that there really were people concerned for my welfare." Clearly, the social worker needs to acknowledge that the woman is not alone in experiencing the abuse and that she is not to blame for it. This may serve as a first line of defense against the problem.

A recent study by a Korean family legal counseling service in Los Angeles ("Korean Battered Women," 1990) found that wife-abuse is the most serious of all domestic problems occurring in immigrant Korean families. That few Korean women seek professional help indicates not only that, culturally, Korean immigrants reject the idea of professional help, but also that there must be many untreated, unrevealed cases of abuse in the Korean population in major urban centers throughout the United States. The problem may also extend to other Asian women.

Social work practitioners need to assess the situation and help clients recognize that denial, rationalization (making excuses for the batterer and blaming herself), and pretending that battering is not as serious as it really is are coping skills they have developed. In fact, most of the battered women in the current study reported that they did nothing and "hoped that time would take care of the problem." Once these battered women face the truth of their victimization, social workers can help them enhance their perception of themselves and the way in which they live. No matter what they have experienced in the past, they have the right to make new choices.

Most important, social workers need to focus on the strengths of attered Korean women when intervening. Social workers are encourged to help these women see that the incredible strength they have hown in enduring their problems may be constructively rechanneled o improve the quality of their lives. There is much reason to be ptimistic regarding battered Korean women if culturally sensitive ntervention is provided.

REFERENCES

dler, A. (1966). The psychology of power. *Journal of Individual Psychology, 22*, 166-172.

andura, A. (1977). Self-efficacy: Toward a unified theory of behavioral change. *Psychological Review, 84*, 191-215.

aum, A., & Singer, J. E. (Eds.). (1980). *Applications of personal control: Advances of environmental psychology.* Englewood Cliffs, NJ: Lawrence Erlbaum.

rane, P. (1967). *Korean patterns.* Seoul: Hollym.

avidson, T. (1978). *Conjugal crime: Understanding and changing wife beating patterns.* New York: Hawthorn.

utton, D. G., & Browning, J. J. (1988). Power struggles and intimacy anxieties as causative factors of violence in intimate relationships. In G. Russell (Ed.), *Violence in intimate relationships* (pp. 163-175). New York: Russell Sage.

elles, R. J. (1972). *The violent home: A study of physical aggression between husbands and wives.* Beverly Hills, CA: Sage.

ondolf, E. W. (1985). Anger and oppression in men who batter: Empiricist and feminist perspectives and their implications for research. *Victimology: An International Journal, 10*, 311-324.

orean battered women: Increasing significantly. (1990, September 23). *Korean Times,* p. 6.

anger, E. (1983). *The psychology of control.* Beverly Hills, CA: Sage.

acLeod, L. (1980). *Wife battering in Canada: The vicious circle.* Ottawa: The Canadian Advisory Council on the Status of Women.

artin, D. (1983). *Battered wives.* San Francisco: Volcano.

agelow, M. (1984). *Family violence.* New York: Praeger.

erlmuter, L. C., & Monty, R. A. (Eds.). (1979). *Choice and perceived control.* Hillsdale, NJ: Lawrence Erlbaum.

leck, J. H. (1981). *The myth of masculinity.* Cambridge: MIT Press.

rescott, S. L., & Letko, C. (1977). Battered women: A social psychological perspective. In M. Roy (Ed.), *Battered women: A psychosociological study of domestic violence* (pp. 72-96). New York: Van Nostrand Reinhold.

oy, M. (1977). A current survey of 150 cases. In M. Roy (Ed.), *Battered women: A psychosociological study of domestic violence* (pp. 25-44). New York: Van Nostrand Reinhold.

eligman, M. E. (1975). *On depression, development and death.* San Francisco: Freeman.

Strube, M. J., & Barbour, L. S. (1983). The decision to leave an abusive relationship: An economic dependence and psychological commitment. *Journal of Marriage and the Family, 45,* 785-793.

Strube, M. J., & Barbour, L. S. (1984). Factors related to the decision to leave an abusive relationship. *Journal of Marriage and the Family, 46,* 837-844.

Walker, L. E. (1979). *The battered woman.* New York: Harper & Row.

Yim, S. B. (1978). Korean battered wives: A sociological and psychological analysis of conjugal violence in Korean immigrant families. In H. Sunoo & D. Kom (Eds.), *Korean women struggle for humanization* (pp. 171-199). Memphis, TN: Korean Christian Scholars.

Yu, E-Y. (1980). Koreans in America: Social and economic adjustment. In B-S Kim (Ed.), *The Korean immigration in America* (pp. 119-137). NJ: Association of Korean Christian Schools.

Chapter 13

KOREAN ELDERLY:
Policy, Program, and Practice Implications

PAUL K. KIM
JUNG-SUP KIM

The number of Korean elderly living in the United States is estimated to be approximately 75,000 and is increasing. Korean elderly not only face similar economic, health care, and social plights as Euro American elderly, but they also must deal with the additional problems of being ethnic minority group members with limited English language skills.

This chapter presents the following: (a) a description of demographic and social characteristics of Korean elderly; (b) a discussion of the three major problems that confront the elderly—economic insecurity, poor health, and mental health problems, including racial discrimination; (c) policy and program recommendations to alleviate the plight of the elderly; and (d) social work practice implications in relation to the values and traditions of Korean elderly.

HISTORY AND CHARACTERISTICS

The first group of 101 Koreans was admitted to the U. S. territory, the Hawaiian Islands, in 1903 through the Korean American Treaty of Amity and Trade (Hurh & Kim, 1984; Kim, 1981; Kim, 1971). Unlike the previous Asian immigrants from China and Japan, early Korean immigrants were not disadvantaged by various discriminatory exclusion acts. On the contrary, implementation of the 1882 Chinese exclusion law resulted in a shortage of incoming cheap laborers, and hence a desire for Korean immigrants to replace the Chinese in the sugar cane fields. Later, however, under the U. S. immigration quota system, only 100 Koreans were allowed to immigrate each year between 1952 and 1965 (U. S. Department of Justice, 1964-1980). The 1965 immigration law eliminated the selective immigrant quota system, resulting in substantial increases in the admission of Koreans to the United States.

Over the past two decades, an average of 33,000 Koreans annually have entered the United States as legal immigrants, with approximately 51% of them settling in Pacific Coast states (U. S. Department of Justice, 1964-1980). In 1980 there were an estimated 355,000 Koreans in the United States, including an estimated 20,000 who were elderly (U. S. Bureau of the Census, 1980). However, the Korean embassy in Washington, D.C., estimated between approximately 800,000 and 1 million Koreans were living in the United States in 1989, including more than 75,000 elders. This increase is explained by limited participation of Koreans in the 1980 census, the presence of illegal aliens, and the increase in numbers since 1980.

Although the Korean culture and traditions are built on the teachings of Confucianism and Buddhism, more than 80% of Koreans claim to be Christians. They maintain a Judeo-Christian life-style in the United States, and their family and friends are Korean neighbors and fellow Christians.

Korean families enjoy a higher income than the average American family. In 1976, two-thirds of Koreans in the Los Angeles area earned an annual income that exceeded the national median income for the year, and more than 85% earned an income that exceeded the median income of other ethnic minorities. The reason for the higher income is that the majority of Koreans live in nuclear families in which most of the family members earn an income. A study of Koreans in the Greater Atlanta, Georgia area indicated that approximately 86% of individuals older than age 20 are married. It is not uncommon for both husband and wife to be in the labor force. In general, Koreans appear satisfied with their immigration to the United States and feel that they are making satisfactory progress as planned (Hurh & Kim, 1979, 1984).

Despite a common religious affiliation with the larger American society and a comfortable economic status, Koreans experience social and emotional problems. In two separate studies, Hurh and Kim (1979, 1984) found that 36% and 47% of Koreans, respectively, stated that they felt powerless and lonely, and 84% experienced serious language problems. Married Korean women, in particular, pay the heaviest toll in the family by working up to two or three full-time jobs. In addition, Korean immigrants have the highest incidence of depression among their Asian counterparts (Kuo, 1984). Nonetheless, Korean families are being modernized and Westernized at a faster rate than other Asian groups, and the number of Korean nuclear families is increasing. The number of Korean elderly who are 60 years of age or older is also increasing. This population is particularly susceptible to stress.

METHODOLOGY

To examine the levels and causes of stress and its consequences for the Korean elderly, a review of the literature and three studies were conducted. This chapter is based on the literature review and the three studies.

Sample participants in all three studies were residents of New York City and its surrounding communities, and were contacted through ethnic, social, cultural, and religious organizations in the area, as well as through local ethnic newspapers. Koh interviewed 151 elderly Koreans in 1983, while Kim interviewed 538 in 1987 and 69 in 1988 with a structured questionnaire.

The 1983 and 1987 studies were both designed to examine social and demographic conditions of Korean elderly, and utilized structured questionnaires with similar items. The 1988 study, on the other hand, was intended to prioritize social programs needed by Koreans in the New York area, and thus the questionnaire for that study was not completely comparable to the questionnaires used in 1983 and 1987. Nonetheless, respondents in 1988 cited perceived "problem areas." For the analysis presented here, variables from the three studies used for a trend analysis are age, sex, marital status, religious affiliation, number of years in the United States, socioeconomic status, and problems and prospects facing elderly immigrants.

CHANGING DEMOGRAPHIC CHARACTERISTICS
OF THE KOREAN ELDERLY

The median age of Korean elderly in New York shifted during the period of 1983 to 1988 from 73 years to 66. In 1988 approximately 10% more elderly were in the age 66 or older category. Middle-aged immigrants who came to the United States in the late 1960s and 1970s are

now in their early sixties. Additionally, many elderly persons are among
the recent immigrants who followed their children. Consequently, the
segment of older Koreans is growing rapidly. Moreover, the female
elderly in 1988 outnumbered their male counterparts 2:1, a significant
change from 1983, when the ratio was nearly 1:1. The number of
married elderly persons has decreased by 33% since 1983. In addition,
both the number of Korean elderly who are widowed and the number
of unmarried single individuals are increasing, statistics that are similar
to those in Korea (United Nations, 1984). In the 1988 study, information
regarding the elders' perception in the following areas was obtained:
occupation, attitudes toward family life, marital satisfaction, racism;
self-confidence, futuristic outlook, leisure activities, neighbors; and
local, state, and federal governments. With the exception of attitude
toward marriage, all of these categories are statistically significant at
the level of $p<.001$. This indicates that levels of satisfaction in marriage
are almost equally distributed, in that 24% indicate high satisfaction,
and 22% indicate dissatisfaction.

SOCIAL ISOLATION AND
SEPARATION FROM FAMILY

Most elderly Koreans live in rented apartments, and nearly half are
married and live with spouses. As their children grow older, choose
careers, and move away, the parents are left to themselves. Consequently, the elder's expectation of living in an extended family generally is not met. Since 1983 the trend has been that fewer elderly persons
are living with their children; instead, an increasing number of older
Koreans are living alone or with other relatives or friends.

Separated from their children and handicapped by the language
barrier, many Korean elderly live in, or close to, places known as Korea
Town—Olympic Boulevard in Los Angeles, Lawrence Avenue in Chicago, and Flushing in New York. Here the elderly can meet other
Koreans, converse in the same language, and maintain social, economic, and religious ties.

The children of Korean elders who have moved away communicate
with their parents. Forty-two percent of elderly persons receive phone
calls from their children at least once a week, but their children visit
only two to three times a year. Older persons accept separation from

their children, and the subsequent loneliness, simply to promote their children's happiness; however, some blame their children's lack of filial devotion for their low life satisfaction, yet most of them accept or endure their children's neglect.

Unlike the Japanese elderly, who maintain a strong informal support network among their cohort group members, the Korean elderly appear to be independent and too proud to ask for help from persons outside their immediate family. They seem more concerned about the tradi-tional value of *che-myun,* or face-saving, and therefore tend to internal-ize their personal problems. Koreans are highly competitive, even among family members, and thus their mutual support systems are much weaker than those of other Asian groups. Of those in the study, only 21% of Korean elderly receive some financial support from their chil-dren; 55% prepare their own meals; and 3% have meals provided by daughters-in-law (J. S. Kim, 1987).

MAJOR PROBLEMS FACING KOREAN ELDERLY

Korean elderly face the three primary problems of economic inse-curity, poor health, and racial discrimination, for which they require social work intervention.

Economic Insecurity

While young Korean families seem to be comfortable financially, the condition of Korean elderly can be characterized as poor. Forty-seven percent of Korean elders received Supplemental Security Income (SSI) in 1983 and 1987. From 1983 to 1988, the number of elderly persons in New York who lived under poverty (an income below $3,000 per year) apparently increased by about sixfold, from 12% to 70%. Economic poverty among the Korean elderly can be attributed to several causes: low Social Security payments; ineligibility for Social Security benefits; unemployment or underemployment; loss of the spouse responsible for partial financial support; an increased cost of living, especially in housing; and forced withdrawal from the labor market because of poor health. Most of the Korean elderly studied in 1987 were dissatisfied with their low income level.

Poor Health

As a natural process of human aging, Koreans experience poor health in their old age. Most Koreans today perceive their health as "fair" or "poor." The proportion of elderly who described their health conditions as "fair to poor" increased substantially, from 38% in 1983 to 86% in 1988. Major health-related complaints include poor eyesight, diminished hearing, and high blood pressure. While health problems related to nervous and digestive systems were prevalent in 1988, they were even more apparent in 1983. According to a World Health Organization study (Andrews, Esterman, Braunack-Mayer, & Rungie, 1986), Koreans are likely to develop vision and dental problems in their old age. Whenever they need to see physicians, more and more elderly persons—88% in 1988—prefer Korean doctors. Only 4% wanted to be treated by local herbalists. Fifty-two percent of elderly persons have Medicare or Medicaid coverage, and the remaining 48% indicated no health insurance whatsoever.

Mental Health and Attitude Toward Racism

Racial discrimination is one of the most serious mental health problems for the Korean elderly. Although the civil rights movement of the 1960s brought significant progress, at the cost of noble lives of outstanding Americans, the prejudice against ethnic minorities still affects the lives of immigrants. According to the 1988 study, 48% expressed a strong negative feeling about racism, 20% indicated "as anticipated," and 34% had "no opinion." Those who indicate "no opinion" may be hesitant to express their opinion, or may not yet have experienced much interracial animosity because they have not associated with mainstream American society. A significant proportion of the Korean elderly have limited English language capabilities; hence, they generally mingle among themselves in social, economic, cultural, religious, or political activities.

Increasing numbers of Korean elderly are living in ethnic enclaves, apart from their adult children. A high proportion have poor physical and mental health. Nonetheless, by effective use of entitlement acts and resources, these problems are not insurmountable because the problems of the elderly have surfaced relatively recently. Perhaps these problems are even preventable, with appropriate and timely intervention. The United States should deal with the growing social problems facing newcomers from Asia. The following recommended policies and programs

Table 13.1

Health Care Needs Among Korean Elderly

	1983	1987	1988
Perceived health conditions			
Excellent-good	62	17	14
Fair-poor	38	83	86
Choice of health care providers			
Korean American doctors	66	85	88
Herbalists	8	5	4
American doctors	19	7	8
Others (clinics, emergency rooms, and so forth)	7	3	0
Health insurance			
Medicare/Medicaid	46	56	52
None	54	44	48

are applicable, perhaps not only to elderly ethnic minorities but also to all elderly persons who experience similar problems, regardless of their ethnicity.

POLICY AND PROGRAM RECOMMENDATIONS

Income security for older immigrants should be guaranteed. Although the Social Security program was not meant to guarantee sufficient income for older Americans, most retirees depend on it. Some elderly persons have considerable assets at retirement, but inflation and recession can quickly deplete these resources. Thus, many American elderly face economic poverty for the first time during retirement. Although the SSI program claims to have reduced American poverty in old age by more than 60% in the past two decades, 12% to 14% of elderly citizens in the United States still live below the poverty level (U. S. Senate, 1986).

Economic deprivation is most prevalent among first-generation immigrant Asian elderly. Many recent immigrant Korean elderly have not participated in Social Security long enough to qualify for benefits at retirement. Therefore, they will receive a reduced level of monthly Social Security benefits. Others, who worked part-time or at menial jobs, could not pay into the Social Security fund. For example, a large proportion of elderly persons today were in their mid-fifties at the time of their legal admission to the United States and entered the country with no command of the English language. Often their only source of employment was small businesses run by Koreans, many of whom did not contribute to Social Security. Another example is employees who paid their portion of the Social Security tax (as though they were self-employed), but their input into the system was rather meager due to low wages. As a result, their benefits are inconsequential.

Similar problems have been reported for other Asian groups in the United States. For example, approximately 25% of Filipino elders are still employed, and 15% indicate they are suffering from economic poverty. They seek help from their children when they are sick and when they need transportation, financial assistance, and physical assistance (Peterson, 1978).

To reduce this financial misery, the Social Security minimum period of employment requirements should be individually assessed. It is suggested that at the time of immigration, all individuals over 55 years of age be assigned a minimum number of quarters to be eligible for the full benefits entitled by the Social Security Act upon retirement.

Culturally effective forms of public education, including multicultural information brochures describing the rights and privileges of individuals in the American social services system, should be developed and implemented. Although the number of SSI recipients has increased, many Korean elderly who qualify for benefits are still unaware of the SSI program or are unwilling to apply for it because it is perceived to be a welfare program. Koreans consider receiving such a handout to be personally disgraceful and an indignity. Some Koreans do not apply for SSI benefits because of an alleged rumor that no welfare recipient can petition on behalf of any family members (primarily their children) who wish to immigrate to the United States. Consequently, many poor Korean elderly persons endure the fate of living in poverty and hiding behind the superficial model minority wall.

A law, which might be called Parents' Retirement Account, could be enacted to relieve the financial burden children have to support their parents, and to alleviate the economic plight of elderly persons. Like the philosophy of an Individual Retirement Account (IRA), a PRA would provide adult children a tax credit for contributions to their parents' retirement fund. A maximum amount of tax credit and the minimum age for parents to withdraw from the account should be determined. Similarly, the IRA should be instituted for all interested individuals. The assumption is that the more savings one has, the more income one has at retirement, and the less the government will spend on old age programs.

In addition, to maintain family unity and enable adult children to support their parents, a system of tax relief similar to the one being implemented in Singapore must be realized. Individuals who provide care for older family members should receive a predetermined tax credit. Other programs could lessen the financial burden on children who provide parental support. For example, children who finance their aged parents' health insurance should be granted tax deductions or credits. This policy would help relieve anxiety over high health care costs and would help the parents maintain independent living.

Aside from addressing the economic problems of the Korean elderly, policies are needed also to address their health care issues. Korean elderly are not guaranteed health services because the United States is the only industrialized and developed country in the world that does not have a national health policy.

One health program that is perhaps culturally appropriate for the Korean elderly as well as other Asian elderly is home health care. This program allows nurses or other health professionals to visit elderly persons in their homes. Such visits would allow adult children to fulfill their filial obligation to their aged parents until institutional care is required.

Like the Korean elderly, other Asian elderly share problems such as isolation and "poor" or "no" English language skills. For example, two-thirds of the older persons living in Chinatown in San Francisco are in poor health, which subsequently limits their physical activity. Many regularly visit doctors, including herbalists. Their problems are similar to those of American inner-city elderly in that health, economic poverty, substandard housing, and so on, are eminent. Likewise, more than two-thirds of the Filipino elderly have fair-to-poor health status, suffering most frequently from high blood pressure (Peterson, 1978). Among the Asian group, the Chinese elderly experience the lowest level of depression than other elderly (Kuo, 1984).

Policies also must address the problem of racial discrimination. Although there has been significant progress, nevertheless racism prevails in the United States. Legal services to combat racism and discrimination are urgently needed for Koreans and other Asians, who, through culture and tradition, remain silent and forbear. Consequently, Asians need lawyers and advocates to vocally protect them from exploitation and discrimination in the labor market based on race, sex, age, and language ability. Asians also need help in being heard and represented in the public sector. Legal services workers should be advocates for the elderly, particularly in dealing with dysfunctional, and at times inhumane, systems. All legal residents should be aware of and have access to their entitlements. Information should be provided in languages and in terms that can be understood.

Protective legal services should mandate the employment of qualified bilingual ethnic minorities for professional positions rather than merely as interpreters. In the judicial system, Koreans can benefit from the presence of Korean professionals who can serve as their advocates and support their cause.

SOCIAL WORK PRACTICE IMPLICATIONS

Social service practitioners who work with and for Korean elderly persons should understand the cultural and value-related factors of family pride, primogeniture, and empathy, warmth, and respect.

Family Pride and *Che-myun*

Although the Chinese and Japanese value highly and have invested in friendships and patriotism, Koreans are generally more private and family-oriented. Koreans seem to be highly self-motivated for individual and family growth; at times they are extremely competitive and self-centered. They are overly concerned about personal as well as family grace and celebrity, or *che-myun*—an internalized reaction to the probably externally imposed social, psychological, and behavioral prescriptions.

Koreans protect *che-myun* at all cost, and generally Korean elderly will put their *che-myun* at stake only as the last resort. For example, although the Korean elderly are unhappy with their Westernized children, they may not admit this simply to protect their pride in family unity and filial relationship with their children. They may be poor and living at a substandard level, but they may instead pretend they are being well supported by their children. This behavior is to save their children's and their family's face. They never want themselves, their children, or their family to be disgraced. In a way, *che-myun* is the heart of the Korean elderly. They smile and express their courage and stamina, but this behavior is not necessarily congruent with reality.

Practitioners should be sensitive to nonverbal behaviors or unarticulated needs of the Korean elderly. They should not make any hurried assessment or decision on behalf of these elderly persons. Instead, practitioners should probe the reality of the elderly persons' situation while respecting their dignity and *che-myun*. Social workers should appreciate the opportunity the elderly person has given them to discuss their problems, an act not usually done. The elderly person has come a long way and is very courageous to come even to the point of meeting.

The Loss of Primogeniture

Many Asian elderly in the United States brought with them the traditional and cultural law of primogeniture. This law prescribes the relationship between the aged parents and the oldest son. In this unwritten cultural law, parents expect the family of the oldest son, or other children, to care for them as they grow older. In return, the son has the right to inherit the parents' wealth.

Much to the elders' surprise, such a law is apparently inappropriate in the United States where customs, language, and life-style differ from those in the home country. Although the family of the oldest Korean son might have brought their aging parents to the United States under pressure of this cultural law, many of them are unable economically to maintain and honor the law. In many families both husbands and wives work, and some work at additional jobs to meet their needs and aspirations. Many immigrants move from place to place, seeking employment opportunities or a community that offers better education for their children and an improved living situation. Meanwhile, the older Asians remain in areas such as Chinatown, Little Tokyo, Korea Town, and Little Saigon, where they can use their own native language and meet people like themselves. Thus, the law of primogeniture is being endangered in the United States.

Many Korean elders are suffering from the loss of primogeniture. Older persons did not expect to be completely dependent on their children during their old age, neither did they expect the insecurity of living alone and subsequent mental health problems such as anxiety, stress, and depression. There is an old Korean saying: "Children are untouchable investments for old age." Korean elders, especially the first-generation immigrants, have based their expectations of security on supports from their children. The loss of their dream here in the new world is a tragedy, triggering some to return to Korea while others remain and cope with reality as best they possibly can.

Practitioners should appreciate these dreams and expectations of Korean elders. It is imperative that social workers educate both the young and older Koreans and cultivate a realistic understanding of growing old in the United States.

Genuine Empathy, Warmth, and Respect

Many Asian elderly are skeptical and distrust the American government due to former discriminatory laws and the incarceration of Japanese citizens in the United States during World War II. An old Korean warning is: "Don't be deceived by Russians, and don't believe Americans." Korean elders believe in genuine empathy and a sincere motivation to help when asked. In return, Korean elders in the United States ask for unconditional respect and need equal treatment. In other words, they want to be treated here by Americans just as the Koreans treated the Americans during the Korean War.

Practitioners should attempt to understand the frustration, distrust, and resentment many Korean and other Asian elders feel. Bureaucratic, discriminatory, and insincere behaviors are easily detected by Korean elderly persons.

CONCLUSIONS

In recent times, the 1965 immigration law reopened the door for large-scale Asian immigration. South Koreans have immigrated to the United States by the thousands, representing people from all walks of life, who encountered a variety of problems in the new country. This paper proposed measures to lessen the newly emerging problems of Asian elderly immigrants: a change in eligibility requirements to qualify for full Social Security benefits; tax credits for adult children who pay into their parents' retirement fund or who pay the premium of their parents' "medigap" health insurance policy; and humane implementation of civil rights policies. For service providers, it is imperative to appreciate traditional values of Asian elders, their unavoidable losses, as well as their pride and dignity.

REFERENCES

Andrews, G. R., Esterman, A. J., Braunack-Mayer, A. J., & Rungie, C. M. (1986). *Aging in the Western Pacific: A four-country study.* Manila: World Health Organization.

Hurh, W. M., & Kim, K. C. (1979). *Korean immigrants in the Los Angeles area: A sociological study.* Macomb, IL: Western University Press.

Hurh, W. M., & Kim, K. C. (1984). *Korea immigrants in America.* Cranberg, NJ: Associated University Press.

Kim, I. (1981). *New urban immigrants.* Princeton, NJ: Princeton University Press.

Kim, J. S. (1987). *Korean-American elderly in New York: Problems and prospects.* New York: Korean-American Senior Citizens Society.

Kim, W. Y. (1971). *Koreans in America.* Seoul: Po Chin Chai Printing Co.

Kuo, W. H. (1984). The prevalence of depression among Asian Americans. *Journal of Nervous and Mental Disease, 172,* 449-457.

Peterson, M. (1978). *Philipino elderly.* San Diego, CA: San Diego State University Center on Aging.

United Nations. (1984). *Demographic yearbook 1982.* New York: United Nations.

U. S. Bureau of the Census. (1980). *General population characteristics* (PC80-1). Washington, DC: Government Printing Office.

U. S. Department of Justice. (1964-1980). *Immigration and Naturalization Services.* Washington, DC: Government Printing Office.

U. S. Senate Special Committee on Aging. (1986). *Aging in America: Trends and projections.* Washington, DC: Government Printing Office.

Chapter 14

ASIAN AMERICANS IN THE FUTURE

SHARLENE MAEDA FURUTO
KENJI MURASE

This final chapter represents an amalgam of the thinking of the four unit editors, as interpreted and integrated by the Chief Editor. We begin this chapter with a look at the future role of Asian Americans in both the international and national arenas. This is followed by a discussion of the implications for the United States of recent population projections concerning Asian Americans, the priority problem areas these people face in the future, and the professional roles and responsibilities demanded of Asian American social workers in response to the challenges presented. We then look at future policies and programs that Asian Americans must be prepared to support. The chapter ends with a delineation of issues for future research and with our conclusions.

ASIAN AMERICANS IN THE INTERNATIONAL AND NATIONAL ARENAS

As we look at what lies ahead for Asian Americans, the future appears ominous as portended by the recent rise of anti-Asian hostility and violence directed at Asians nationwide. Historically, Euro American sentiment about ethnic populations has been heavily influenced by the economy and the character of U. S. foreign relations. Likewise, ethnic minority groups also seem to target particular minority groups based on the economy and international relations. The most compelling example of U. S. reaction to international events is the internment of Japanese citizens in concentration camps 50 years ago. Today, as American hostility is again directed against Japan, the Japanese and other Asians are being victimized further in all states. Revival of the "Yellow Peril" threat embodied in racial slurs, demeaning caricatures in the media, verbal and physical abuse in the streets, vandalism, arson, and even mob killings of Asians in, for example, California, New Jersey, and Michigan occur regularly.

The prospect for any immediate abatement of anti-Asian hostility is not promising in light of a continuing trade imbalance between the United States and some Asian countries. The complexities of international trade are not easily understood, and prominent "experts" in the media, in their haste to find simple solutions, often pander to the ingrained xenophobic bias of some Euro Americans. In the case of Japan, attacks in the media have gone far beyond the claim that the Japanese do not behave fairly in trade. Increasingly, as the Japanese character becomes the target, references are made to the "ugly Japanese" who are "sinister," "unprincipled," and "selfish." These characterizations are then generalized to apply to the Japanese in the United States. Moreover, since other Asians are not differentiated from Japanese Americans, they too become the target of the new wave of anti-Asian resentment in this country. The recent blacklisting of India as a trade partner carries the same sentiment.

The challenge to Asian Americans is to: (a) clarify to the general public the rightful role of Asians as contributing citizens of the United States in economics, education, science, technology, and so on; and (b) try to mediate the tensions arising from differences in the legitimate self-interest of the United States as a whole and Asian countries. With their knowledge of Asian languages and cultures, Asian Americans have a unique opportunity to provide other Americans with a greater understanding of the realities facing Asian countries.

POPULATION PROJECTIONS

By virtue of being the fastest growing ethnic minority population in the United States, Asian Americans comprise an increasingly important sector of the American mosaic. Recent reports of the U. S. Census Bureau (1988) identify certain significant trends in the population growth of this country. Between 1990 and 2000, the West is expected to grow by 13.7%, a sharp increase compared to other parts of the United States. California, the most populous state in the Union, will have between 37 million and 38 million people in 2010, or about 30% more residents than in 1990. Of the new residents, one-third, or about 3.5 million, will be immigrants, mainly from Asia and the Pacific Islands. These estimates are conservative since they assume that immigration will be much slower between 1990 and 2010 than it was in the 1980s. The Asian and Pacific Islander population is expected to continue to grow the fastest (U. S. Census, 1988).

In another report, the Census Bureau (1990) states that during the period from 1980 to 1988, the national Asian and Pacific Islander population grew by more than 75%, from 2.7 million in 1980 to 5.5 million in 1988. According to the 1990 Census (Dunn, 1990), there are now 7 million Asians in the United States. In contrast, the growth rate of the Euro American population from 1980 to 1988 was 6%; blacks, 13%; Native Americans, 19%; and Hispanics, 34%. Immigration continues to be a major factor in the growth of the Asian and Pacific Islander population. More than 1.1 million people emigrated to the United States from East and Southeast Asia between 1982 and 1988, plus another 304,000 from and around the Indian subcontinent.

It is clear that the continuing growth of the Asian American population in this country, largely made up of immigrants and refugees, poses a challenge to American public policy and programs with respect to the future integration of this population into the mainstream. In the following section, we will discuss some of the priority problems to be confronted, the desired policies and programs, the roles and responsibilities that social workers must be prepared to undertake to meet this challenge, and issues for future research.

PRIORITY PROBLEM AREAS OF THE FUTURE

As Asians look to their future, a number of current and emerging problems will require priority attention in the United States. These problems reflect the consequences of the demographic trends cited earlier, particularly the expected continuing influx of immigrants and refugees from Asia and the Pacific Islands. The following are among the problem areas most likely to require response.

Economic and Social Integration

The ongoing problems of economic and social integration will continue for all Asians. While some Asian households have comfortable incomes, many more have multiple wage earners and consist of individuals who are underpaid and/or work at several jobs. New immigrants and refugees will continue to suffer the most economically and socially. Assistance in the early stages of transition to a new country will be a critical factor in influencing the process of adaptation and integration of newcomers. Although mutual assistance associations have developed among Asian immigrant and refugee groups, the main source of help with immediate problems of survival will continue to be the established public and private social service agencies. Resources available to support such agencies have been diminishing in recent years, and there is the danger that public apathy will lead to diversion of funding to other areas.

Newcomers must be oriented to the U. S. economic and social systems through educational programs. Social workers must continue to monitor and advocate for basic economic assistance and social services for both immigrants and refugees.

Differential Impact of Poverty

Much media attention has been given to the "model minority" stereotype of Asians based on their academic and economic achievements. However, these achievements are largely attributable to the Chinese and Japanese populations, who have the longest history in the United States. They do not generally apply to other Asian American groups, whose history in this country is shorter and who have not yet developed a viable economic base in their communities. Among the more recent populations of Koreans, Filipinos, Southeast Asians, and Pacific Islanders, there are pockets of severe poverty and related pathology of mental illness, chronic health problems, family breakdown, and delinquency. The populations most affected by these problems are unskilled new immigrants, refugees, the elderly, and single-parent families. The notion that Asians no longer qualify as an underrepresented or disadvantaged group and need no further protection under Affirmative Action laws must be dispelled.

Children, Youth, and Families

The problems of Asian children, youth, and families vary greatly depending upon their level of adaptation and integration into the United

States. For example youth who reject their own culture and accept the American cultural ways may have intergenerational conflict with their traditional parents. The opposite is also true for those youth who maintain their traditional culture, reject the host culture, and suffer rejection by classmates at school. Furthermore, those who are bicultural and have achieved in academic and extra-curricular activities, may be rejected by Ivy League universities with a growing proportion of Asians.

Asian immigrants and refugees experience severe stress in the process of moving to a new country and coping with culture shock and acculturation. The disruptions in the continuity of family life create enormous pressures that destabilize normal family relations and individual role performance. As the acculturation process takes place, there is increasing intergenerational tension and alienation between parents and children. Internal conflicts are then manifested in gang affiliation, drug use, and delinquency. Parents, reacting in accustomed ways, often resort to physical punishment and sanctions that are not acceptable in this country.

For many newcomers, the social organization of American schools presents another alien world to which they are unable to adjust. Both parents and children may have unfulfilled expectations of the American educational system. Immigrant parents are likely to expect schools to teach their children principles of moral behavior, as did the schools in their home country.

Parents preoccupied with their drive for economic survival and independence are unable to provide adequate guidance and support that is needed by their children. Increasingly, many youths turn to their peer groups for support. Youth gangs have developed in response to the alienation of youth from parents and community.

Refugee children, in particular, have serious health problems related to malnutrition, anemia, and parasitosis, in addition to severe behavioral and emotional problems. The consequences of experiencing the trauma of war, their perilous escape on the high seas, and prolonged periods of deprivation in the refugee camps frequently take their toll in such manifestations as nightmares, fear, guilt, and acting-out behavior. Amerasian children, who survived in the streets back in their home country without the care and support of families, face special problems of adaptation and integration. This population will make special demands on service agencies as few are equipped to meet the extraordinary needs of this client group about which very little is known at this time.

Women

By far the majority of Asian service users are women. Recently arrived Asian women seem to be thrust either into isolation and loneliness, as nonworking women who speak little if any English, or into a highly technological society, as overburdened women underemployed at multiple jobs, keeping house, and raising a family. Husband-wife relationships become strained when, as is often the case, the woman locates a job before her husband or earns more than he does due to multiple employment. A strain in the marital relationship, compounded by adaptation and integration difficulties, is manifested in other family relationships as well, oftentimes resulting in a dysfunctional family.

Refugee women often bring with them unimaginable experiences of repeated rape incidents, death of spouse and children, extreme hunger and hopelessness. Frequently these women need mental health and economic assistance before they can compete adequately in employment and gain financial independence.

On the other hand, Asian women who were either born in the United States or lived here for a number of years face other problems: intermarriages and ethnically mixed children, being passed by for promotions, discrimination in admission to preferred universities or programs, relegation to low-status and dead-end jobs, and stereotypical treatment or sexual harassment in their places of employment. The diverse population of Asian women requires equally different services.

The Elderly

The Asian elderly population is growing rapidly and generally living longer than non-Asians, creating problems that stem from their alienation and isolation, physical illness, and the need for long-term care. This is particularly true among the Chinese, Japanese, and Korean communities. Since high value is placed on the status of the aged among Asians, families make every effort to care for the elderly in their own homes rather than in institutions. However, it is becoming increasingly difficult for Asian families, especially in urban areas, to care for the aged in their own homes. Expansion of in-home supportive services is needed, as well as long-term care facilities.

Mental Health

The need for mental health services will continue to increase, especially among the population of immigrants and refugees. Prominent among mental health problems will be major mood disorders related to stress over loss and grief for loved ones, disrupted family relationships, social isolation, status inconsistencies, prolonged or repetitive trauma, cultural shock, and acculturation conflicts.

A condition found frequently among Southeast Asian refugees is that of post-traumatic stress disorder, which is manifested by intrusive and recurring memories of traumatic events, repeated nightmares and dreams, intense distress at exposure to symbolic or similar events of the past, acute shame or survivor guilt, and internalized rage. Also likely to be found are psychotic episodes among immigrants and refugees who have been isolated or separated from relatives for prolonged periods or who are unable to cope with the stress of their migration experience and the pressures of acculturation in this country.

Discrimination

Unless major changes occur in a number of areas, including the national economy, the relationship between the United States and foreign countries, and how non-Asians react to the achievements of Asians, the level of discrimination against Asians is likely to increase. Since the end of 1990, the United States has been in an economic recession. This recession, coupled with an unfair trade balance with Japan and the war with Iraq, could place a severe strain on the already fragile U. S. economy. This recession, which has been predicted to last between several months and several years, will erode consumer buying power and will lead Americans to an uncomfortable standard of living.

The war in Iraq and political changes in the former Eastern Block Communist countries will probably lead to thousands of refugees and immigrants from those areas to the United States. Most of the refugees shall require financial assistance, and the need for an expanded social welfare budget shall compete for already limited federal and state funds. A cut in health, educational, and social programs can lead to frustration and anger.

In addition, it seems to be an American attribute to cheer for the underdog. In fact, it is not unusual for non-Asians to react with disdain or jealousy when apprised of the success of an Asian. Non-Asians need to understand that Asians succeed largely through tremendous effort, extended family support, and nurtured talent. Non-Asians must realize that they too can achieve largely by following this Asian model. The government and media have a responsibility to make the non-Asian cognizant of how the success of Asians will benefit all Americans.

When the economy and the buying power of individuals drop, when individual attitudes toward Asian success are negative, and when government services are curtailed, the stage is set for anger, hostility, and discrimination. Ethnic minorities are easy targets for discrimination, and Asians in particular due to their success.

Service Delivery

In response to the problems outlined above, there will continue to be the issue of cultural and linguistic relevance in service delivery. This means that ongoing attention must be directed to the need for both bicultural and bilingual staff in order to assure sensitivity to cultural differences, appropriateness of response, and access to services.

In addition, staff who are less familiar with the Asian cultures must be given the opportunity to learn about Asian values and life-styles through educational programs. However, it is not sufficient for the staff alone to be responsive to cultural differences among clients. Practice needs to be augmented by parallel institutional policy and procedures in order to maximize effective service delivery to ethnically diverse populations.

PROFESSIONAL ROLES AND RESPONSIBILITIES

It is clear that the traditional social work practitioner role must be re-examined if we are to respond to the future needs of Asian communities in the United States. For Asians and other minorities, the typical practitioner role of helping clients to achieve self-fulfillment and the realization of their human potential through individual change is insufficient. Efforts directed to achieve client conformity to established norms of behavior in the American culture must be extended to efforts directed to client initiation of improvement in his or her social and economic environment.

Individual change must be supported by structural and institutional changes that redistribute power, resources, and authority locally and nationally in economics, politics, education, and social welfare. The practitioner required in Asian communities in the future must not only provide services to help clients function more effectively in their environment but must also seek to help clients deal directly with those institutions that deny them the right to self-determination and equal opportunity. The practitioner must therefore be prepared to assist clients in their own efforts to organize themselves into effective advocacy groups that will ultimately enable them to acquire and exercise power on their own behalf. The practitioner should not only facilitate conformity or adjustment of clients to the American culture but, more significantly, the practitioner must also help empower clients to act collectively to control decisions, projects, and programs that affect their reality.

The government will never provide enough social services for all, let alone service for ethnic minorities. Therefore, it is crucial that the practitioner either initiate or organize and help to develop Asian community organizations. Service providers could use a three-pronged approach:

(a) sensitivity to cultures of origin by knowing and understanding these cultures and their strengths, such as family effort in achievements accomplished by family members and the family collectively;

(b) support to ethnic community organizations by recognizing the role these organizations play in maintaining the culture and traditions; providing a base for identification in the host country; and giving Asians an audience for positions, problems, and solutions; and

(c) empowerment of the Asian family within the Asian worldview.

Both as individual citizens and as professionals, Asian social workers must actively participate in the process of formulating public policy at the local, state, and national levels. Both individually and collectively, Asian social workers must become involved not only in their own communities but also on the state and national levels in electoral, legislative, and regulatory processes. Asian social workers should also participate in social action campaigns such as rallies, marches, and demonstrations. This challenge is great—the opportunity awaits and the responsibility cannot be denied.

POLICY AND PROGRAMS

Asians have a vital interest in the promotion and advancement of sound public policies and programs to meet human needs and improve he quality of life for all Americans. Cultural diversity is both a social trength and an imperative element in policy design. Therefore, they aave a stake in local, state, and federal legislation that seeks to combat all forms of discrimination, promote Affirmative Action laws and auman rights, and facilitate unimpeded access to needed services. Asians join with other Americans in calling for an integrated national ocial policy, which will assure that each individual and family will eceive the health, mental health, social and economic services and ntitlements necessary to achieve their maximum level of functioning.

More specifically, Asians support the following, among other, concerns:

(1) a public educational program to counter personal and institutional racism;

(2) reforms in the public welfare system to provide national minimum benefit levels to assure a healthful standard of living for all;

(3) a more responsive, accountable, and effective public school system to meet basic educational needs of all low-income, minority, and exceptional students;

(4) efforts to counteract and resist English-only legislation and to support the expansion of English as a Second Language educational programs;

(5) a national policy and program for universal and comprehensive health and mental health care;

(6) a comprehensive and meaningful nondiscriminatory national employment program that would create both sufficient jobs paying living wages and safe working condition;

(7) local, state, and national public policy and programs to assure a clean, safe, and healthy environment;

(8) freedom of choice in women's reproductive health at local, state, and national levels; and

(9) with the end of Desert Storm and the war with Iraq, there needs to be a shift in national priorities from world military ascendance and power to world peace and disarmament, which would then provide the necessary resources for human service needs, affordable housing, mass public transportation, public works, debt reduction, and other critical domestic needs.

ISSUES FOR FURTHER RESEARCH

There is a great need for Asian ethnographic research to be conducted. A review of the chapters in this book suggests a number of areas for future research on Asians in the United States. Among the issues that have emerged are the following.

Relationship Between Socioeconomic and Minority Status

Much of the literature on the "model minority" status ascribed to Asians has been based on the status of Chinese and Japanese, whose educational and economic achievements now outstrip their Euro American contemporaries. However, it should be noted that among all Asians, the Chinese and Japanese have the longest history of settlement in this country, and their early experience is characterized by racial oppression and severe economic hardships. Similarly, recent immigrants and refugees from Korea, the Philippines, and Southeast Asia endure poverty and deprivation in their early experiences in this country. Many must rely upon public assistance or relatives for their survival.

However, after the initial period of struggle for survival, some recent immigrants and refugees become successful entrepreneurs in small business enterprises such as restaurants, grocery stores, dry cleaning shops, produce markets, auto repair shops, and various personal services. Some children of these families excel in school, complete a college education, and secure high-paying employment in the professional and technical fields. Many of these families today achieve, in two generations, educational and economic achievement levels that took earlier Chinese and Japanese immigrants three or four generations.

It would be instructive to study the experiences of these few newcomers from such countries as Vietnam, Cambodia, and Laos to identify the specific factors that contributed to their educational and economic success in a relatively short span of time, despite the obstacles of language, culture, and racial discrimination. A delineation of the personal and cultural, as well as institutional, factors that facilitate economic independence and upward mobility may suggest policies and programs that could be helpful to other minority groups facing similar problems of poverty and dependence on public assistance for survival.

Social/Cultural Resources and Coping

The successful adaptation of Asian immigrants and refugees to their new environment is often attributed to their capacity to cope with stress. Their ability to deal with stress is due to a number of reasons, one being the availability of American and indigenous social and cultural resources within their communities. While there is need to study the manifestations of stress and the specific processes that create stress among Asians, there is also the need to identify those unique social and cultural resources to which the newcomers have access. This includes the informal and natural support networks, which not only function as mechanisms to identify persons in need of help but also direct them to the appropriate resources.

An integral part of the support network is the kinship structure, which should be studied to better understand culture-specific influence processes and obligatory helping roles and responsibilities. For example, since the critical kin dyad among Asians is frequently not husband-wife but parent-child, the network models developed for mainstream or other minority groups are not directly applicable to Asians.

Ethnic Identity, Acculturation, and Racism

There is need for further empirical study regarding the role of acculturation, individual and multiple group identities, and biculturalism in the adaptation and integration of Asians. Such studies may not only challenge the concept of the "marginal man" but may also provide useful insight to the coping strategies and potential sources of social support for ethnic minorities.

There also continues to be the need for further analysis of the relationship between such structural variables as racism and cultural diversity and their consequences on the quality of life of Asians. At issue is the question of the extent to which Asians, in order to gain security and fulfillment, must continue to remain within the protective confines of their ethnic enclaves.

Asian Americans in Non-Urban Areas

A new set of research questions is raised because of the increasingly rapid dispersal of Asians away from urban areas where, historically, they have been concentrated. This movement to non-urban areas is a consequence of pressures for economic mobility and the ongoing processes of acculturation. The result is that individuals and families become isolated not only from kin but also from their ethnic organizations and communities. There is need to study the impact of such isolation upon individual and family functioning, particularly in terms of mental health implications. There are also public policy implications regarding the issue of dispersal of families in the resettlement of future populations of refugees.

Clearly much research is needed in a wide variety of areas and in differing degrees to better plan for working with Asians. Practitioners and academicians must increasingly collaborate to provide the information officials should have when making program and policy decisions. Only then will Asians use the social services available to meet their specific needs, thus enabling them to help not only themselves but also others.

CONCLUDING REMARKS

Asians have come a long way since they first arrived in the United States more than 150 years ago. Like other immigrants, Asians struggled, and continue to struggle, with problems related to acculturation, housing, income, and health. However, they suffer from the additional handicap of discrimination because few if any laws protected them even into the first half of this century.

Although today Asians and other Americans in general are more aware of basic human rights and the system for protecting these rights, there are, nevertheless, indications that: (a) Asians do not enjoy equal opportunities that Euro Americans take for granted; (b) refugees, most of whom are Asians, require not only the same services as immigrants but also additional sensitivities and services due to the nature of their unique experiences; and (c) the recent increase of anger and hostility against Asians across the nation is compounding their already tenuous status.

Collectively, Asians must unite beyond their traditional values into the realms of basic human rights, politics, education, and social service programs. Inequality and our differentness require that we stand together for our mutual benefit—united as Asians rather than separated as Chinese, Filipinos, Asian Indians, Japanese, and so on. Asians also need to form coalitions with groups that share our interests and issues. Only when we are empowered will we be able to influence institutions, elected leaders, and the wider community in matters related to the rights and needs of this minority group.

Then shall we be able to read about Asians in terms of integration of all into the American society, not marginalization or separation of some youth and elderly; adequate income, not poverty or want; equal opportunities, not prejudice or discrimination; available services staffed by qualified, bicultural personnel, or staff trained in the Asian culture, not inadequate services or individuals without appropriate credentials, and so on.

To promote a more equal life-style for Asians and therefore for all others, there must be a greater coming together of all Asian and non-Asian Americans in joint endeavors in research, micro and macro social work practice, politics, and education. The time is now. We are the workers. Perhaps the focus of this book shall encourage us to do our part. Our effort can be a token of appreciation to our ancestors and a legacy for our children, for we are made wise by responding to the future.

REFERENCES

Dunn, W. (1990, November 28). Asian wave is changing U. S. scene. *Honolulu Star-Bulletin*, p. A-24.

U. S. Bureau of the Census. (1988). *Projections of the population of states, by sex, and race: 1988-2010*. (Current Population Reports, Series P-25, No. 1017.) Washington, DC: Government Printing Office.

U. S. Bureau of the Census. (1990). *Population estimates by age, sex, race, and ethnic origin: 1980 to 1988*. (Current Population Reports, Series P-25, No. 1045.) Washington, DC: Government Printing Office.

AUTHOR INDEX

SUBJECT INDEX

Acculturation: definition of, 68; of Chinese immigrants, 68; of Filipino immigrants, 68; of Japanese immigrants, 68; of Korean immigrants, 68; of Southeast Asian refugees, 68

Adaptation: definition of, 46; of Amerasians to U.S., 54; options for Asian immigrants, 48, 49; outcomes, 52-59

Adler, A., 70

Asian American movement, 20-21

Asian Americans: adaptation to American society by, 2, 45-61; advancement of programs by, 248; advancement of public policies by, 248; children, 244; cultural commonalities among, 28, 46; cultural commonalities with Euro American culture, 2; cultural differences between Euro Americans and, 28-43; during World War II, 15-18; economic integration of, 243; economic patterns of, 55-56; elderly, 245; families, 244; future of, 240-253; geographic concentration of, 145; history of, 3-23; importance of family to, 144-146; in Hawaii, 4, 8; mental health of, 246; population figures for, 1, 3; population projections for, 241-242; poverty of, 243; priority problem areas of the future for, 242-247;

racist discrimination of, 1, 2, 23, 55, 57, 59-60, 69-70, 198, 240-241, 246-247; residential patterns of, 53-55; restriction of immigration to U.S. by, 11, 12, 13; second-generation formation of, 14-15; service delivery to, 247; social integration of, 243; social stability of, 57-59; war brides, 17; women, 245. *See also* names of individual Asian American groups

Asian Indians, American, 1, 3, 14, 22; average-performing adolescent, 192; career choice of adolescent, 196; cultural collectivity of, 32; high achievement of, 186; identity crises of adolescent, 194-196; in Bellingham, Washington, 12; Muslim identity of, 57; overachieving adolescent, 190-191; population figures for, 12, 18; problems of adolescent, 189-201; racist discrimination of, 12, 22, 57; residential patterns of, 54; second generation of, 14; socialization choice of adolescent, 197; stress and, 47-48; underachieving adolescent, 192-194; women, 146, 147, 152, 154, 158, 160

Asian Indians, immigration of to U.S., 11-12, 45

ABOUT THE CONTRIBUTORS

RENUKA BISWAS, D.S.W., received her degree from Columbia University in 1971. She is currently Chairperson of the Department of Sociology, Anthropology, Social Work, and Geography at Lock Haven University of Pennsylvania. Her areas of interest include community organization and administration.

DOUGLAS K. CHUNG, PH.D., received his degree from The Ohio State University in 1981. Currently Professor in the School of Social Work at Grand Valley State University, he also serves as the Chair for Research Sequence. His other areas of interest include Confucianism, Christian social work, universal generalist social work, and religion and social work. His articles have appeared in *Evaluative Research, Social Problems*, the *Journal of International Social Work*, and the *Alliance of Information Referral Systems.*

ROWENA FONG, ED.D., received her degree from Harvard University in 1990. She is currently Assistant Professor at the University of Hawaii at Manoa. Her areas of interest include Asian American social work practice and mental health of Chinese American children and youth.

SHARLENE MAEDA FURUTO, ED.D., received her degree from Brigham Young University in 1981. She is currently Professor and Social Work Program Coordinator for Brigham Young University, Hawaii. Her areas of expertise include cross-cultural practice and Asian and Pacific Islanders. Her most recent publication is *Family Violence Among Pacific Islanders* (1991).

SHANTI K. KHINDUKA, PH.D., received his degree from Brandeis University in 1968. He is currently Dean of the George Warren Brown School of Social Work at Washington University. His areas of interest include international social development and social work education. He has served as editor of *Social Work in India* (1965), and as co-editor of *Profiles in International Social Work* (1992) and *Social Work in Practice* (1976).

JUNG-SUP KIM, PH.D., is Executive Director of United Service USA. She received her degree from Atlanta University in 1986. Her areas of interest include social planning and development and social administration. Her articles have appeared in the *Journal of Korean Gerontological Society*.

PAUL K. KIM, D.S.W., is Professor of Social Work and Clinical Professor of Medicine at Louisiana State University. He received his degree from Tulane University in 1972. His areas of interest are social work research, program evaluation, and gerontology. His most recent publication is *Serving the Elderly: Skills for Practice* (1991).

CHI KWONG LAW, D.S.W., received his degree from the University of California at Los Angeles and is Senior Lecturer at the University of Hong Kong. His area of expertise is children and youth work.

JON MATSUOKA, PH.D., received his degree from the University of Michigan in 1984 and is currently Assistant Professor at the University of Hawaii at Manoa. His areas of interest include cultural issues in mental health theory and practice, impact of social change, and stress on mental health of ethnic minority groups. His most recent publications are *Differential Acculturation Among Vietnamese Refugees* (1990) and *Peace and Development: An Interdisciplinary Perspective* with Daniel Sanders (1989).

KATHLEEN M. McINNIS-DITTRICH, PH.D., received her degree from the University of Wisconsin, Madison, in 1987. She is currently Director of and Associate Professor in the Social Work Program at Marquette University in Milwaukee. Her areas of expertise are social welfare policy and refugees and immigration. Her most recent publication is *The Hmong in America: Providing Ethnic-Sensitive Health Education and Human Services* (1990).

PAULINE MEEMEDUMA, D.S.W., received her degree from Howard University in 1988. She is currently the head of the Social Work Programme in the Department of Social Work and Community Welfare at James Cook University of North Queensland, Townsville, Australia. Her areas of interest are cross-cultural social work practice, social work education, and refugee and immigrant populations. Her most recent publication is *Support Networks of Asian Women in North Queensland* (1990) for the Office of Multicultural Affairs.

BRIJ MOHAN, PH.D., received his degree from Lucknow University in 1964. Formerly the Dean of the Department of Social Work, he now serves as Professor at the Louisiana State University, Baton Rouge. His areas of interest include mental health, social policy, and international and comparative social welfare. His most recent publications include *Global Development: Post-Material Values and Social Praxis* (in press); *Unemployment Today* with Hooper, Briar, and McKay (1991); and *Glimpses of International and Comparative Social Welfare* (1989).

NOREEN MOKUAU, D.S.W., received her degree from University of California at Los Angeles in 1982. She is currently Associate Professor at the University of Hawaii on Manoa and serves as Chair of the BSW Program. Her areas of expertise are cross-cultural practice and native Hawaiian issues. Her most recent publication is *Handbook of Social Services for Asian and Pacific Islanders* (1991).

KENJI MURASE, D.S.W., received his degree from Columbia University in 1961. He is currently Professor Emeritus at San Francisco State University. His area of expertise is social policy research. His more recent publications are *Ethnic Minority Mental Health Clinical Training Programs* (1989) and "Education for Social Work Practice in Asian and Pacific American Communities" in Chunn, Dunston, and Ross-Sheriff's *Mental Health and People of Color* (1983).

FARIYAL ROSS-SHERIFF, PH.D., is Associate Professor at Howard University, Washington, D. C. She received her degree from the University of Michigan in 1972. Her area of expertise is displaced populations, and her work includes *Mental Health and People of Color* with Chunn and Dunston (1983).

LEONARD SCHNEIDERMAN, PH.D., Dean of the UCLA School of Social Welfare, received his degree from the University of Minnesota in 1963. His area of expertise is social welfare policies and programs.

JUDITH SHEPHERD, D.S.W., received her degree from the University of California, Berkeley, School of Social Welfare in 1980, where she taught until 1988. She was a Beatrice M. Bain-affiliated scholar at UC Berkeley in 1989. She is currently with San Francisco's General Hospital Family Health Center Refugee Clinic. Her areas of interest include child welfare and cross-cultural issues in immigration and mental health.

YOUNG I. SONG-KIM, PH.D., received her degree from The Ohio State University in 1986. She is currently Associate Professor at the California State University, Hayward. Her area of expertise is immigrant families and women. More recent publications include *Silent Victims* (1987) and *Americana Mosaic* (1991).